4 Feb. '96
Israel

For Gay Nacca,
My special 'barerah' !

Stephen Langfur

Stephen Langfur
Ma'agelei Yavneh 7
Apartment 23
Jerusalem 93582
ISRAEL

Phone and Fax 972-2-792270

CONFESSION FROM A JERICHO JAIL

CONFESSION FROM A JERICHO JAIL

STEPHEN LANGFUR

 GROVE WEIDENFELD / NEW YORK

Published by Grove Weidenfeld
A division of Grove Press, Inc.
841 Broadway
New York, NY 10003-4793

Published in Canada by General Publishing Company, Ltd.

Dylan Thomas: Poems of Dylan Thomas copyright 1939 by New Directions
Publishing Corporation. Reprinted by permission of New Directions.

Excerpt from "Love Song: I and Thou" copyright © 1961, 1962, 1968, 1972,
1973, 1974, 1983 by Alan Dugan. From *New and Collected Poems, 1961–1983*,
first published by The Ecco Press in 1983. Reprinted by permission.

Franz Rosenzweig quotes reprinted by permission of the Journal of Philosophy
and Phenomenological Research, copyright 1947.

All translations from the Hebrew Bible are the author's.

Library of Congress Cataloging-in-Publication Data

    Langfur, Stephen, 1941–
        Confession from a Jericho jail / Stephen Langfur. — 1st ed.
            p.   cm.
        ISBN 0-8021-1482-2 (alk. paper) .
        1. Jewish-Arab relations—1973–   2. Intifada, 1987–
    —Conscientious objectors—Israel.   3. Langfur, Stephen, 1941–
    I. Title.
    DS119.7.L285   1992
    956—dc20   91-41555
                                                            CIP

Manufactured in the United States of America

Printed on acid-free paper

Designed by Christine Swirnoff

Map by Arnold Bombay

First Edition 1992

10 9 8 7 6 5 4 3 2 1

For Noga

CONFESSION FROM A
JERICHO JAIL

1

November 1989.

WHEN I WAS ten years younger and full of hope, I departed the U.S.A. with wife and daughter and moved to Israel. What follow are notes from an army cell, to which I have been sentenced for refusing to go into the West Bank against the Palestinians. The term is twenty-one days. At its end they may order me back to the same place (this is even to be expected) and I shall probably refuse and be sentenced again. Thus it will go—two rounds, three rounds. Next year it can start all over. We reservists get called till age fifty or so. The screw can turn and turn.

This round is easy. It is not even a real prison. I missed the car to prison, so they found me a place in a little army camp near Jericho. It includes a military police station, cells for Palestinians on two sides of a courtyard, and just around the corner a cell for problem soldiers, us.

"Why is Steve making problems?" our next-door neighbor asked my wife.

Ahab to Elijah, I Kings 18:17—"Is it you, you troubler of Israel?"

Did I come to Israel to be a troubler of Israel?

We came, as I said, full of hope. Sadat had just visited. A door had opened. I felt sure that Israel would rush through. I kept in my heart an image of Israelis as reluctant conquerors, restless occupiers, who sat upon another people in the West Bank only because they had no choice. There had been no one (or so it had seemed) with whom to make an agreement that would give the Jewish state, at last, security and acceptance. And then came Sadat, flying into Tel Aviv like the falcon of Horus. I heard myself gasp, in a living room in Houston, when that bird touched down. I had never heard myself gasp before.

A decade later I sit under arrest in the shadow of three Herodian fortresses. We are on Wadi Qilt, a unique cut in the cliff between Jericho and Jerusalem. This was a vital pass in antiquity—hence the fortresses. It is still a possible pass for guerrillas from Jordan—hence our little base now. A few miles deep into the wadi is the Greek Orthodox monastery of St. George, where an old servant shows a cave with the very crack through which the ravens flew to feed the hidden Elijah. He had proclaimed a drought in the name of the Lord because Ahab and the people had gone over to Baal. After three rainless years he presented himself to Ahab, and Ahab called him a troubler.

Of Israel. What is Israel? A people. A country.

When one of our children falls from a chair, my mother-in-law, who grew up in Jerusalem, cries out, "Elijah the Prophet!" He is the rescuer—until the day of redemption. The troubler, the rescuer.

No Elijahs now. No prophets now. But ninety oddball troublers (in the two years of intifada) have gone this route before me. I am, I believe, the only American among them. I have two citizenships, could always leave, have where to go. And because of this fact my mere presence in Israel amounts to a constant implicit choice. It is a tacit "Yes"—Yes to being here, Yes to the country and the people. Going to jail in the present circumstances is a way of adding a "but" to the "Yes." If that troubles Israel, so be it. It is a needed troubling.

HAVING WASHED a thousand dishes, I go to the main yard during break time—it is perhaps 2:00 P.M. There are Arab prisoners, fifteen or so, sitting blindfolded on the ground. The blindfolds look like bandages, bright white in the Jericho sun, as if they had eye wounds. I have seen such things on TV, but this is different of course. Even here there is a kind of screen. A row of metal barricades divides our section, which belongs to the military police, from the east side of the yard, which belongs to the regiment whose prisoners these are. Some sit with their backs to the wall of the wing on our right—we can see the lower parts of their faces—and others sit against the barricades, their backs to us. One sits alone in the middle of the yard. They are separated so that they cannot whisper. Young men between fifteen and thirty. But there is also a boy maybe ten years old against the wall. He is not blindfolded. And sitting straight-backed against a barricade—yet not leaning on it, slightly turned, in red-and-white headdress, there is a man of delicate features, of great dignity, a beduin perhaps, holding his son of three or four in his lap, and they are not blindfolded either.

How relaxed they are, all of them. Perhaps they have been here for hours already, and fear has given way to boredom. But it is not boredom. There is no restlessness. As if they have been through it all before. No fear. Not even the ten-year-old. But they have not blindfolded him, nor the father and son, perhaps to spare them fear. A fat bearded reservist fights sleep on the threshold of a doorway in the same wall, a rifle across his knees. On the other side of the yard to the left two soldiers stand chatting by a jeep. The prisoners cannot know how lax the guard is, so they will not try to lift their hands, which are unbound, to remove the blindfolds. The sun throws no shadows. No fear. There is even a certain dignity and grace.

They have been caught doing whatever they were doing, or perhaps not doing anything; in what is called "administrative detention," they can be arrested on the suspicion that they might one day do something. How long will it go on? At the signature of the local commander, they can be held for six months uncharged, and this can be renewed for another six months, and then perhaps they will be tried. The time before them is so uncertain, and possibly so long, that they can put any thought of freedom, of family, off into an unreckonable future. And what will happen to them until then? One reads of torture, not of high-tech torture but of the primitive ad hoc type requiring no special equipment: cigarette burns, or being tied into painful positions for hours, or beatings, or the occasional negligence on Sabbath, when the officers are away and the guards may not bother to bring water. Surely they know about these things. Surely they have heard far worse, whether true or not. But no fear. Perhaps it is the famous fatalism, a part of the famous Arab mentality. Or is it the blindfolds? They are so helpless, there is no point in fear.

The one in the middle, probably baking. But it is the kind of posture that we, in the sixties, used to call "cool." Part yoga, part sprawl. He hasn't lost his cool.

My fellow problem soldiers are busy repainting the walls of the police side white. But two are taking a break on the gray-slatted wooden bench in front of the police office, even while the police (still boys almost) stand and watch it all and joke with the policewomen (girls becoming women). So apparently it is all right to sit. I take a place on the bench. My back and legs ache from leaning over the sink. The Arabs, one guy tells me, were stopped crossing the Allenby Bridge coming back in. They are suspected of contacts with terrorists in Jordan. Could be. One of the rules in the army is never believe anything.

The other guy says they were caught laying mines by the Damya Bridge north of here. Well, that ten-year-old wouldn't have been laying mines. Nor father and son, so calm. Sitting, all of them, directly on the asphalt. Sitting calmly on the earth, relaxed and silent and blind, like the earth. No need to move. Not bothered even, as we are, by the flies. Stolid.

Something about the hairline. With the blue-collar and the farming Arabs, there is a kind of dusty indistinctness where the hair meets the skin of the forehead. One of the ways to tell an Arab. When I first began to live here, I could not fathom how my friends and neighbors could distinguish them from us. Now I too have a system of signs. A touch of racial consciousness. One does not live here and stay unblemished.

Out of the office behind me more police emerge with another Arab, a different sort, upper-class, nineteen or twenty. It is clear where his hair stops. He has a white shirt on and narrow-cut gray slacks and black loafers. Old-fashioned by Israeli standards. (Another way to tell an Arab.)

A roar, a screech.

Ami, a jailer, dark and small, has backed up the police van and, slamming the brake, has blocked my view of the yard. He comes out with a chain and bends down before this upper-class one, lifts his slacks, shackles his ankles. He rises and goes and opens the back doors and motions him to get in. "I'm taking a hostage," he says to the policewomen. A joking swagger. On the one hand, Ami knows he is short and skinny and can't possibly impress anyone, so he makes a joke out of it, but on the other hand, he really is taking a hostage. He is apparently going into dangerland and wants nonetheless to impress them. The youth has to hop around to the back. He looks in and says something in Arabic. Ami: "Who speaks Arabic?" A soldier comes. A Yemenite (one can tell). They talk in Arabic. "He says his clothes will get dirty." Ami seems puzzled. Looks into the van. "Bring some newspapers," he says. One of the girl-women goes into the office and brings a newspaper. They spread it on the floor of the van. Now what is this for Israeli brutality, if they worry about the clothes? Then the youth gets in, but lying down, so how can he be a hostage? I suppose if Ami is surrounded by a mob, he can have him sit up and point a gun at his head. Indeed, now a reservist gets into the back with a rifle. "If he moves," another policeman says, "put a bullet in him." He is joking. It is like a new toy for them. The military police are responsible for Israeli soldiers, not for West Bank Arabs. New, to have an Arab.

They drive away. Again the courtyard is revealed. No one has moved.

The two reservists chat by the jeep. Then one crosses and beckons to the ten-year-old, who stands up. He is a strapping kid with brown skin, a part descendant of Sudanese, either those who came up with the Mamluks in the thirteenth century or those who came with Muhammad Ali's army in the 1830s. Both groups settled in Jericho because it was as like as they could find to home (nestled deep in the Rift Valley that runs down to Africa). Before he takes a step he thrusts his chest forward and his shoulders back like a soldier. The real soldier goes and places a hand on him, paternally almost, and guides him across to the jeep. The boy stands there. Then the soldier lights a cigarette, goes to the cool one in the middle, and puts it in his mouth. He must have asked for it when he heard them pass.

That ten-year-old might be the very kid who threw a stone at the bus in which I was guiding (I am a tour guide by profession) maybe six months ago, a hundred yards south of here by the refugee camp. I saw him running and he looks like him. He had two smaller girls with him. It almost killed us. It didn't hit—it whipped across in front, the size of a softball—but it almost killed us because the driver saw them coming with it and braked and swerved, and if there had been anything else on the road the swerve could have killed us. Over my shoulder I saw them running, laughing, back into the mostly deserted camp. If it had hit, then too it could have killed someone.

He stands at attention facing the jeep like a soldier. My own boy is nine. So let's make him eleven or twelve. But what do you do with him? What do you do with any of them that age? They're just kids, and probably without meaning to be, the moment after they've let the stone go they can turn out to be killers.

And we Israelis will not forget what happened two miles to the north of here a year ago. Some men about the age of the blindfolded ones waited in a banana grove at a bend in the road. When the bus from Tiberias came into view, they lit the wicks on bottles full of gasoline and glue. The bus slowed at the bend, they came forward and threw the bottles, and the fire got inside. The driver opened the doors and everyone made it out except a woman named Rachel and her three small sons. A young soldier heard her cries and went back in. Half-blinded by the smoke, he counted seats to the back of the bus. Then he saw her with two of the children and pulled on her head, but she resisted and cried, "What about my baby? I have another baby here!" He could not stand it any longer, and just barely made it back out himself, counting seats.

The killers in this case were caught—or so the authorities assure us. (The judicial system in the Territories does not inspire confidence.) But firebombs are often thrown. A hundred had been thrown precisely there. They don't usually get inside or catch. Some of these prisoners, sitting now in restful dignity, had possibly thrown firebombs too. They could just as easily have been the killers. And we Israelis cannot get those deaths out of our minds. Even the accident of the woman's name conjures up for us a biblical image which belongs to our essence. Her brother evoked it before the funeral:

> Thus the Lord has said:
> "A voice is heard in Ramah,
> bitter weeping and lamentation—
> Rachel is weeping for her children."

This is Jeremiah 31:15–16, and it goes on:

> *"She will not be comforted for her children,*
> *because they are no more."*
>
> *Thus the Lord has said:*
> *"Keep your voice from weeping,*
> *your eyes from tears;*
> *there is a reward for your labor"—*
> *word of the Lord—*
> *"and they will come back*
> *from the enemy's land."*

This comes from a time when the children of Israel, forced to leave Jerusalem, are walking north toward exile in Babylon. They pass the town of Ramah, near which the matriarch Rachel is buried. (Her grave is not near the Bethlehem of today, where we guides have shown it for centuries.) She sees them from her tomb and weeps. But no, the Lord says, they will return. And they have, twice so far. Some tens of thousands returned out of that Babylonian exile. But then came new conquerors (Greeks, Romans, Arabs, Crusaders). Rachel's children left the land again. And now we have come back again. And now—now this Rachel. This Rachel and her three sons and how many others? And what about Hagar and her children—the more than hundred Arab children killed so far in the intifada? So here we are, the heirs of prophecy, ancient Rachel's children, and we are sitting on Hagar's children, and they are our prisoners, and we . . . I am tempted to say that we too are prisoners. Of history. Of prophecy.

It is unique in history that a people, dispersed among others for centuries, does not politely blend in. No one forced us to keep our identity. On the contrary. In Europe, until the Nazis defined a Jew in racial terms, our persecutors were happy to accept "new Christians" (though still with suspicion). In the Near East and North Africa the door into Islam was open. Yet two thousand years passed and still there we were. Jews. Poverty-stricken, most of us, but Jews. When pogroms broke out in Russia, a million of these Jews—my great-grandparents and grandparents among them—headed for America. A minority sought a more radical solution. They came here.

It is easy with hindsight to accuse them of arrogance. Did they really think they could build a Jewish state when several hundred thousand Arabs, increasing all the time, lived here, worked the land? They saw the Arabs all right, but not as a political force. They persuaded themselves that the Arabs would accept a Jewish state in return for the material benefit it would bring to all.

Wishful thinking. Many of the early Zionists shared in a widespread transformation of consciousness which had begun to take place among oppressed and colonized peoples. Yet they do not seem to have credited the Palestinian Arabs with the capacity for also sharing in it. In fact, they proved to be the catalyst: for every step they took toward achieving a state, Arab political consciousness crystallized in opposition.

Here was an impossible situation: a people, having refused to assimilate, came back out of the mists. A husband, long missing, returned to his remarried wife.

The problem was sovereignty. Where Jews lived, nearby lived Arabs too. This is easy to forget. We see no trace today. We ride through the plains and talk about the "pioneers." But more than three hundred nonpioneering Arab towns and villages have since then disappeared from our midst.

So the problem went deeper than land. Both Jews and Arabs had been dominated for centuries—the Jews in foreign parts, the Arabs here. Now they lived next to each other. Neither people was about to give way.

The UN proposed partition. The Jewish leadership accepted, while pointedly declining to acknowledge the borders. Groups of local Arabs went on the attack.

In the course of the ensuing war, in 1948, more than half of the Palestinians went into exile—or what they call their *nakbah*, catastrophe. If the historian Benny Morris is right (and his is the most comprehensive research we have) the flight did not begin by design. The Jewish forces had a plan, indeed, to destroy hostile villages which dominated the roads and refused to surrender, but they envisioned nothing on the scale of what was to happen. Nor did Arab leaders order their own people out of the way. The event was rather a result of circumstance and timing. The Arabs had created no infrastructure, as the Jews had, to replace the withdrawing British. The latter could no longer promise protection, but until they left, the armies of the Arab states could not join in. It was during this interval (April 1948) that flight became massive. The Jews began to decide on objectives, move troops, and attack. It was exactly the sort of thing which the local Arabs, lacking coordination, could not do. Each neighborhood or village had to fight back on its own. In many places the leaders had already left. There was no general policy about going or staying.

And then came a massacre. A Jewish fringe group massacred the villagers of Deir Yassin near Jerusalem. When the Arab radio played this up, the propaganda backfired, spreading fear.

In Tiberias and Haifa—as soon as it seemed clear that the Jews were winning—the Arabs called a cease-fire, arranged with the British for a peaceful departure, and left. That became an example to others. It became, too, a temptation to the Jewish commanders, who learned how to frighten (by mortars or rumors) whole communities out. Apart from a few big exceptions (Ramle, Lydda), the work could be done without rounding them up and pushing. And so they left, hoping to come back soon: to Lebanon, Syria, and Iraq; to Gaza; to Transjordan; to Nablus, Ramallah, Bethlehem, Hebron—the West Bank of today. And to Jericho.

The boy stands at attention in front of the jeep. A third-generation refugee. I am fairly sure he's the one. Ran back with his sisters into the partly bulldozed camp just to the right beyond the wall where the other prisoners are sitting. The UN is responsible for the camps, and it finally gave the Israelis permission a few years ago to level those huts which were empty. At their busiest, when Jordan ruled here (1948–1967), the ones around Jericho held eighty thousand people: five per room, fifty per toilet, no electricity, one faucet per street. An oven during the summer. And right next door flourished the green, lush oasis, resort town of the sheikhs. Most of the inhabitants fled across the Jordan River during the 1967 war. But this boy's family stayed. There they are still. Now he is a soldier in the intifada.

We Israelis . . . should I say "we," I who immigrated so much later? Well I suppose, in a sense, I inherited the whole history up to that point, its pride and its shame, as a man inherits his father's coat:

cloth, patches and holes. We Israelis took over the roughly two million acres and hundred thousand houses which the Palestinian refugees left behind in 1948. We did not allow them to come back. We made evasive, highly conditioned offers of compensation, on which we never had to deliver. We have arguments to justify this, but they do not wipe out a measure of guilt.

The vast majority of the refugees were innocent people caught in the middle. We try to soothe our conscience with numbers and precedents, but human beings are neither. A dispossessed Jewish refugee from Morocco does not equal a dispossessed Arab refugee from Jaffa, nor is he greater or smaller, for the simple reason that you cannot do arithmetic with human beings. You can only do arithmetic if you bracket their humanity.

We took. We had no choice? Of course we had a choice, many choices. But to try to be just would have made things much harder for us when we were very hard put indeed. The clearing out of the Arabs—their catastrophe—was our "miracle" (Chaim Weizmann). It resolved the impossible situation—the new husband was out—at least for the time being and maybe forever. So we chose to turn our backs on them, even as the Arab states did. Yet conscience is never interested in how hard something is, or in the bad things other people are doing, or in arithmetic.

I live, for example, in Jerusalem, in what was an Arab neighborhood called Dejaneeya just south of the old German Colony—though our block is part of what people call the German Colony today. Those who lived here became refugees and we Jews got the houses. Over the years we expanded them, often adding upper stories. There is hardly a piece of real estate in Israel more valuable today than an Arab house in the German Colony. When someone says "Arab house," a light comes into the eyes, as if he had just named the bearer of ultimate well-being. Curious, because the name "Arab" has such negative connotations otherwise. The same people who do not hesitate to call the Arabs animals, or to call poor craftsmanship Arab work, are very proud to have part of an Arab house. The word "Arab" here is neutralized. It does not refer to people, but rather to a style of building. One somehow puts out of mind, by a little click in which we are all practiced, that it was Arab people who built this way.

Where I live, there was an Arab house with a huge garden, but a contractor turned it into an apartment complex with a parking lot. So I drink coffee on the porch in the morning and look out over the Arab houses, and those who live in them look at our ugly building. I do not usually think about the refugees. No one does anymore. It came as a jolt when a Palestinian bus driver said to me—we had stopped at a traffic light while taking a tour group through the neighboring Greek Colony—"Do you see that over there?" He pointed out a beautiful ornate structure on what is today a busy corner. "That was our house." He did say "was."

A section of my building sits on pillars; cars are parked under our living-room floor. One evening two weeks ago, as I was building a booth for Succoth on the porch, three cars were set on fire. There had been many such torchings already, over a hundred, but it was the first time that such a thing had happened so deep within the Jewish part of Jerusalem. The fire department reached us in time to save the building. Then came Palestinian workers from the West Bank to clean up what Palestinians, presumably, had wrought. The government is to pay for it out of a fund for victims of war. My wife and I worked side by side with the Palestinians, repainting and cleaning, right up to my mobilization day.

Only now as I look at that boy, standing while the soldiers chat, a fantasy plays through my mind: a scion of the Arab family that once lived there comes back to torch the cars under the modern building in order to restore the honor of his people and burn the abomination down. Could be. But my wife has a more prosaic theory. The Arabs were watching us for months. They were working in the buildings on all sides of ours—putting up extra stories, redoing interiors. Only ours provided no employment.

If Israel's modern history were an archeological tell, then you would find, at the level just above that of the 1948 war, a thin fermenting layer of guilt. Well buried.

History moves sluggishly at Jericho. The boy stands. The others sit in their blindfolds. The one in the middle puffs on his cigarette. The father holds his son and looks ever so slightly upward. My fellow inmates paint by the club. The two on a break still sit beside me, chat. The military policewomen pass to and fro between the office and their quarters. Pretty, in this setting, all of them. I avoid following with my eyes, like a boy who does not look at the impossible sweets in the shop window. We are eight hundred feet below sea level. The sun does not blink here even in November.

This compound was originally British, if my guide's eye serves me right, and then Jordanian. For when the smoke lifted in 1948, Jordan occupied the West Bank. The term is misleading. It refers to the bank of the Jordan River, but this "bank" extends up over the central mountain range, both north and south of Jerusalem, in the north almost brushing the Mediterranean. The State of Israel is at one point only nine miles wide. And precisely on that narrow waist of coastal plain between Tel Aviv and Haifa live about two-thirds of the country's Jewish population. Before 1967, therefore, these people had Jordanian tanks and artillery at their backs. Unlike the Syrians on the Golan Heights, who often shelled the Jewish towns just below them during those years, and unlike the Egyptians, who supported guerrilla raids from the Gaza Strip, the Jordanians for the most part loomed quietly. But the danger was clear. A push of nine miles, and they could have divided the Jewish population on the coast. By crossing a similar strip to the south, they could also have cut off Jerusalem.

In the war of June 1967, Israel took the entire West Bank from Jordan as well as Gaza and Sinai from Egypt and the Golan Heights from Syria. Twenty-two years later, only the Sinai has been given back.

The soldier who brought him to the jeep now takes him by the shoulder and turns him around and walks him back the same way, and the boy has his chest out and his shoulders back and marches, and when they get to the wall he doesn't turn around. He just stands there at attention facing it. The soldier says something and touches his shoulder again, and now he turns around. The soldier makes a sign, and the boy squats, leaning against the wall. The soldier returns to his friend. So what was that all about? They were maybe thinking to release him, and then they decided not to. The boy is squatting in the same position he was in before. He is smiling.

It goes across my mind again. How they passed in front of the cool, smoking one. Chest out, shoulders back. Outsoldiering the soldier. He had thrown a rock. He threw a rock at me, my countrymen!

That smile. You will never beat them. They belong to the earth. You can't beat the earth.

What crossed through my mind as they marched across:

"The force that through the green fuse drives the flower. . . ."

At a certain age a boy needs to become a man, a girl to become a woman. One needs to establish and to find an identity for oneself. A young person (I am paraphrasing Erik Erikson) must learn to be most himself where he means most to others—those others, especially, who mean most to him. And what ways are open to them, these blindfolded here? Except maybe for the patient, unblinking father, who holds his patient son in his lap, they can none of them remember a time when they did not live under our occupation. So what channels did we open for them? The sense of identity is made of love and work. What kind of work is open for them? We let no industry develop in the West Bank. There are no future captains of industry here, or designers of buildings, or chemical engineers. There are West Bank universities, it is true, although they have been shut down for two years, and what are they supposed to do with the education they got or were getting there? So then there are no channels for them, no passageways from boyhood to manhood, except the one for which they are sitting blindfolded here. "They can leave. They can find careers elsewhere." Is that your justice? And what about those who can't leave? We Israelis can become, or aim to become, doctors, lawyers, professors, engineers, architects, contractors. They can aim to become, at best, masons, carpenters and house painters, largely under our contractors, and they will also be our street sweepers and our garbagemen. Well, all work should be holy, but there are some jobs for which you have to be a saint to find the holiness, and these are no saintlier than we; these are boys needing to become men. Anybody with drive in him is not going to find his identity working for contractors. So what channels are open to them—except that one for which they sit blindfolded here?

A sense of identity is made of love and work. What about love then? That is not closed to them. They can marry, have children. Many of the young men who can leave do. The young women stay, practically all of them, with the young men who could not leave. So romantic love comes hard—for the young men who find no channels to self-respect and for the young women whose single channel is prescribed and who outnumber and often "outclass" the young men. But suppose love, or the form of love, happens. They bear children. And now comes the decisive thing. These young men, sitting blindfolded before me, grew up watching their parents bend their necks. They resolved that they would never let their own children see them bend their necks like that.

"At this point," writes Freud in *The Interpretation of Dreams* (translated in freedom, one month later):

> . . . *I stumble across a particular youthful experience which even today exerts its power over all these emotions and dreams. I may have been ten or twelve when my father began to take me with him on his walks and reveal to me, in conversation, his views about the things of this world. Once he wanted to show me how much better the times were into which I had come, compared with what he had gone through. He said: "When I was a young man, I went for a walk one Saturday in the streets of your birthplace. I was dressed up and had a new fur cap on my head. Then comes a Christian and with one swipe he knocks my cap into the mud and yells: 'Jew, off the sidewalk!' " "And what did you do?" "I went into the street and picked up the cap," came the calm answer. To me that seemed unheroic on the part of the big strong man who held little me by the hand. Over against this situation, which was so unsatisfactory, I set up another that fit my sensibility better: the scene where Hannibal's father, Hamilcar Barca, makes his son swear before the household altar that he will take revenge on the Romans. Hannibal has had a place in my fantasies ever since.*

We Israelis, by administrative and military means, have been knocking their fathers' hats off for most of their lives. So what do we expect?

"The force that through the green fuse drives. . . ."

They will not bow. A boy must find a way to become a man, a girl to become a woman. No use, in the long run, sending troops against that.

Their parents bowed. Their parents had the memory of King Hussein, who had occupied them for the nineteen years before us. He had brooked no demonstrations. But these blindfolded do not remember the rule of Hussein.

The submissiveness of the fathers once lulled us into thinking that those who live in the West Bank accept our occupation. Troubles, we thought, always had their origins among the PLO and its splinter groups outside. So until December 1987, most of us Israelis had come, against our better knowledge, to accept the occupation as a normal state of affairs. We called it the status quo, and a status quo has by definition something static about it, something which human beings apparently can live with. The picture of the at-home Palestinians was one of a people that was willing to settle for peace, quiet, and comparative well-being. But the sons and daughters were not willing. And when they went into the streets (their own streets), the parents followed. The crowds of them, standing up with stones against armed soldiers, revealed at last the ugly picture to the world: one people, a supposedly democratic people with a strong ethical tradition, sitting on top of another. And now they are trying to shake us off—that is the literal translation of "intifada"—and our leaders continue to regard this uprising as abnormal. It is normal! It is nature itself, and it will not go away. The twenty years of submission—that was the abnormality.

We do not understand that. It will take more than two years to undo the effect of twenty. The Arab workers come each morning to sweep our streets or pick up our garbage or tend our gardens (conceivably the gardens of their parents or grandparents), and they are bent, quiet, they have learned to make themselves invisible. We, the masters, are so used to it that it seems natural. We have no idea therefore of what we are up against in this intifada: not merely a political will, but nature itself, a different nature from what they show us during the day, nature as the push toward being a full human being, nature persistent and irresistible. Perhaps they don't recognize it either for what it is: the force that works in them, upward through the legs and torso and arm that throws the stone. In the blinding glare of this courtyard, they sit blindfolded against the wall and against the metal barricades, except for the one smiling boy, and the father and son looking patiently, ever so slightly upward.

2

MOON OVER JERICHO. A sliver tonight. I can see it from my bed, by the door. I have just finished the first letters to my kids. They will be seeing the moon from Jerusalem. Or no, Benny, the nine-year-old, will be watching TV, the huge earphones on his head so as not to disturb his mother. And Talya, eleven, will be with her friends in the city on a Thursday night, hanging out, playing video games or eating felafel or waiting at the bus stop. Not noting this moon, not thinking of me at the moment. I love her even more for just being there, chattering away, not thinking of me. To a parent, all a child has to do is be.

To me, anyhow. But of course my timing is different. "You missed a generation," my father said on his deathbed. I was thirty-seven when Talya was born. I could almost be her grandfather. This has made a considerable difference, because I was past some of the struggles. I was able to concentrate on her in a way that would not have been possible had I been, say, twenty-seven. But still, I know it's true for younger parents too: when a child is there, the question about the meaning of life loses its force.

And then a day turns up when, to the young man or woman, doing is suddenly important. Where does that come from? Our parents? When mine were dying, I had still achieved nothing, but it didn't matter.

18

Yet I go on trying. Ambition is my curse, distracting me from those I love.

I noticed this the day before I left. I thought I'd probably be going to jail, so I was making it a point to be with the kids. I sat across from my son watching him eat. I gathered him in for a while, but then my mind wandered off to an essay I had written. I pulled my attention back to him. I had almost missed what he was asking—the avocado, would it make him big?—and so it went, back and forth, like a camera changing focus. Of course, if he had *appeared* in the full importance which he has for me, my mind would not have wandered. We humans seem to have a problem with full presence. But let me not universalize. I for one require a certain distance—a certain absence—in order to feel someone else's importance. The distance, for example, between Jericho and Jerusalem, as relayed by the moon.

It shines nowhere else so brightly. The name Jericho hints at this. In biblical Hebrew, a dialect of Canaanite, the city is called *yereekho*, and the principal word for moon is *yarayakh*. Nowhere else is the sky so clear when the wind blows from the west, as it mostly does. For we are deep in the earth's crust here, thirty-two hundred feet below Jerusalem, which tops the mountain range west of us. In winter, clouds blow in from the sea. They let out their water as they climb the west side of the range, then break up over the heat of this valley. They form again on the other side, on the heights of Jordan.

Thus we have a spell of exceeding clarity. As if God had taken a rag and polished the moon. It is the white of wet ivory, a tusk dipped in some African river. I shall be glad to see it at the full, and I suppose I'll be here long enough. I don't know if it's waxing or waning. That's the trouble with being so out of touch with the Hebrew calendar. Orthodox Jews know exactly where they are in relation to the moon.

I could ask Yigal, the Orthodox one on the lower bunk across from me. But I'm afraid to embarrass him. I suspect he's not really Orthodox. He wears a white, gold-braided yarmulke which does not quite settle on his head, the sort that Christian tourists purchase in souvenir shops. So I suspect he ran out and bought the paraphernalia because he figured it would lower the work load. His prayer shawl and gold-edged, touristy prayerbook lie upon the black metal surface of what once was a sink in the corner near his bed. They are obliged to give him time to pray. And Jewish prayer, especially the morning service, can take a long time.

Yigal has blond hair and a poor wisp of beard—an excuse not to shave, I think—and dull, shifty green eyes. He is tall and skinny, frail even. He was the first prisoner I talked with. He was alone stretched out on his bunk reading a newspaper when I came into the cell, newly walletless and watchless. I said hello and he grunted a return.

"Where should I sleep?"

He nodded toward a lower bunk across from him.

"That's on vacation."

I sat on it, and the thing sank about a foot. My God. I lifted the mattress and saw that there were supposed to be hooks to hold the springs to the metal frame, but a good third of them were missing. Everybody must have raided this bed for hooks. I could maybe shove my duffel bag under it to boost it on one side. But how could I ever sleep on that? Something like that, as elementary as that, I hadn't thought of. It had all sounded very good when I had thought of Dostoevsky saying every writer should do time in jail, or when Thoreau said, "Under a government which imprisons any unjustly, the true place for a just man is also a prison," or when Richard Lovelace wrote from jail, "Stone walls do not a prison make, / Nor iron bars a cage." But bedsprings do a bed make, dammit. That's dualism, all that about how they may torture the body but the spirit is happy. On that bed, that first one (which thank God I did not in the end have to sleep on), it would have been the extremest dualism. Fakirism. And all that in Thoreau, about how they thought they were keeping him behind prison walls, but they couldn't, because that was just the body, and his mind was free. Dualism, dualism! But didn't I just write to my daughter, "I am one of the freest men in the Israeli army . . . "? And it's true. I feel a definite lightness. It infiltrates, it bears me up. For years I've wanted to express my feelings about the situation. I wrote articles, I demonstrated, I argued, but none of it did much good. Now the army has shown me the way. The army has made it very simple. My head is as clear as that sliver of moon.

Maybe I could have slept on the hookless bed. But I shall not now offer to exchange. The jailers brought in a new cot, with springs and hooks intact, and placed it by the door. A single, not like the others.

They didn't say it was for me. They just said, "We're getting some new boys." I was quick enough to shove my bag under it. There's altruism for you. And of course I don't smoke, and the others all do, and it's by the door. And from it I can see the moon, this visible link to the outside world, to the life before and after, to all the faces that ever beamed down on me.

Next day. Cooks' room.

It is 10:30 A.M., I have been told. The jailers took my watch. I remember a Faulkner character who gave his son a watch and said, "I give it to you not that you may remember time, but that you might forget it now and then for a moment and not spend all your breath trying to conquer it." But for me it is part of the great unburdening not to have one. A watch implies the responsibility to plan one's time. And here I do not have that responsibility. Time is not at my disposal. I wake up when they wake us, usually at five. I shave and get dressed as I am supposed to and go to breakfast with the other eight. We eat with the military police and the reservists who check bags at the Allenby Bridge. Then I walk through a gutted building to another kitchen and dining room, which belongs to a different reserve unit, the one that fights the intifada. Here I wash dishes and help the cooks. I know that seems odd. We are in the West Bank. I am imprisoned for refusing to serve in the West Bank, and here I am, serving in the West Bank.

Maybe I'm wrong to wash their dishes. I am a man of conscience, but I am not, by impulse, a good man. When a situation takes me by surprise, the baser parts of my character are likely to sway me. The draft notice did not take me by surprise. I had known for two years that it might come and that I would refuse. But it had never occurred to me that I might be shipped off as a prisoner to Jericho—to the West Bank. For a few moments, in fact, after they disburdened me of wallet and watch, I sat alone and the question came, "Should I work here?" If I refused they would add days to my term. And then I remembered my political position about the Jordan Valley. (I cannot envision a peace agreement in which Israel does not retain some kind of presence in it.) I let that sway me.

If I really think it through, I should not work here until there is a peace settlement.

And yet . . . am I not being too finicky after all, too principled, too pure?

Thus it goes, the argument with myself, as I stand over the sink and wash their dishes. Blue dishes for dairy. Orange for meat. There is a sink for the dairy, a sink for the meat. There are racks for the dairy, racks for the meat. There are pots for the dairy, pots for the meat. Those are our kosher laws.

But Time is the topic now. Watchlessness. So I show up in their kitchen early and wash the blue breakfast dishes as they bring them in. That is a responsibility. Then I help the cooks peel potatoes or cucumbers for lunch. That is a responsibility. Some of the meat pots are ready, and I wash them in the meat sink. A responsibility. Then I ask what time it is, and they tell me, "Ten-thirty. Go take a rest in our room." The great advantage of resting in their room is that I don't have the jailers standing over me. Strictly speaking, it is forbidden. This whole arrangement with their kitchen is something special, something not quite kosher perhaps. One of the reserve regiment's commanders is good friends with someone in the police, so he said to him: "Give me a prisoner." We are not supposed to associate with the reservists at all. I felt uncomfortable at first about going to their room. But then I came up with a good reason: being watchless, I have to rest with them in order to know when it is time to get up and go back.

We eat from 11:30 to 12:00. I wash the orange dishes and the meat pots until 2:30. Then there is a long rest in their room. At 4:30 we have dinner: blue dishes again. After that I go back through the gutted building, suffer through an inspection, and then I can read or write or sleep.

I like the narrow definition of responsibilities. I have just enumerated most of mine. We must also remember to say "commander" to the jailers. We must fold our blankets in a certain manner. We must have our hats on when not under a roof. We wear the same work uniform as regular soldiers, but we alone must wear the hats. This has quickly become automatic. The hat is like a bloated pancake on a string. I throw it on or off with aplomb upon crossing a threshold.

All this is a great lightening. Not like having to build an experience for a tour group. Not like having to educate a child. Not like having to answer letters or write a book. The hours of break time arrive like gifts. It's time that you don't have coming to you, because time is not at your disposal. And so it's not that you're obliged to do anything worthwhile. Undeserved hours are sweeter.

With so-called freedom comes an illusion that the day is mine to plan. I forget that I came from nothing and can drop dead any minute—that time is not, never has been, never will be my own. The wristwatch, by which one views the rest of the day in advance, is an accessory to this forgetting. That Faulkner character was right in a sense: a watch helps one forget time—real time, the time that is not one's own. They took my watch and gave me time.

So too I avoid putting day headings on these entries. I don't want to count the days. It's getting toward Sabbath, I know that, and I suppose if I really thought about it I would realize it was Friday. But I would find it oppressive, I'm sure, to think of the time that lies ahead of me. For of course I'd much rather have my kids jumping all over me like a baboon or a lion or any major beast of the jungle. To imagine a sum of days, say, fifteen more days, would be to burden myself unnecessarily, when all that is required is to get through this one. Besides, from all that I hear, the day of liberation will be that of reimprisonment.

For the others liberation is really that. No one else is here for my reason. They count the days indeed. They ask one another and me: "When are you getting out?" They scratch calendars onto the walls and put another X each evening. And not only the prisoners. The reserve soldiers too. I am lying here in the cooks' room, the kitchen crew are sacked out around me, and just about every other bed has a calendar on the wall above it. Of course they are most of them old and fully X'd. The reservists come in and go out together, so they need only one calendar per room per service. The present calendar is half X'd through, eight empty boxes to go. Not on the wall, but in the mind, the boxes become longer as they get toward the end.

One of them, a cook they call Hanina—it's his last name, meaning

Mercy—said to me, putting his hand on my shoulder, "It will pass." "Everything will pass," I answered, "but what good does that do?" To which he merely smiled. But then others started to say it: "This too will pass." "It's not so awful," I said. And they say it of themselves, "The time passes." And my fellow prisoners, kids all, lie back on their bunks and cry, "Oh, let it pass!" Finally, last night, it got on my nerves. We were lying around waiting for sleep, and one of them moaned, "Let it pass, O God!" So I sat up and said—they like riddles and such—"Suppose God gave you a choice. How long are you in for?" "Sixteen more days." "All right. God says: Either I erase these sixteen days from your life, and you live sixteen days less, or you live the sixteen days in this prison. Which do you choose?" They all listened very solemnly, and they all agreed, "Life is always better." (They are kids after all.) So I said, "Then why do you want the time to pass?"

That has stopped them momentarily. But maybe they are right. "Doing time" is the slang for what we are doing. As if there were nothing but time.

And time by itself is burdensome. The mind runs in neutral, has nothing to feed on. So if you are clever, and if you have been brought up to traipse around with books, you invent some task which will connect you to the world of love and work. You keep, for example, a diary. But the diary creates obligations. And one day, trying to capture the whole experience, you realize you haven't time.

WE ARE GOING to lunch. I dozed a little. But getting up off the bunk just now, I reached (out of long habit) to pat my pocket, my wallet, and it isn't there. I panicked for a moment.

3

Same day. Afternoon break time. Cooks' room.

FEWER PEOPLE NOW. Most have gone home for Sabbath. Even four of the eight prisoners got leave for the weekend. That's like two days off your sentence: Friday afternoon, Sabbath, Sunday morning.

One named Dubi told me that I should not expect Sabbath leave. "In our case it's an act of mercy. But you—if you need mercy so much, you didn't need to come here. And you're famous. Your name's been in the papers and on TV. You think they want your neighbors to see you while your unit's in the field?"

HERE IS the story of how I wound up here.

First comes the draft notice, upon which is written, "Area of Judea and Samaria."

I go to see my commander.

"I refuse to support what we are doing in the Territories."

Dark and burly, he bends to the side, glancing past three dark and burly officers toward his secretary at the end of the table, and it seems to me that there is between them a silent rollicking laughter. Finally he recovers, straightens, settles.

"Stephen!" he reads my name from the draft notice. It is, of course, a foreign one here. I wanted to change it to Shai, meaning "gift," but my mother told me not to. There was a time in America when lots of Jewish couples gave their children Christian names like Stephen and Richard. The Israelis have fun with it. The only Stephen they know is Steve Austin, the six-million-dollar man, and lots of them call me Steve Austin. It gives them a chance to practice their English. But this commander takes particular relish in my name, I think, because it signifies that I am a spoiled American, and cannot therefore have the slightest idea of the mentality in this part of the world. My refusal belongs elsewhere. A little reality—and it will dissolve. Americans have a reputation for being soft. "American soap," the Israelis call us. There are three billion dollars in foreign aid to prove it.

He shakes his head. He does not look at me but at the piece of paper. "The notice stands," he says. "The place remains the place. You are to report on schedule. If you still want to refuse then, the army has procedures." And now he bends back away from me again. "However! If on that day it appears that I have filled my requirements in the Territories, I will arrange something for you in Jerusalem."

"I hope you will remember me," I say.

"I will remember you," he says.

Comes the day, two months after that.

I arrive seven minutes late. The taxi driver insisted on picking up an old lady at her house. Having inquired and heard my position, he told me that I would be going to jail. "It's a possibility," I said, Bogart style. "And then you'll get another notice in your hand to the same place." "It's a possibility." When I pulled my huge duffel bag out over her knees, the old lady spoke for the first time, with a push in her voice—she had mustered her courage: "May God be with you." I was surprised. She looked at me. I would not have expected support from a stranger in this oddball thing I was about to do. "Thank you," I said. I did not exactly believe in that God. There had been too many innocent people with whom he had not been. But I believed in the old lady, who believed in that God.

Seven minutes late. It bothers me. I know from experience that people will still be arriving two hours from now. But I want everything to be by the book, so that my disobedience will be clear and clean.

Schneller, the base is called. A German Protestant missionary of that name founded an orphanage here in the mid-nineteenth century. The Turks had been ruling for more than three hundred years, and to them the land was Lower Syria. The arriving soldier-to-be, therefore, is confronted by a building that looks like an illustration from a tattered copy of Brothers Grimm, with the faint traces of an inscription reading *Syrisches Waisenhaus*, and nearby another: *Jesu, lieber Meister, erbarme dich unser* ("Jesus, dear master, have mercy on us"). The extremists among our Orthodox might take exception to being greeted thus, but I don't think they ever enter Schneller, since they have student deferments until a hoary age.

There are bell towers and Old Testament quotes too chiseled over the doors in Gothic script, and upon each building the name of the German city whose Protestants financed it: Koeln, Stuttgart, Petersburg, Halle. The modern asphalt goes up to these old buildings, as if it would invade and undermine them and clip them off. Along the stretches of asphalt appear wooden signs, couplets in black-stenciled Hebrew, the elegance and pithy wisdom of which are scarcely to be rendered: SOLDIER! HEALTH IS THE GAIN/ WHEN YOU KEEP YOURSELF CLEAN! A THOUGHT FOR TOMORROW/ SAVES AN OCEAN OF SORROW. WHEN EQUIPMENT GOES TO WASTE/ IT'S YOUR UNIT YOU'VE DISGRACED! This was the language of the Psalms.

Given the buildings and the Hebrew signs, one has the odd impression of a quaint German city which has been emptied of its burghers and occupied by an army of Jews, as in a nightmare of Josef Goebbels.

The buildings are crumbling. Stone sits upon stone, but bulges here and there forebode collapse. The drainpipes are askew. Some of the tile roofs are three-quarters gone, bare innards exposed to the heavens. Occasionally, near the entrance, the asphalt stops short and there are the remains of a pitiful attempt at a garden, long since given up. But on the left as you go in there is a duck pond about two yards square, with an actual mother duck and her babies flipping water from their tails, and a bit of green grass around it, and a bench. These are the only cheerful beings in sight. The duck pond must be the brainchild of the base commander, an attempt to change the atmosphere, but so patent a ploy that it serves rather to acknowledge how depressing the place is. A few droopy soldiers guard the entrance, open the gate for authorized vehicles, check your identity papers, wait for their time to pass. On the insides—although I do not at first go inside, but I know from experience—there is the smell of damp decaying plaster, the latest flakes still on the floor. The fresh-faced soldiers, girls and boys—boys some of whom have been assigned to the offices here, rather than to fighting units, because their fathers or brothers were killed in our wars—tack up pictures of movie stars or singers, and the plaster crumbles under the tacks as the generations of soldiers, stars, and singers age and pass.

A guard directs me where I am to go. I am full of energy for the ordeal. The huge bag weighs nothing on my shoulder. I fight the depressing effect of Schneller by reminding myself that it is, after all, a place which has war as its central concern. It would be a kind of obscene euphemism if it looked like an Ivy League campus.

I round a curve and there they are, only a few of course at this appointed hour, behind metal barricades which have been set up to enclose the yard between the reserves building and some warehouses. An opening is left in the barricades, and on the inside stand a few officers. *Shalom!* they say to me. Warmly. As if they knew me. Each makes a point of saying it. Eye contact. *Shalom,* I answer. Surprised. Awed. How nice of them. A welcoming committee. It seems I have entered a gate from which there is no going out.

> *You're in the army now,*
> *You're not behind a plow;*
> *You'll never get rich,*
> *By digging a ditch,*
> *You're in the army now;*
> *Go to your left, right, left;*
> *Go to your left, right, left.*

I go to my left and sign up at the table. Now begins the long wait.

Others come in. They all seem to know each other. I know no one. Apparently a mistake has been made. My file got shuffled into the wrong group. These are all longtime Israelis, veterans of former wars. And each of them has a little bag, the size of an airline bag, which you can shove under the seat in front of you.

Yet no one laughs at my bag. No one seems to notice it or me.

Three hours later I am standing there in uniform with two huge bags, the new one full of equipment, and an Uzi submachine gun. The dark and burly commander did not remember me. When I reminded him of my position he did not have a fit of laughter. He said I should get equipment. So here I am. Buses have pulled up, and there must have been an order to board, because someone said, "Come on, gang!" and there was a surge toward the first bus. As soon as it was full it moved forward a few yards and stopped, and the second has moved up and is filling. I have resisted so far the natural pull to get on. It seems the simplest thing in the world, to get on a bus. And thus it might happen. I might so innocently get on. No one has said where they are going. I haven't even heard an explicit order to get on. It is as simple and natural, therefore, as every previous step: handing in my draft notice, filling out, for the umpteenth time, the form for my address and phone number, changing into uniform, signing for the Uzi—and now getting on the bus. The simplest thing in the world, and I could find myself, an hour or two from now, exactly where I do not intend to go. By default. Just as by default I came into this life, so by default I could wind up in the West Bank.

Officers are running to and fro, shouting at people: "Why aren't you in uniform?" "Why aren't you on the bus?" But no one shouts at me. I am invisible. The yard is still populated. A few are even still arriving. There is a big crowd in the entrance to the reserves building; it is the line for the doctor. An old woman comes, someone's mother, and makes a fuss, and is refused, and starts crying. The officers are embarrassed but hard. Yosi—for that is my commander's name—is about to walk by me, and I ask, "Do I get on the bus?"

"If someone tells you to get on the bus, you get on the bus. If no one tells you to get on the bus, you don't get on the bus."

"No one has told me anything," I say.

He keeps on walking.

I look at the buses. They have almost filled the second one now. The yard is beginning to empty.

Finally there is someone I know. Danny, the father of a friend of my daughter's. I know he is in my unit. So there has been no mistake.

"Come on, Steve, let's get on." He wants company.

"I don't get on till someone tells me specifically to get on."

He nods, smiles. Goes to the second bus.

It seems so contrary and untoward a thing, what I am doing, or rather not doing. Freakish even. The orderly succession that begins with the *"Shalom"* of the officers and would end by landing me in the Territories is rather like a wave, a great wave that carries everybody to shore, and there they are onshore, looking at me from the bus windows, two and a half busfuls now. What is this strange figure there, flailing against the wave? There is a saying: "You spit on the army, the army drowns you." Perhaps they are thinking that. Or: Who is this misfit, this miscreant? Doesn't belong to our unit. Never seen him before. Nor will Danny say he knows me. All kinds of strange types in the world, even here, this oddball. Those waiting for the doctor they understand. But someone who defiantly stands there, showing no limp, seems selfishly assertive, exalting himself, for whatever principles, like a raised fist toward the State of Israel.

There is no seam in this process, no identifiable place of which one can say, "Here is the line." And so I draw the line. That is the hardest part. To assert oneself that much, to say, "Here, quite arbitrarily, I stop and draw it." I decide, for my purposes, that the buses are going to the West Bank, and I will not get on.

The third bus is filling. Those in the first bus have sat there for at least an hour.

The truth is, I don't feel the push of that wave. I am rather like a sieve. I feel that it is there, but it goes right through me. If I were younger, then I would feel it, and to resist would be an act of courage. I would think: Surely all those guys can't be wrong. They must know what they are doing. Why should I trust my half-informed opinion against the weight of all the experienced, heavy-jowled wisdom sitting unquestioning on the buses? No doubt there are aspects that I haven't thought of. I have lived in this country only ten years, after all. I have fought in none of its wars. I should go this once, and see what it's like, and there I'll have time to think about it.

I have a tendency to credit any roughly normal-looking stranger with wisdom, until it is proved otherwise. But I have lived long enough—and it has been proved otherwise often enough—that I have learned to correct for this tendency as for an optical illusion.

I stand, therefore, amused. It is an ancient scene. One alone against a multitude. If I were to look with inner vision, I know I would find myself in good company, on the shoulders of giants. But it is amusing that I, little Stevie Langfur from Cedarhurst, Long Island, who did in the privacy of his home, and sometimes secretly in public places, things of which any decent human being would be rightly ashamed, should nonetheless be granted the honor of playing this part here.

Yet these men are also old enough, have suffered enough in life, from a woman or a friend or a child, that to resist the army and pay the price, for conscience's sake, is comparatively no great matter. Have been riddled through enough that to be a sieve against the wave is no great matter. And surely among these hundred and fifty or so—I know it from the surveys—there must be fifty who believe that what we are doing in the West Bank is unnecessary and therefore immoral. And among these fifty, there must be twenty or ten or five or three or two— two more than I!—who feel as strongly about it as I do. So why does no one else think to draw the line here? Why am I standing here alone?

Yet I can understand why—or partly. Two considerations, financial and moral, work together. These are old-time Israelis. They don't have the security of well-stocked families abroad. Both husband and wife work, and if they are careful they manage to make it through the month. During reserve service the National Insurance pays the husband's salary, but not if he's in prison. (The movement called Yesh Gvul— "There is a limit"—helps the families of soldiers who take the course that I am taking, but few are aware of that.) Another thing: one doesn't know how long the screw will turn, and when they finally stop sending you back to prison and give you an assignment you can accept, there's that time too. What employer will put up with so indeterminate an absence, especially if he is against refusal, as practically everyone is? Or if you have your own business, your clients will need to go elsewhere.

And then, as the clincher, comes the moral consideration: I should go to the West Bank in order to restrain the violent ones among our soldiers, the trigger-happy, the beaters, the bone breakers. I should go there to save Arab lives.

There is truth in this. The Palestinians are thankful for the kind ones.

And if these two considerations are not enough, there are others: we are a democracy after all. As a citizen one can vote. One can demonstrate. But as a soldier, one must obey the orders of a government which represents the will of the majority.

So one may be totally against the occupation, and even in favor of a Palestinian state in the West Bank and Gaza, but one gets on the bus.

In my case the financial pressure is not there. I work for a Palestinian tour agency. I guide Christians through the Holy Land.

On the other hand, people do refuse, so why not these? In the two years of intifada ninety Israelis have stood as I do now. Most were under financial pressure. Despite this and despite the moral argument and the point about democracy, they chose jail. There have probably been others for whom the army (which is sensibly wary) changed the assignment. And there must be thousands like those who are waiting for the doctor. The number of refusers is small, but we are a small country.

It is well to remember too that until a few years ago our army was something holy for most of us. It had become a symbol, perhaps the principal symbol, of our resurgence as a people after the Holocaust. In moments of great anxiety it brought such swift deliverance that it took on a biblical aura. Through it we tasted again—or thought we did—the ancient miracles, the parting of the waters, the drowning of Pharaoh's army, the tumbling of the walls. There is no healing, no consolation ever, when a soldier falls in battle. But there was a time, even without consolation, when one could say that he had fallen for something meaningful. To his family one could say that the abysmal and surely endless pain they were feeling was the strength of their bond to him, and that this bond was part of the bond which bound our whole people, the bond for the sake of which he had fought and risked and fallen, and that the whole people would always be with them in their loss. And it was so. I discovered this in 1972, when I was here as a student, on the day after our athletes were slaughtered at the Munich Olympics. The mourning was not only in the media. It was in every face, in every back, in every word. That's when I discovered that there was a community here, a wholeness, a being-with-one-another which could face those deaths and in its sorrow be more powerful than death, be, in very sadness, an affirmation of life over death. With that kind of connection, who would refuse the army? It was practically unheard of.

And now look at us. In Lebanon the army lost any glimmer of holiness. It was—after its first few days—a different kind of war for us. It was not a war to defend our very life. It was rather politics by another means, an attempt to fulfill an ex-general's vision of a new order in the Middle East. And now another unnecessary war: this futile attempt to suppress the intifada. The distance between the men on the buses and me is the rift that has opened up within our people. Our brokenness shows in many places, but nowhere so strongly as in the fact that ninety of us so far, in the two years of the intifada, have refused and gone to jail—a thing unheard of! unheard of!—and that I too stand here, not picking up my bags, not moving toward the third bus.

There are, in fact, a few others standing about, but not for my reason apparently. A group of officers, including Yosi, has been going around visiting them one by one. Each becomes the focus of a conference. Then the soldier picks up his army bag and his airline bag and his Uzi and moves either to the line for the doctor or to the third bus, and the conference changes venue. Mopping up.

"What about you?" Gruffly. A lone officer from the buses behind me.

"I do not go to the Territories."

He is tall, kindly-looking, with a wrinkled face. He has put on gruffness for the occasion.

"You can go to Bethlehem. With my bus."

"Bethlehem is in the Territories." I have to muster my courage and make it clearer. "I refuse to go to the Territories. On grounds of conscience." This is a slogan, a category. It will register.

"There's no such thing as refusing to go to the Territories. You are refusing an order."

"So I'm refusing an order."

Then suddenly he melts:

"I respect your opinion."

And he goes away. I am left to ponder this.

The conference moves toward me. They are talking about me. The kindly one joins them.

"I respect your opinion," he repeats in their hearing.

Yosi: "I understand the issue of conscience." He looks down at me through his sunglasses. A large man with an intelligent air, a certain personal force. These sayings—"respect your opinion," "issue of conscience" (unexpected from the mouths of officers)—are also mere slogans. It is not the living man who talks in them. When surprised by something basic, we are reduced to slogans.

"As I told you in our interview two months ago, I am ready to serve anywhere in the State of Israel and in all of Jerusalem." Prepared text.

"Where do you live?"

"In the German Colony."

"Where's that?" he asks the others. "I'm weak in Jerusalem."

"South," I say. "Near the railroad station."

Perhaps he wants to arrange a night watch for me on my block.

"You can be in Bethlehem!"

All approve. He has solved it.

"Bethlehem is not part of the State of Israel, and it is not part of Jerusalem."

He was thinking that I might just want to be near home. Conscience and all.

"Give him Mount Gilo," he says to the kindly one.

"Now wait! I can't promise him Mount Gilo."

The kindly one does not understand, I am sure, but this is a trick. The idea is to persuade him to give me Mount Gilo, and I am supposed to accept with relief. Only during the bus ride, after we have passed the Jerusalem neighborhood called "Gilo," will I, ignorant American soap, begin to learn the difference between it and Mount Gilo. The latter is a Jewish settlement in the West Bank; it looks down on the Jerusalem neighborhood. (This neighborhood is also in the West Bank, but after the Six-Day War the government declared it to be part of Jerusalem, in which—all of which—I have stated my willingness to serve.) Once I am sitting in the guardhouse of Mount Gilo, I'll be ashamed to say what a fool I was. How could I claim to know enough to refuse the army, if I don't know the difference between Gilo and Mount Gilo? Guarding the settlement gate, chatting with the women, sipping coffee and munching homemade cake, I'll see how pleasant and harmless and interesting it all is.

"Mount Gilo," I say, "is in the Territories. Look"—with a gesture of helplessness now—"whether it's Bethlehem or Mount Gilo or Hebron or Maon, a border is a border. There is a border." In Hebrew, Yesh Gvul.

He removes the sunglasses.

"You know, this means jail."

"I know."

"You're ready?"

"I hope so."

He calls someone over. Decision taken.

"Make out a"—and he says a number—"for this man."

Man? Already a man?

The fellow, short, thin, and bald, shakes his head and says mournfully to me, "You need this?"

The conference has moved away. I give my name and the bald fellow moves away. I look down at the two bags. So there will be no alternative arrangement in Jerusalem. It is done. I am going to jail.

I sit down on my own bag. Noon. I have been on my feet without noticing it for five hours. Should I pull out Faulkner? Should I finally read? I do not.

The first two buses drive away.

A group of officers. One is glaring at me. It is the first look of hatred I have encountered. A large man with short-cropped red hair. But the eyebrows are thick and wild. Bright flames. From beside him another, dark and deeply lined—we are middle-aged men here—calls me. I rise and walk toward him, avoiding the redhead's eyes.

"Prepare your soul," says the wrinkled one, "for a trial."

"I think my soul is prepared."

That is all. Apparently this is something he is required to say.

"Now?"

"No. We'll call you. A few minutes."

I go back and sit down. "Prepare your soul." In Hebrew it sounds quite natural. "Prepare yourself soulwise" would be a literal rendering. So what am I supposed to do? Think grave thoughts? Go over my arguments? I have lived with the grave thoughts and the arguments for years.

The third bus is half full. It is waiting for those whom the doctor does not discharge. And it is waiting, theoretically, for me.

The wrinkled one comes. It is time.

"After me," he says.

He disappears into the crowd that has filled up the hallway in front of the doctor's room. How am I to do this? Perhaps he expects me to leave the bags down here. Well, I won't. I stand, thrice widened, the Uzi slung from my neck, before the solid wall of the supposedly sick.

"Excuse me!"

Not even a glance. Invisible. There is nowhere for them to move anyhow. This is a curious kind of waiting. Normally people try to sneak ahead in line. But here the hope is that the third bus will pull away before one's turn comes. Thus there is a kind of curious restraint, a pale, sweating lethargy. These men are careful each of his place in order not to go in prematurely. They will not part for me. That would shuffle whatever complex order they are keeping track of. I put down my bags.

Suddenly a vibration, a quiver in that mound. It is my wrinkled officer, cursing as he shoves and squeezes. He is spewed out.

"Where the hell are you?"

I bend and lift the bags.

"Leave them here."

"I will not leave them here." There is such definiteness in my voice that he doesn't argue. He takes the army bag and hoists it above his head—I take my duffel bag and do the same—and he simply throws himself against the wall until it parts (Nachshon, think I: there is a legend that the Red Sea would not part until one man leaped in in the faith that it would, and that was Nachshon). And one after the other, he shouting, I excusing, a groundhog and a snake, we wend a way through the rooted bodies, past the dull unsurprised faces, my co-refusers, gray refusers (when the mobilization is for service in Jerusalem, not only is there no line for the doctor, there is no doctor), then up through and over those on the stairs, up to the first landing, and it is free. They do not want to be visible from the offices.

Nachshon tells me to put the bags down outside the door. I don't want to. If mine is stolen, I'll be stuck in Atlit without long underwear. It'll be all right, he insists. I picture myself raising a fuss, being carted off without my underwear. What is his "all right" worth once it's gone? Can I wrap myself in his "all right"? Will it keep me warm?

"Give me your weapon."

This I am glad to get rid of. I haven't the faintest idea how to use it. I last had an Uzi in my hands six years ago for maybe four hours of my life.

"When you go in, you will salute. To every question you will answer 'Yes, commander' or 'No, commander.' If you are acquitted, you will salute and leave with me. If you are found guilty, you are not to salute. Do you have a hat?"

"Yes."

"Put it on."

I dig it out of my pocket and put it on. My heart is pounding. All this formality. Should have prepared my soul.

"What about my bag?"

"I told you it'll be all right."

"Will you watch it?"

"No one will touch it."

It is dark brown. It is lying under the army bag. But it is so heavy. Anyone stealing it would have to take it down through the crowd at the doctor's office.

I am led to an inner door.

"Not yet," he says.

It opens. I peek through. There is a small hall, and another open doorway, and there at the desk of Yosi's secretary, at the far end, sits the redhead from the yard. He is writing.

"I forget when I am supposed to salute."

"You salute when you go in, and again if you are freed."

"Like in the movies?"

He looks puzzled. I am serious. In my three weeks of training no one ever taught me. So now, by way of rehearsal, I make an imitation of American war movies.

"Like that?"

He nods and blushes and glances around.

A smart-alecky–looking kid comes out. He has just been tried.

"Wait here and I'll call you."

My escort goes in, exchanges a word with the judge, then steps back, turns sideways, pulls himself to attention, and commands:

"The soldier will enter!"

A last glance at my brown bag in the hallway and I enter. Stop.

Snap my heels together and salute. I shouldn't have snapped my heels together. I have combined the American and the Nazi sides out of World War II movies.

"Name?"

"Stephen Langfur, commander."

"Number?"

I give my number.

"Do you want to be tried by me?"

And here he looks up for the first time. Boring through. Hating. I don't quite understand the question. Do I have a choice of judges? Perhaps if I say yes he'll be nice.

"Yes, commander."

He writes.

"When did you last do reserve duty?"

"In September last year, commander."

He writes.

"Where were you stationed?"

"In Jerusalem, commander."

"And before that?"

"Before that nothing, commander."

"Nothing?"

He looks at me in disbelief. He asks:

"How long have you been in this country?"

"Ten years."

"And in ten . . . "

"Commander."

" . . . years you have done reserve duty only once?"

"I did training after three years, commander. Then they called me to a course and canceled it. The next year they called me to a course and disqualified me because of my glasses. Then for two years they didn't call me. Commander. Then they called me and said they didn't need me. Then my father was sick in the States and they postponed it and then never called me. I always reported when I was called. Commander. I never tried to get out of it, commander."

"You are charged with refusing an order. What order?"

"To go to the Territories, commander."

He writes something. It goes on and on. It is perhaps the decision.

Finally he puts down the pen, leans forward over the form, looks up at me, and says softly, "Why?"

This I have not expected. After all, what difference can it make, why? Am I really supposed to persuade him? And now I feel at a disadvantage—because I have to do this in Hebrew, and because I am standing while he is sitting, and because of the tension of ceremony.

"It is immoral for one people to govern another, without the consent of the governed. Commander."

I should leave it at that. But of course it seems so unreasonable. We can't just pull out. I don't want to be a goddamned lily-white do-gooder bleeding-heart idealist. I say:

"There was a time when we had no other choice, because there was no one to talk to." Slogans. The old phrases. No one persuades anyone. No one can hear anymore, because the minute you push the button of a slogan, everyone knows in advance that you have nothing new to say. My voice doesn't feel like it's coming from my own body. It comes from a radio installed in my mouth. "But for years there've been people to talk to, and we've done nothing. That changes the whole picture." I can't help it. "The moment we can do something to end the occupation, and we don't do it, it becomes immoral. Excuse me that my Hebrew is so bad. Commander."

"I have no problem with your Hebrew. Do you know what we're asking you to do?"

"I heard a rumor, to guard Jewish settlements near Hebron."

"To guard Jews!" he bawls up at me. "Not settlements! Jews!"

Well, what the hell are they doing there? I want to ask, but I do not, for I do not, after all, want to antagonize him more. He is glaring at me. Such eyebrows. Crusader. As when I grew a mustache once, and it was red, and my aunt Gertrude said, "That's a Crusader coming out above your upper lip." There was no one then to guard Jews.

"We are not asking you to kill Arabs. You don't have to dirty your hands. You go to a settlement. You get a gate. It's your responsibility for a few hours a day. If you come up against Arabs, it'll be Arabs who are trying to get in through your gate and throw grenades or take hostages. Or do you think terrorists ought to be protected?"

He awaits an answer.

"No, commander."

"No, so then you should go and sit in the gate and protect Jews. We'll forget all about this."

He has lifted his pen. He is poised to release me. I am confused. Defend Jews! Images come to mind, in black and white. Of course Jews should be defended! I have no position left. I forget what my position was. I am grasping for a wisp.

"If you will allow me so much time, commander, the truth is, I am not so much in favor of the policy of the settlements either."

"Do you think we should just leave those Jews undefended?"

"If we were doing all we could, and the Palestinians were the ones saying No, then I'd be willing to go."

He leans back, shakes his head, looks at me quizzically. For the first time without that hatred.

"But there *are* negotiations going on. All the time. Under the table. We've made a peace initiative. Are you putting yourself and the army to all this trouble because you're not satisfied with the *pace* of the negotiations?"

I feel really stupid. After the first few slogans, it seems, I have nothing to say.

"Yeah, sure I'm not satisfied. Commander. We're acting as if it's a card game and we have to hold the cards close to our chest. If Labor had won the last elections . . . " Now this is really stupid, but having started, I have to continue. I am falling into a vortex. " . . . then maybe we would have gone ahead as we should, and if we were trying all we could, then I could in good conscience go. But unfortunately for me Labor didn't win."

Not exactly the trial of Socrates.

He reddens. He bawls:

"I am a leftist! And I say you are wrong!"

Hard to believe. He is the image of a right-winger.

"I am about to send you to jail for twenty-one days because you are not satisfied with the pace of the negotiations and because you don't want to defend Jews. If we were sending you to run after Arabs, maybe I could understand—not agree, but understand. But to defend your own people, women and children, against some terrorist—"

He goes on. I miss part of it, because I am thinking: Twenty-one days! Is that all?

He is saying that while negotiations go on, we have to defend Jews. Then something new:

"What happens if I don't send you to jail? You're not in jail, and you're not doing your reserve duty. So where are you? A man has to be somewhere. That's anarchy!"

He glares up at me and waits. I say nothing. I am not inclined to defend anarchy.

"You'll sit in the gate of a settlement. You can argue with the settlers. Maybe you can persuade them."

He waits. We are both fixed firm. Even if my arguments were stronger, and my Hebrew fluent, would it make any difference? If he were persuaded, he would have to come and stand where I am and say to someone else, "Yes, commander," "No, commander." And I will not give up (though I feel that my position has been shattered in the burning focus of his eyes) for the simple reason that I would lose the respect of my friends. I locked myself in during the last few months, half deliberately I think, boasting to them, "The army hasn't a snowball's chance to send me into the West Bank."

"Maybe you want to think about it for five or ten minutes."

Why not? I studied philosophy.

"Yeah, sure. Thinking is always good."

"Five minutes to think," he says to Nachshon.

Do I salute?

Nachshon comes and takes me by the arm, so I do not. Another smart-alecky kid is waiting. Out in the hall my bag is still there under the army bag. I lean against the wall next to it. From the side comes an officer, another deeply lined face, but he has many fancy insignia upon him.

"May I have a word with you?" he asks. Friendly.

"I've been given five minutes to think."

"Well, after you're finished thinking, call me. I'll be in here."

He goes into a room on the right.

Why not, after all? I know there are reasons why not, but I could not remember them within that narrow frame: "Defend Jews!" Now, outside, I can push against the frame. The settlements. The Drobles Committee. That was 1979. This committee made a recommendation which became the official policy of the Israeli government. The Jewish settlements are placed where they are with the express intent of surrounding the Arab villages and cutting them off from one another, so that the eighty thousand Jews in the West Bank and Gaza today can help us to dominate the one and a half million Palestinians. And these are the Jews he wants me to protect! They are the heart of a plan to perpetuate the immorality. They will turn out to be the main obstacle to a peace settlement. He wants me to guard the gate of the main obstacle. Worried about their security? So instead of sending me out to guard them in their injustice, let's pull them back into justice. I'll gladly participate in that. Send me to the West Bank to do that!

I am champing at the bit to get back in there. But I remember the officer.

I catch his eye. He comes out and stands before me, brightly bedecked.

"Don't be fooled by what you see here." He points to the signs of rank. I never learned ranks.

"I am a leftist," he says. "I'm Peace Now. He lowers his voice. "I think someday the nations of the world are going to make us a Nuremberg Trial for what we are doing to the Arabs."

My God. I would never say that. I know something about what we're doing to the Arabs, and you may well call it a crime, but to say that!

(Writing this now, I realize what I should have said: "You need a refresher course in the Holocaust." But I was stunned. I had heard, of course, the invidious comparison before—from my German youth groups—but here? Among my own people! At such a level!)

"And in spite of that," he says, "I go to the Territories. It's exactly the ones like us who are needed to keep our own soldiers under control. Understand?"

I nod.

"I always tell them, 'I'm the only one to shoot.' And I shoot in the air. And no one gets hurt. I have saved Arab lives. So you decide, and let me know afterward what you've decided."

"The low gear," I say, "can slow the car, but it cannot change its direction."

He looks puzzled.

"The good," I say, "is sometimes the enemy of the best."

"Let me know what you decide."

He goes off. My escort comes. Again the ceremony. I stand before my judge.

"*Nu?*"

"The settlements are part of a policy—"

"What— Not that. In one word now, do you accept or refuse."

"I refuse."

He writes. He gets up and starts to leave, not waiting for me not to salute. "You're in for twenty-one days." Irritated.

(Only twenty-one days!)

"Where? Commander."

"I don't know." He stalks out.

Nachshon looks upset.

"Are you healthy?" he asks.

"I hope so. Basically."

"Maybe the doctor can find something wrong, and you won't have to go to jail."

4

Sometime in November.

(MY FIRST SABBATH, to be exact. Cooks' room. Morning break. I
am supposed not to have to work on Sabbath, but I found this out
too late. Had already said I'd come.)

I stayed at Schneller two days while they looked for a prison. I
stayed in a room with pictures of Elvis, James Dean, and Sylvester
Stallone, as well as some I did not know. My window allowed a view
northward over part of the plateau which had belonged to the tribe of
Benjamin. I could see the mound of Gibeah, capital of King Saul. It is
easy to pick out, because the skeleton of King Hussein's palace rusts
upon it half built, interrupted by the Six-Day War.

There Saul sat under a pomegranate tree, and he heard the panic in
the Philistine camp, for his son Jonathan had surprised it. He and
Jonathan chased the Philistines westward down to the lowlands, and
they restored this plateau to Israel.

And I can see Nebi Samwil, the supposed gravesite of the
"prophet Samuel." It is a squarish building alone on a higher hill
west of Gibeah and farther away. It has a minaret in Mamluk style
and two old Aleppo pines on its western side. The Crusaders called
the hill "Montjoie" because coming up by the same ridge road down
which the Philistines had fled, they first glimpsed Jerusalem from
there. They built a church to "Saint Samuel," some of which is

included in the present building. For they, as well as the Jews of the Middle Ages, had accepted a six-hundred-year-old Christian tradition that Samuel is buried on this hill. This contradicts the biblical witness, which places his grave in Ramah, today the Arab village of e-Ram, a few miles to the east.

The interest in biblical locations is not just antiquarian. For suppose that we were to sit down at last to negotiate with the Palestinians. I have an idea what our final position would have to be (more than the present government would allow) in order to persuade them to stop fighting. I think I know what theirs would have to be, too, if Israel is ever to be persuaded to make the needed concessions. Between these two theoretical possibilities there is common ground: a Palestinian state without heavy arms, meaning no tanks, no artillery, no military aircraft, and Israeli observers, on the ground and in the air, to make sure that no such arms cross the Jordan Valley. And, yes, an agreement with Jordan—that would have to be part of it—including the provision that no Syrian or Iraqi tanks would be allowed there. That is the only solution I can imagine that would have any chance at all. For the Palestinians will not stop the intifada until they have a sovereign state. And Israel will not let any such state come into being unless it feels secure. The agreement will have to be one, therefore, which requires no trust on Israel's part, but on the basis of which trust can be built up over the decades. And the Palestinians would accept that, I think. It's the only chance, and they surely know it. At least we can't know that they do not know it, unless we sit with them and talk. We should not expect them to proclaim, before coming to the table, that they would agree to such an arrangement. Demilitarization is almost the only card they've got.

If they are to keep the peace, they will need to have something to lose. There will have to be a transition period, with the establishment of a strong Palestinian police force before our army pulls out. Only after they have something to lose will they be willing and able to control their own extremists. Jordan, for example, has had all its agriculture to lose since 1970 (on the other side of the valley), and it has been careful to keep the border quiet. So peace is conceivable. In fact, this solution has been staring us in the face for years. Jerusalem is another matter, but that too is soluble—there are many possibilities, one of which will come out on top during the give-and-take of negotiations. The basic principle of statecraft in our region must be: a unique situation demands a unique response.

There is one thing only for which I cannot conceive a solution, and this thing is bound up with beliefs like that about Samuel's grave.

I mean the Jewish settlements in the biblical heartland. Even if my government were willing to dismantle them, or some of them, how would the settlers be persuaded to go along? They might of course be cajoled into staying as resident aliens in a Palestinian state (fat chance)—but without their Uzis? Remember Yamit. This was an area of Jewish settlements in the Sinai. The five thousand inhabitants, who had established a demiparadise, were supposed to leave as a result of the Camp David agreement. The government offered almost a billion dollars in compensation, that is, an average of about $200,000 per person. Nevertheless the settlers resisted, most of them passively, and the army had to evict hundreds by force. Some stayed on the rooftops and fought the unarmed soldiers with burning tires and bricks. One group threatened suicide, recalling images of Massada. And this was Yamit, which is not mentioned in the Bible. How then would it be in Bethel? In Shiloh? In Ophrah? In Elon Moreh? In Tekoa? In Kiryat Arba above Hebron? Tapuach? Baraka? And tens of others, each with its biblical associations—and each with its roster of martyrs? These are no Yamits. Some of the more flexible settlers have told me that they would undertake passive resistance. But what about the twenty thousand or so hard-core? At the imagined end of the peace process rises the specter of civil war. My government knows this and fears it.

The motives in the hearts of the hard-core Jewish settlers are no less strong than those in the hearts of the Palestinian rebels. "The force that through the green fuse drives the flower" finds a way, with the Palestinians, in intifada—and often it is bound up with Islamic fundamentalism. The same force finds a way, with these young Jewish men and women, in the restoration of Israel upon its ancient land.

The context in which this force appears is often late adolescence, the time between leaving one's first home (or ceasing to feel that one's parents are very important) and not yet having established another. One has no parameters, no bearings. One's behavior, or fantasy, can go to all sorts of extremes, and one knows of nothing sure to stop it, to say,

"Here should be a limit." One is free, and no one has a right to stop anyone, and everything is relative, and the point of life is that there is no point, and everything will pass, and this doesn't matter and that doesn't matter. Life is empty and one is miserable. But why miserable? Why not just drift merrily about in the limitless swamp that is adolescence? The problem is that the force is also there, the force that through the green fuse drives . . . , and it wants direction, it wants to flower. Flowering requires direction and design. Where can one find direction and design? So one is miserable.

And then comes something, religion perhaps. If so, it is often Religion Again, for one may have spurned it before. My clue for understanding the settlers is my own return to Judaism. This happened thirteen years after my Bar Mitzvah (which had signified my last obligation to and final release from the infinitely tedious and insipid singsong that then passed in my town as Judaism) during Christmas break at Drew University in New Jersey. Everyone had left the campus, but I had decided to stay on to continue the search for the meaning of life. "The force that through the green fuse drives . . ." had taken in me a philosophical turn. This too is a story. One can always go farther back. But let it be that crisp, snow-white day.

I was in the midst of trying to decipher Heidegger. The German philosopher offered a great hope to my adolescence, because he talked about "the meaning of Being"—and not on a merely abstract level, but in connection with experiential things: birth, death, conscience, anxiety, escapism. Moreover he was very difficult to understand. His obscurity proved an advantage, because the adolescent need for direction and design could take the specific shape of trying to figure him out. It was as if Heidegger held the Ariadne thread which could lead one out to Life. And he *should* indeed be difficult, because he required a transformation of one's whole way of thinking and being. That's what one wanted: transformation! A new being! A new heaven and a new earth! Not this muddled thing.

There was however a problem with Heidegger. He had published *Being and Time*, his foundational work, in 1927, and six years later he had become a Nazi. He had not stayed a Nazi for very long. But still! If the thread he had held in 1927 had really been *it*, then it should not have led through that door. Only an existence, he had said, whose present living is explicitly informed by the fundamental conditions of birth and death, can see things undistorted, as they are, and make its decisions accordingly. But what kind of decision was that? Was it the result of undistorted seeing? And if Heidegger could be so wrong, how could he guide? (He could analyze our inauthenticity, but how could he help us toward a transformation which he himself had not undergone?) In the speeches he made during that brief but crucial time, as rector of Freiburg University, he proclaimed that the German people under Hitler remained resolute, receiving the revelation—on a global scale—of what was to be done, for the sake of a true life, at that historical hour. The terms in which he spoke of this spiritual mission were central to his philosophy. This was no sideline—and no mere mistake. If one took his philosophy seriously, there were no excuses.

On that Christmassy day the library was warm, the windows steamed up. I happened upon an essay called "M. Heidegger and F. Rosenzweig, or Temporality and Eternity," by one Karl Löwith. I had never heard of Rosenzweig. But I began to read and was fascinated. Here was Löwith, Heidegger's former assistant, daring to compare an obscure German Jewish philosopher with the greatest thinker of the age. Löwith summarized passages from Rosenzweig's *Star of Redemption*:

> *The "wandering Jew" is no invention by the Christian and antisemitic environment but a world-historical fact, contradicted by every other experience of the power of time.*

"The power of time." Here "time," the Heideggerean theme, was meant in a simple, ordinary way. A people had been dispersed among the nations, wanderers all. The power of time might have led to their assimilation, as it had with other dispersed peoples. But it had not. Why hadn't we all converted to Christianity or Islam? How had it come to this, that I sat there a Jew, an unbeliever but Jew nonetheless, in the library of a Methodist university in the State of New Jersey, two thousand years after my ancestors had scattered over the face of the earth?

The essay continued: by the very fact that we Jews remain a community, and marry within it, and thus give birth to more Jews whom we bring up as such, we bear witness to our faith in God's promise to Abraham, Isaac, and Jacob: that we are eternal. Thus an experience of "eternity through community" is opposed to Heidegger's experience of authentic time. (The latter is based on the individualizing effect that the possibility of one's own death has, when one lets it inform one's living.) And then came this:

Who is born a Jew bears witness to his faith by multiplying the eternal people. He does not believe in something, he himself is belief.

That was the beginning of a conversion. Not that after the ten minutes or so I put on yarmulke and fringes. But I was converted in the literal sense of being turned.

I had always had trouble with the expression "to believe in God." If I substitute the word "trust" for the word "believe," then indeed it makes sense. You trust in someone or you don't. But people never seem to mean just that when they ask, "Do you believe in God?" They seem to mean, "Do you believe that God exists?" I was suspicious of this question. It lifted the whole issue up and away into the realm of speculation. In the Bible (the so-called Old Testament, I mean), the relevant question is always that of trust. The question of God's existence never arises. Or take, for example, a little boy balancing on a wall. His father, who stands beneath him, says, "Jump into my arms!" If the boy believes in his father, he jumps, and if he does not believe in him, he does not jump. But it never occurs to him to ask whether his father exists. Such a question would be superfluous. And so to me the question of God's existence seemed—and still seems—superfluous. If you have to ask it, then it is clear that God is not with you as He was with biblical Israel, and the biblically relevant question, of whether to trust Him or not, cannot even arise. Nowadays, for people who believe that God exists, it goes without saying that He is to be trusted; they cannot understand the biblical question of faith, nor does it occur to them that they do not understand.

Into this medley of ideas came the statement quoted above: who is born a Jew does not believe *in* something, he himself *is* belief. That brought the whole matter down from the realm of theory. To be belief.

Whether I believe or not, I am belief. I am it, by the mere fact that I was born Jewish, circumcised, Bar Mitzvahed. I am a testimony. And this testimony that I am is bigger than I know myself to be. So I had better set about finding out what this testimony is that I am—who I am.

When human beings are willing to live and die for their way of life, generation after generation, then there must be something to it, some core of truth, perhaps merely a truth of the psyche, but truth for all that. And I had no inkling what it might be. Growing up in a suburb on Long Island, I had seen Judaism as so much nonsense, wishful thinking easily disproved. Yet my ancestors, despite the persecutions, had not opted out, had married Jews, had kept bearing Jews—and here was I, a Jew in a Christian university, with no idea of what it was that had held them together, with no idea of that to which I was a testimony, not even knowing what I believed, but being belief.

Kierkegaard, Heidegger, and Sartre had analyzed inauthenticity. That shoe had fit me too. But how would it be to live in truth? They had pointed, in response, to the individual who has accepted his mortality and who brings this resolute acceptance to bear on every situation. I suspected that if I were to get back behind my inauthenticity, I would find not myself as an individual, but rather myself in community. It would be indeed the community of my ancestors, but it would demand its own reestablishment in my generation.

Such was the beginning of my way to Judaism. I doubt whether many of our Jewish settlers in the West Bank took so philosophical a route. Yet Rosenzweig's sentence articulates what is essential to them: the feeling of connection to an ancestral community. Orthodox Jews live essentially as their fathers and mothers did. The keeping of the Sabbath, for example: one is never so strongly tied to one's ancestors and one's future descendants as on this day. The words one reads and recites are the words that were and will be; the practices which these words ordain were and will be; one can meaningfully say, therefore (as we do when called to read from the Torah on Sabbath morning), that God "has planted eternal life in our midst." But one does not think of the ancestral community in a vacuum. The successive generations were indeed scattered all over the world, bound and bounded only by books, but all these books came out of the one Book, and that one Book has our ancestors living in places like Shechem, Tapuach, Shiloh,

Bethel, Jerusalem, Tekoa, and Hebron, also called Kiryat Arba. The beauty of what the Jewish settlers are doing, in their own eyes, is this: out of the Diaspora, in which by dint of blood and word and practice God preserved his scattered sheep as one community for two thousand years, they have been brought back, by the miracle of the Six-Day War, to the very same biblical places, with the mission of fulfilling in the present generation that for which the previous generations had prayed three times a day: the renewal of the age-old community upon its original land. They even look somewhat biblical: the beards, the conspicuous fringes, the kerchiefed women with their many children. Abraham and Sarah have come back to Shechem, though they live (for now) on the surrounding hillsides facing the ancient mound. Jacob and Leah have come back to Hebron. Gideon threshes in Ophrah. A boy named Samuel wakes up and goes to school in Shiloh. Amos herds sheep in Tekoa. Our fulfillment, our renewal. God has stretched out his arm once more into history—beautifully, fittingly, precisely here.

You will not rip that out. The settlements are like the caper plants that grow into the wall. You cannot pull them out without destroying the wall.

THERE WAS MORE to my conversion. I read on in Löwith's essay and found a long citation from Rosenzweig. (Transcribed in freedom):

> *The peoples of the world cannot content themselves with the community of blood; they strike roots in the night . . . of the earth and find in its perpetuity the guarantee of their own perpetuity. Their will to eternity fastens on the soil and its dominion, the territory. The blood of their sons flows around the earth of the native land; for they do not trust in the living community of blood unless it be anchored in the firm ground of the earth. We alone trusted in the blood and left the land. . . . Therefore, the saga of the eternal people, different from that of the other peoples of the world, does not begin with autochthony. Earth-born is he, and even he only bodily, alone the father of man-kind: Israel's ancestor is an immigrant, with the divine*

command to leave his native land and to go to a country that
God will show to him. Thus begins his story as told in the sacred
books. Only by exile does this people become a people, first in the
dawn of its dark ages and afterwards again in the bright light of
history in Egypt and in Babylon. And the fatherland to which
the life of a great people accustoms itself by ploughing itself into
it till it nearly forgets that being a people means more than
living in the land—this land never belongs in such a sense to the
eternal people . . . the land belongs to it only as land of its
yearning, as—the Holy land. Therefore, its full possession—
again in contra-distinction to all peoples of the world—is
disputed even when the people is there: for then it is only a
stranger and denizen in his land; "Mine is the land," says God
to it; the holiness of the land kept it from being seized straight-
way so long as the people was in a position to seize it; this
holiness infinitely intensifies the yearning for what is lost and
henceforth prevents the people from feeling at home in any other
country. . . . With nothing external is our life interwoven, we
struck roots in ourselves, without roots in the earth and therefore
wanderers for ever, but being deeply rooted in ourselves, in our
own body and blood.

In every conversion there is something peculiar and personal. The
West Bank and Gaza are full of converts, people who may or may not
have been brought up in Islam or Judaism, but to whom, at some point
during the muddle of adolescence, Islam or Judaism suddenly made
terrific sense.

Before I encountered Rosenzweig on that snow-white day, my idea
of the authentic life had been that of a great creator, and my image of
the great creator in my time had for years been crystallized in the figure
of William Faulkner. I mean literally the figure, for the Cartier-Bresson
photograph of him—standing short and solid, pipe in hand, outside
his Mississippi home—hung on my wall, and what I saw there was how
rooted he was, how rooted those legs were, in the Mississippi earth.
And that was my excuse—why I was not myself becoming a great
creator. It was my excuse and my complaint. I had no Mississippi. No
earth. No roots. I had had the bad luck to grow up in a newly founded,

newly middle-class suburb on the shifting sands of Long Island, where there were no farms or factories, little visible work, no traditions, no local tales, no group of farmers and traders sitting on the porch of Varner's country store chewing tobacco and spinning yarns, no dialect, nothing raw, nothing that had not already been worked over and given form by rooted creators living elsewhere, and presented to us in books or movies or on TV.

And now here came Franz Rosenzweig and told me that this unrootedness was my rootedness, that I had grown up on Long Island of all places, among family and neighbors newly arrived, because I belonged to an ancient, wandering people. It made sense! My life made sense. That's why we had no Mississippi, no Yoknapatawpha County, no local traditions, no yarns, nothing new and raw out of the earth where we lived. Because we did not belong to that earth! Because of the history of the Jewish people, to which we did belong!

It was not then bad luck that I had grown up there. It was my destiny as a Jew that I should be placeless, rootless. But in this very condition, I gathered, there might reside a truth that was deeper than roots; it would have to do with what this philosopher had called "being rooted in one another." The earth did not now appear to be so positive a thing. The possession of it, I heard him say, promotes the illusion of self-sufficiency into which we all, Jew and Gentile, easily fall. It keeps us from experiencing, in full consciousness, that rootedness-in-one-another which is our truth.

Rosenzweig spoke in terms of blood (meaning the blood in the veins, the *Volk*) versus earth. He was no doubt juxtaposing that with the nationalistic, anti-Semitic ideology of blood *and* earth which was rife in Germany when he wrote. But to me, living after the horrors that had happened in the name of racial purity, his point about our Jewish blood simply did not register. I knew enough about Judaism to think of us as a People of the Book. So now instead of "blood versus earth" I heard "words versus earth." The rootedness-in-one-another of which Rosenzweig spoke would have been created and sustained by words, as in "Hear, O Israel . . . !" Perhaps the words could have full binding power only when a certain distance was kept from the earth. If I studied the Bible with this theme in mind, I might penetrate to the foundational experiences of ancient Israel. For I suspected that my ancestors had known what it means to live rooted-in-one-another, without the illusion of self-sufficiency, and that this knowledge had been lost, had been covered over by the wisdom of the earth-rooted Greeks. If we too—we rootless moderns, living after the final collapse of Hellenistic dualism—could learn again to find roots in one another, we might come into contact once more, perhaps in very different terms, with what the ancient Israelites had experienced as God. Or would such contact prove to be, instead, a prerequisite for discovering our roots in one another? Thus began, with all the force that through the green fuse drives . . . , my plunge into Judaism, not for the sake of the Jewish people only, but for all the modern wilderness wanderers—a mission for all.

That was conversion. My life had been shaping itself into a vast complaint. Suddenly this was lifted: there was a point in my having grown up as I had, and there was at last something for me to do. Direction and design.

IF THE Jewish settlers had shared those last minutes of my conversion, we wouldn't have the problem of the capers in the wall.

I AM LYING on the cot in the cooks' room. It is Sunday afternoon. (So I am naming the days.) People are back. Noga (my wife) and Rami Hasson of Yesh Gvul visited yesterday. Rami has done one hundred and forty days in Jail Six for refusal. He wore a T-shirt on which was written "Down with the Occupation!" Nervy of him to wear it here. I even had the petty thought that it might get me in trouble. Unlike me, he seems to have no fear. He is quite clear about what he means, and he really means it.

I SHALL pick up again at Schneller. I did not start this diary there. I was busy reading *Light in August*, my first Faulkner in almost thirty years.

Now and then I looked away from Yoknapatawpha County and out the window toward Nebi Samwil. I did not think then any of those thoughts about the settlers or my conversion. All that just came to me while writing. In Schneller I had simply the same little feeling I always get when I look at Nebi Samwil. Such a feeling is like a dense ball of yarn, and when you unravel it you find the associations that compose it. I go up there with groups a lot. I have a map ten feet long, which I lay out on the ground, and we look back and forth between the map and the places around us. If it is clear one sees the high horizon of Gilead to the east, on the other side of the Jordan, and to the west the coast and the Mediterranean—the whole breadth of the country. Spreading before us is the Benjamin plateau. The Arabs wouldn't call it that. But I am with American or German Christians who have been attracted to this land by the Bible, and it is in biblical terms I speak.

There is Gibeah of Saul. Silhouetted against the morning light, Hussein's unfinished palace looks like the Wright brothers' airplane just landed on that hill. There is the Arab village of e-Ram, biblical Ramah, from which Rachel wept for her children as she watched them pass toward Babylon and exile. It was in Ramah, about five hundred years earlier, that the people assembled and said to Samuel, "Give us a king to lead us, as with all the nations." In front of the Arab city of Ramallah, there is the hill of Mizpah, where Saul, the tallest, was chosen king. Farther out on the horizon, beyond Ramallah, are two humps with what look like two barrels sticking up. It is Baal-Hazor, the highest mountain in the region, and as long as the modern Israelis have any say in the matter, there will be no peace settlement unless we or our surrogates have a lookout station there. It was this mountain, according to tradition, on which Abraham stood (though he was still called Abram then) after Lot had chosen Sodom. And the Lord said to Abraham:

Lift up your eyes, and from where you are, look north and south, east and west. All the land that you see I shall give you, to you and your offspring forever. And I shall make your offspring like the dust of the earth, so that if someone can count the dust of the earth, then your offspring too can be counted. Rise up and walk the land, its length and breadth, for to you I am giving it.
(GEN. 13:14–17)

Just below the two humps there is a slightly diagonal line of white houses. It is the modern Jewish settlement of Bethel. The people living in the houses believe in the twofold promise; they are doing their utmost toward its twofold fulfillment. And below them, not quite visible, is the Arab village of Beitin, smack on the tell of ancient Bethel, where the offspring of Abraham by his wife's handmaid are doing their twofold utmost too.

Bethel. Jacob used a rock for a pillow and dreamed of angels going up and down on a ladder. Then he anointed his pillow and called the place "Bethel," the house of God. In the time of the Judges the ark was there. So Bethel had a tradition of holiness, which is why the rebel Jeroboam could persuade his subjects, who had seceded from the Davidic union, that it was not necessary to go to Solomon's Temple in Jerusalem. At Bethel they had a golden calf, and God could ride upon its back (the seceders thought) as well as He could upon the wings of the golden cherubim in the Holy of Holies in Jerusalem.

"Go to Bethel and sin," spoke God through Amos. But neither Jeroboam's people nor today's Jewish settlers were drawn there only by the memory of holiness. The generous plateau which stretches before us comes to a narrow finish at Bethel. Beyond that is the winding watershed-road up to Shechem. So it was and still is vital to those in the north to have this foothold on the plateau—and to be able to ambush, at the neck, any army coming toward them. What is more, Bethel sits on the only continuous ridge road leading down east from the plateau to me here in the cooks' room in Jericho, and from Jericho one can cross the Jordan. It is the road which Jacob would have taken when, leaving Bethel, he fled "to the land of the eastern peoples." And Joshua and the army would have taken it going up from here toward Ai.

With a turn of the head you can see, while standing on Nebi Samwil, the whole stretch of this plateau from Jerusalem to Bethel, with the mounds of Gibeah, Ramah, and Mizpah between. But you have to overlook much urban sprawl. The Arab villages are surrounded by Jewish neighborhoods, assembled during the past fifteen years by Israeli contractors and Palestinian workers. Concrete bulwarks faced with gleaming stone.

5

Sometime in November. Cell.

EVENING. He has locked the outer gate. My cellmates are talking about a new Israeli jet that you can stop in midair and fly in reverse.

I came back from the blue dishes, and they all had white specks on their uniforms. They are still scraping and repainting the courtyard. It is very hard work. They tell me how lucky I am to be in the regimental kitchen. Indeed, I would hate to be doing that work under the eyes of those jailers all the time, just as the jailers would hate— would be embarrassed—to have someone their fathers' age always under them, saying "Yes, commander, no, commander." I think it embarrasses them every time I call them that, and I do, every chance I get, with gusto.

After dinner we had an inspection. It was Ami who made it. That was a problem—it's always a problem with Ami—because he doesn't fit the part, and he knows it, and we know it, but there's this ceremony to be gotten through. We tidy the room and button up and stand in front of our beds, hats on, tense because we know what to expect. The monitor is Yoni, a small, wiry paratrooper who left his weapon in the barracks when he went to dinner and was sentenced, therefore, to twenty-eight days. Yoni watches for Ami. At last he speaks.

"He is coming."

We straighten up. Ami pauses before the door.

Yoni: "Detainees will prepare to receive the commander! Detainees will come to attention! Two, three . . . !"

And everyone stamps his right foot and cries out: "*Kshev!*" that being the last syllable of the Hebrew for "Attention!" But inevitably something goes wrong. We don't all stamp together. Or someone's voice comes out high-pitched. Or it isn't loud enough. Or enthusiastic enough. So Ami appears in the doorway and says, "Again," and withdraws.

Yoni: Same speech. "Two, three . . . !"

"*Kshev!*"

And he comes in. There is silence. At my first inspection with Ami I thought it was like in the war movies: that the tension was because he might find some speck of dust and make us stand up to our chests in cold water all night. But it's not that. It's worse in a way. He comes in, and the silence, the waiting for him to speak, is just too much. He knows it, we know it. He knows that we are about to explode, and we know that he is, and each side knows that the other knows. He gets all red-faced, he can't even look at us, he cannot speak. And then, if someone on our side does not mercifully start, he does. Trying to get a word out, he reddens even more, and bends over the useless sink as if he were about to throw up. And then, if we haven't started, he lurches about and heads out the door, shouting behind him, hysterically, "Ten minutes!"

So it goes, and at some point we pass through the wave of laughter. I hate this part, because I am, after all, forty-eight years old, with silver in my sideburns, and it is unseemly for me to be breaking to pieces with the others. Yet they do not seem to notice.

I sort of like Ami. Vulnerable of body, dark and shy. I could perhaps help him. The best thing for him, of course, would be to find another position. But as long as he has to put on this farce, he should cut the "*Kshev!*" business. It's the "*Kshev!*" that does it, and the abrupt silence that follows. He should just come in, and laugh a little, and ask if there are any problems, and warn the rapscallions, and give assignments for the morning. But of course, then we might not be afraid of him. So he puts on this act. He even carries a swagger stick, like Chaplin in *The Great Dictator*. It is not a real swagger stick, and I'm sure he's not aware of what he is doing, but he always comes to inspections with something pointed in his hand: a broken-off antenna, for example, which he telescopes in and out, or a knitting needle, or a metal rod, or, failing anything else, a ballpoint pen—something, anything that he can wave about, the ancient symbol of authority, the shepherd's staff, eternally erect. When finally we have gone through the first wave of laughter, the big wave, he goes out again, and comes in again, to the same ceremony, and this can go on, with ten-minute pauses, until we are all so sick of it that nobody laughs, and then he takes his position, still red and sweating, and taps the swagger stick into his palm: "Any problems?"

Well, tonight he had the very unpleasant task of confiscating shampoo. After no one mentioned problems, he tapped again and told us to open our bags.

"You have to give me your shampoo," he said. "You aren't supposed to have any. We didn't even know about this."

But I knew about it. Rami Hasson had told me to take only shampoo in tubes, because plastic bottles were not allowed. But my anti-baldness shampoo is in a bottle, and I had brought it also, in case I did not have to go to jail.

I started to ask, "What about tubes?" But "tubes" is an immensely complicated word in Hebrew: *shfoferot*. I couldn't quite get through it, and Dubi—a reservist, maybe ten years older than the others—said:

"He has a special shampoo."

"Not you, Stephen," said Ami, not looking at me.

Then each of them brought his bottled shampoo, all glorious expensive brands, and Ami wrote down on a piece of paper his name and the name of the brand, for each would get his bottle back on the day of freedom.

Then he went around and stuck his antenna into each bag, as if poking into garbage.

Why no bottled shampoo? I suppose because they can't see what liquid is inside.

I wanted to do them a favor. I had three or four tubes. But I wanted it to be all right.

"What about *shf-f-f* . . . ?"

"Not you, Stephen."

So I shut up. When he had gone, Dubi said:

"Stephen! Don't ask questions!"

"Yes, I know." You can always tell an American by the fact that he asks questions.

Then I decided not to say anything about my stock. I might need all of it. For they all knew the date of freedom, but I did not.

THE SAD TRUTH is, I find nothing interesting to say about my fellow inmates. Here am I, whose whole thought, for the past quarter century, has been bound up with Martin Buber's philosophy of I and Thou, and yet each of them seems to me like a wall, like one of the walls of this prison. And because "walls do not a prison make," I escape, via this diary, to memories of standing with a group on Nebi Samwil. One should have to do, first of all, with those who are near, actually, physically near.

But they are arguing about this damned airplane that stops in midair and flies in reverse. Now what am I supposed to do about that? Yoni and Yigal are trying to convince Shlomo that there is such a thing. But Yoni insists it's Israeli, and Yigal says it's French. How does one get from here to the I-Thou relation? Or to anything?

Shlomo doesn't know whether to believe them. He has a face that at first appears intelligent, but on second look the features empty out. He has told me and everyone that he got himself put in jail on purpose, because he has a heart condition, and his commander wasn't taking it seriously. He hopes that in jail they will take it more seriously and lower his medical profile so that he won't have to be in a field unit. He goes each day to the doctor and tries to get a referral to an army hospital so that they will check his heart. The doctor sends him back. He smokes. I say, "If you really have a heart condition, you should stop smoking." He has never heard this. "How can you not have heard this? It causes lung cancer and heart attacks." "No kidding." He accords this the same measure of doubtful belief that he is presently according the plane that flies backward.

Well, here I am writing about Shlomo, and there is Shlomo. It's like talking about someone to someone else while the person is in the room. A sin. I should rather, à la Buber, put down the pen and have to do with them. But what do I want with nonexistent airplanes?

I too shall escape. Walls do not a prison make. Here I am, locked up for the night in Jericho, where the walls fell down, but I am recalling the two days at Schneller, in a room from whose window I looked out at Nebi Samwil and had a feeling in my gut, because I remembered how it was to stand up there and survey the plateau of Benjamin. So tell me: Where am I?

___ At home, unraveling my prison experience.
___ In Jericho.
___ In Schneller.
___ On Nebi Samwil.
___ All of the above.
___ None of the above.
_X_ All of the above.

Nor iron bars a cage.

We have been looking into the distance at Bethel, etc., but at our feet is a hill with the Arab village of El Gib on half of it. This preserves the ancient name of Gibeon. The Gibeonites had four cities, but the one in front of us was the grandest. "Like one of the royal cities," the Book of Joshua says. There is a story connected with this hill. The Book of Deuteronomy says that God ordered the children of Israel to kill every non-Israelite in Canaan, men, women, children, cattle, everything that breathes (Deut. 20:16–18). Or as the Book of Joshua puts it: to devote them to the Lord. But scholars date these books to a later period than the times about which they report. On a closer look— and taking the Book of Judges into account—one gets a motleyer picture of the so-called conquest. Within the vast area of Manasseh, for example, from the Jezreel Valley to Shechem, there isn't a single battle story from this time. The eponyms of three Canaanite cities get listed among the great-grandchildren of Joseph's son Manasseh. Perhaps the Israelites settled down side by side with the Canaanites and gradually absorbed them, with the result that these later appear as children of Israel.

But the Gibeonites were not absorbed, and so the writers of Deuteronomy and Joshua had a problem. They believed in the "devotional" version of Joshua's conquest. How then could the Gibeonites have survived as a distinct people, name intact? What is more, these same Gibeonites had held the holy ark in one of their cities for a generation. The Israelite tabernacle and the bronze altar had been set up on their high place. They had received the sacred functions of cutting wood and hauling water for the altar of the Lord. The writers of Deuteronomy and Joshua must have been hard put to explain all this. But I imagine the following process: one night one of them has a dream, a vision. It is a good story, and he tells it to the others, and they are persuaded that its inspiration is divine: The Gibeonites heard how the all-conquering Israelites were devoting everything that breathes in Canaan. So they took old, worn-out sacks for their donkeys . . .

> *and frayed wineskins, cracked and patched. The men put on tattered, mended sandals and ragged clothes, and their whole bread supply was stale and moldy. Then they went to Joshua, to the camp at Gilgal [near Jericho], and they said to him and the men of Israel, "From a far-away land we have come, and now make a treaty with us. . . . This bread of ours was warm when we took it from our houses on the day we set forth to go to you, and now look how stale and moldy. And these wineskins when we filled them were new, and now look how cracked, and these clothes and sandals of ours—look how frazzled they are from the length of the journey." The men took from their provisions and did not ask the Lord. And Joshua made peace with them and entered a covenant with them to let them live. (J O S H . 9 : 4 – 1 5)*

The Gibeonites were in fact a mighty people by local standards. Their cities dominated the western part of this plateau. Around the mound of Gibeon still spreads the fertile land, well watered and well drained. They had a good spring. They sat where the ridge road from the west comes up unbroken. By the treaty with them, therefore, Joshua could control the whole plateau, which became a staging area for spreading north, south, and west. The Canaanite king of Jerusalem understood the danger, called up his allies, and laid siege to Gibeon.

The Israelites responded at once, coming up from Gilgal by night to rescue the alleged deceivers. At dawn they surprised the Canaanites and drove them down that western road. It went so well that Joshua prayed:

> *O sun, stand still over Gibeon,*
> *And moon, over the Valley of Ayalon.*

This valley is down at the end of the ridge road and leads to the cities in the south and west, which the Israelites—says the Book of Joshua— conquered on that long day.

In fact most of the area to the south and west remained Canaanite enough to prevent the tribe of Dan from coming into its inheritance. We know this from the Book of Judges. It seems, moreover—from archeological surveys—that the mountain region south of Jerusalem was almost empty of towns. Into it streamed the Judahites. The Benjaminites settled on the eastern part of this plateau, founding the cities I have mentioned. It is doubtful whether they had to drive anybody out: for the prior two centuries it had been, except for the Gibeonites, unsettled. The Ephraimites may have had a battle at Bethel, but aside from that there was hardly anyone else around: only four Canaanite towns in the whole of their territory. They cut down trees and hewed out cisterns, founding more than a hundred settlements. Farther north, in Manasseh's relatively green and pleasant land, there were about twenty-five Canaanite towns, big and small, mostly on the edges of the broad valleys. The Israelites came in great numbers and lived beside or even among them. Eventually they absorbed them. But we find no battle stories here.

Where then did Joshua fight? Here at Jericho? No one has yet found convincing evidence of a walled city here then. At Ai? Again, no city then. Up north at Hazor? But several generations later Deborah has to lead the fight against its Canaanite king. For a long time we guides were swayed by the great archeologist Yigal Yadin. He judged that the first Israelite settlement sprang up at Hazor upon the smoking ruins of the last Canaanite one. But now one among a new generation of archeologists, Israel Finkelstein, looks at the pottery and tells us that the Canaanite ruins just lay there, unsettled, for more than a century.

The case is similar with other cities of the plains which Joshua is supposed to have conquered: Yokneam, Megiddo, Taanach, Dor, Gezer, Lachish, and twenty or so others. These are the best-situated towns in the country. They dominate good farmland and international roads. If Joshua had conquered them, wouldn't the Israelites have preferred to live there? But they did not live there. Instead they went up to the unsettled mountains and cut down trees and eked a living out of the rocky ground.

Where then did he fight? Here on the plateau of Benjamin perhaps. For there was indeed a king of Jerusalem then, who would have felt threatened. But as for the main thrust of the Book of Joshua, it is a later schematization. Over the centuries the fiction was harmless enough, even uplifting to a downtrodden people, but now—whose beard do you suppose that is, the full beard on the face of the settler with the Uzi? And who are the five thousand of Gush Emunim, the Bloc of the Faithful, and the fifteen thousand or so who have followed their lead deep into the biblical heartland? They are the reincarnation of the people of Israel as it appears in the Book of Joshua. They are following the God who wiped out their enemies from before them, as in the Book of Joshua.

6

Sometime in November. Cooks' room.

MORNING BREAK. Blue dishes done. Aching back. I lie on my side. Don't want to write about the Bible. Have to admit I am writing this diary for others. I wouldn't write all that to myself. A witness. A testimony. I am a testimony.

The radio goes all morning in the kitchen. That is supposed to be an advantage. But in fact, what it amounts to is cheap music and the news, basically the same news every half hour. This morning the main news was that the army has informed the family of the soldier Ilan Sa'adon, who disappeared several months ago, that it has concluded that their boy is dead. So this kept coming at me every half hour as I washed the blue dishes. He had hitchhiked. Almost all the soldiers hitchhike. It is the custom. There are even hitchhiking stations built for them, and they stand in line—there are girl-woman soldiers whose job it is to keep order in the line—and people consider it their patriotic duty to pick them up. They don't hitchhike with Arabs, of course, but Arabs can pose as Jews. This is what happened to Avi Sasportas even before it happened to Ilan Sa'adon, whom they talked about this morning. While looking for Sa'adon, the police found Sasportas' body, and they claim to have caught some of the gang. Others escaped abroad. They are said to be Islamic fundamentalists from Gaza.

65

So every half hour, the abyss.

I studied philosophy. Shouldn't I be able to think of that family without just falling into the abyss? I have nothing I can say to them. Nothing to save them, help them. No consolation.

I think for example of the waiting. The not knowing. The terror. How can one go on living, not knowing? This terrible shrieking emptiness in the center of one's body. The being pulled apart. Everything pulling one apart. In all directions. How can one stand it? How can they stand it? When will it be over? How can it ever be over?

What good is all my philosophy? If a philosopher has nothing to give them, then he might as well just wash dishes. We use halved tangerines to stop the drains. There is a washing sink and a rinsing sink. The blue dishes come with the leavings of cottage cheese and jam. The blue cups—they are plastic of course—come with coffee grounds. The table clearers throw them into the suds, and they color the water brown. I hate that. I change the water. When I wash the cups, there are cigarette burns in them.

"We should put out ashtrays," I said to Uzi, who is in charge of the washing.

"They do," he said.

There are little metal ashtrays, but every third cup on the average has a deep unwashable black spot inside.

Cigarette burns. Who was it told me that? They had gone out to the YMCA in Beit Sahur, the Protestant Shepherds' Fields, where Palestinian kids are being treated for trauma. One of the kids showed them his cigarette burns.

It was Dorothea Walling's group. Dorothea teaches religion in a German high school, and she brings a youth group every summer. Originally she had wanted them to work as volunteers on a kibbutz and then see the country. But the kibbutz movement couldn't accept them for some reason, so she hooked up instead with an institution in Ramallah. For two summers they worked there, repairing the building, and this year they worked at an Arab Christian school in the Old City. So they lived each summer for three weeks among Palestinians and saw some things. And each time I was the guide during the touring part and had to explain the Israeli point of view. This year they brought me cigarette burns.

I do the cups without a sponge. I just run my fingers over the insides while they are still in the soapy water, and occasionally I feel the rough spots, the burns. Then I look quickly and dump them into the rinse water. One has to go very fast.

"We are no better or worse than others," I said to them. "We have good people and bad. The occupation itself is bad. It may be better than a unilateral withdrawal—at least someone can argue that—but even as the lesser of evils, it's still bad. And in a bad situation the sadists come to the fore. They seek out opportunities. You have seen some of the results in Beit Sahur. There is no way to identify the sadists and be on top of them all the time. The only real way to stop them is to change the situation, but that requires an agreement from both sides, not just from ours."

But then I had to qualify and say that we have not been forthcoming enough. We should be moving a lot faster to change it, doing a lot more from our side, and yet most Israelis do not agree. We are a divided people. But by the argument made above, those who keep us from going forward bear a measure of responsibility for the burns.

If I could somehow communicate that! Not to the German group—that was easy—but to my people.

With the German group something awful happened. I should have known—I had invited it. I had used the word "responsibility."

"I see a parallel," someone said. "In the Third Reich the government gave evil men the opportunity to exercise their evil. And you are saying that the same kind of thing is happening here."

I wanted to bury my head in my hands, sink into the ground, run from the room, anything. What had I done? I tried to stay calm. It would not do any good to get excited. They would put me in a category. I said:

"In the Third Reich sadism was national policy."

"That's true," said Dorothea.

"Ten thousand Jews a day," I said. "In 1944. Ten thousand Jews a day, every day, day after day. Death factories."

That was arithmetic. Arithmetic doesn't work. They hadn't seen the smoke of Auschwitz. They had seen the cigarette burns in Beit Sahur.

But I couldn't say any more. I was tongue-tied. Too upset. We went on to other things. There is a German expression, *Treppengedanken*. These are the thoughts one has after a confrontation, when one has left the room and is going down the stairs. What one should have said. So now, bending over the coffee-brown water, I had my *Treppengedanken* for this German group. "We don't . . . we don't deport Palestinian families in trains to death factories. We don't separate them and gas them. We don't throw babies alive into burning pits to save on gas. We don't force parents to choose which child is to die and which is to be spared temporarily. We don't rip the condemned child out of the mother's arms. We don't force the mother to watch. We don't play music while this goes on. We don't perform medical experiments on them. We don't make lampshades out of the Koran or Palestinian skin or soap from their fat or wigs for our ladies from their hair. No comparisons. No invidious comparisons. Excuse me. It upsets me. I have heard it before, and it always surprises and upsets me."

Silence. Silence there, in the fantasized room, and here the radio, some Israeli rock group.

The seeker of parallels speaks: "There wasn't any of that in 1935 either." He has to defend his status after such a put-down.

"I'm sorry. I shouldn't have lit into you like that. The comparison upsets me terribly."

"Because it was your people. But this is their people."

"Are you really going to go on with this? Yes, because it was my people, I have a special awareness of it, just as you should have a special awareness of it, because it was your people that did it. Are you really going to compare? During the Lebanon war, there was a massacre of Palestinian refugees at Sabra and Shatila. Christian Phalangists did the killing, but it was Israeli officials who let them into the camps. A few days later four hundred thousand Israelis came to Tel Aviv to protest, and they forced Begin to appoint a commission, which threw Sharon out of the Defense Ministry and replaced a bunch of others. It was the beginning of the end of our Lebanon war. Four hundred thousand Israelis, that's more than one out of ten. What if one out of ten Germans had come out on November 11, 1938, to protest Kristallnacht? When they didn't come out, it was a clear signal to Hitler. It showed him he had a free hand. You could say that when your parents or grandparents didn't come out, the seeds of the horror were already there. But don't tell me that you see here the seeds of the same thing. We came out and we keep coming out. What you see here is what usually happens when one people oppresses another and the oppressed reach a point where they won't stand for it anymore. What happened in your country was something unique: all the means of technology were harnessed to exterminate, with the utmost efficiency and cruelty, a people that had done nothing and threatened nothing and wanted nothing more than to go on living as before. And yet you latch on to this comparison. Not just you. I hear it over and over. It's almost gleeful: the Jews too! The Jews too! Even the Jews! Excuse me, but I think you are manufacturing for yourself a cheap, glib irony in order to escape from shame."

I am still trembling, crouching to save my back, working the dishes like a machine.

"But I think I know," I go on, for no one is saying anything. "It's not just escape. There is a kernel of truth in what you say. The kernel is that the suffering of a Palestinian mother is no less than that of a Jewish mother. Yes, but you see, there is no comparing the two, for the simple reason that suffering is not amenable to comparison. I think what gets me, what has aroused this anger in me, is the light way you said, 'I see a parallel here.' There are no parallels! Try saying that to the Palestinian mother, or the Jewish mother: 'I see a parallel here.' There is a basic principle in theorizing about suffering: whatever you would be ashamed to say in the presence of the sufferer should not be said at all."

That much was *Treppengedanken*. At the real meeting, in fact, as I was about to leave, someone blurted out—out of context—"I can't help it that I was born German."

I said: "I don't believe in collective guilt. Guilt clings to the person who did the deed and to those who benefit from it, but it does not extend beyond. Shame is something else. I can feel ashamed for something I did, but also for something someone else did, someone in my family or my country. One should not try to escape from shame. It can be very useful. It sharpens against indifference. I am ashamed because of what you saw in Beit Sahur."

7

Sometime in November. Cooks' room. Then cell.

AND NOW WE HAVE washed the orange dishes. And the pans, the great meat pans. The radio news is still of Ilan Sa'adon, but Uzi tells me that there are riots in Jericho today because these guys whose dishes we wash sealed up four houses. They came in to lunch in small groups, dusty, weary, short-tempered. The yard is probably full of blindfolded prisoners, but I did not go. I came straight to the cooks' room. Out of sight, out of mind.

For I am no great soul, no "mahatma," let it be admitted.

I shall memorize a Yeats poem, and I shall say it to myself as I do the dinner dishes. Something far, far from the abyss in which that kidnapped soldier lies, and into which those who love him will follow him forever. And will the moon send them silver apples there? And will the sun send them golden apples there?

O God, how are we to live, if such things can happen? What is this life that you have given us? What is it that we fail to understand—that would make it all right, that would heal our wounds? What are the magic words?

"Has the rain a father?"

That is from the Book of Job. From out of the whirlwind God answers Job with a question.

"Has the rain a father?"

The words sweep like rain across a tin roof.
"Has the rain a father, the rain a father?"

Cell. Evening.

Lockup. The other jailer, a muscular kid named Rafi, did the inspection. No nonsense with him. He did it outside in our little courtyard, so we did not have to look at each other, and that helped. Before dismissing us, he twirled his car keys around his index finger and announced with a smile that he was going on a week's vacation. He wanted envy, but I suspect we mainly felt relief. We'll be with Ami. Despite the awkwardness of his inspections, Ami is easier.

Rafi sent them to the cell but called me to him.

"The American consul is coming to visit you Thursday."

"How come?"

"Commander."

"How come, commander?"

He shrugged.

"He heard about you. So you won't go to the kitchen Thursday. You'll sit and wait for him."

"Yes, commander."

The American consul! Uncle Sam to the rescue! Will he spring me? But it's probably just routine. The consul always visits prisoners.

I go into the cell and lie down. Should I tell them? I do not. I shall savor this. I picture the consul galloping in, leading a cavalry charge. Headline: AMERICAN CONSUL CAPTURES JERICHO! Liberates U.S. citizen! Corrects obvious mistake. Sets things right.

West Bank—Near the Jordan River, where Joshua "fit the battle of Jericho," U.S. consul Elijah Doolittle rode in today at the head of a trumpeting cavalry unit and made the walls come "a-tumblin' down" for an American citizen, Stephen Langfur, Ph.D., Religion and Culture, Syracuse University, 1976, Most

*Distinguished Soldier in His Tent, Army Training (three weeks),
1982. Holding Dr. Langfur by the scruff of the neck, the consul
declared, "This man is the first fruits of the new American age."*

I shall take advantage of my present expansive mood and try to get
interested in the people around me.

Counterclockwise, starting from my feet, there is Ronnie, the
formerly absent tenant of the hookless bed. He has been back two
days. A short, serious kid. I don't know why he's here. Or how he
sleeps on that bed. (He could put his mattress on the floor at night.
Some do.) He stretches out with his feet toward me, so I have had
to turn around and put my head near the door and my feet toward him.

Above him is Gadi the Lazy, who grins most of the time. He has
just finished basic training for the infantry, and already he is in jail. I
can guess why. They tell him to do something, he doesn't move. He
has developed the skill of selective hearing. He remains with that
grin on his face until they go up and shout at him, and then he starts
to cry.

Against the back wall, on the lower bunk, there is Dubi. A
reservist, maybe thirty. He has a wife and kids. He is Moroccan, dark,
with long curly black hair and a broken nose. He drives the Egged bus
from West Jerusalem through East Jerusalem and up to the new Jewish
neighborhoods on the north side. He used to be left-wing, he told me,
but in Lebanon he learned that you could not trust the Arabs. They
drink coffee with you, and when you turn your back they stab you.
Since the intifada began, his bus has been stoned so often that he has
stopped counting. One night a Molotov cocktail got inside and burned
it. There were only three passengers, and they all managed to get out.
"I am against you and everything you stand for," he said. But he has
been very warm and helpful, even protective, as when he told me not to
ask questions. He is exhausted tonight. I gather he does the lion's
share of the painting. He seems to be the only one who knows how to
mix mortar and fill in and paint.

Above him is another Gadi, Gadi the Cheerful. Asleep already. He
works in the kitchen on this side, where the police and the prisoners
eat, as well as the reservists from the Allenby Bridge. He has charmed

the cooks into giving him free run of the kitchen and its storeroom, so the prisoners eat better than anyone else. At breakfast, for example (I eat breakfast with them), we are the only ones to get avocado. He brings small lemons from a tree outside. What is most important, there is a phone in the kitchen storeroom, and Gadi has charmed the base operator into letting him use it whenever he wants. You can call home through Gadi and stay on the line as long as you like.

Against the opposite wall there are two sets of beds. Back in the corner are Yoni, up above, the little paratrooper who forgot his weapon, and Dror, down below, tall and strong. Across from me is Shlomo, up above, with the heart condition. He has the paper open.

And there, on the front page, is that soldier's mother, arms outstretched, mouth open in a cry. In the garish color of the most read newspaper in Israel.

And Yigal under him, with the white yarmulke. That is the round of us, eight plus me.

All disciplinary cases. All good boys, basically, you would think. One evening we were allowed into the courtyard. I happened to be standing near Yigal when two Arabs were brought in blindfolded. A reservist whom I call Taxi Driver brought them in. There is a Scorsese film called *Taxi Driver* about a Vietnam vet who shaves his head and trains himself to kill and goes berserk in the city. Well, this guy has a shaved head and looks very muscular, and he wheels in these two Palestinians bare-handed. I say "wheels in" because he holds them each by an arm—their hands are bound behind—and pushes them along in big strides, putting his back into it like a porter pushing two luggage carts at once up the ramp of a railway station. He stands them against the wall and unlocks the cell door. Yigal says to me, "I'm gonna hit them." And he flounces over there, white yarmulke bobbing, and raises his arm. Taxi Driver snaps something at him. Yigal just stands there frozen with his arm raised while Taxi Driver undoes first the hands and then the blindfold of the one and pushes him in, and then of the other and pushes him in, and locks the door.

Or Ronnie, for example, a sweet kid, quiet, efficient, does his work. Yesterday I visited the courtyard during a break and he was washing down a car. The Arabs in the cell nearby—the same cell, and two of them were the ones Yigal had wanted to hit—were crying,

"Water!" Their cell door was covered by a tin sheet, which had a truck tire up against it to hold it. There was an open space on the side, and they had placed three empty plastic cola bottles on a crossbar there. I saw their eyes, crowded up behind the bottles.

"Why isn't someone taking care of them?" I asked Ronnie.

"Let them die," he said.

So I went up to Ami and asked him to let me get them water, and he said, "They know they'll get water soon." But then he changed his mind as usual and let me. I couldn't get over it. That quiet, sweet kid saying that.

When I went and took the bottles and filled them and handed them through the opening, their eyes changed. A kind of "Ah!" in their eyes. Even happiness. And they looked, close up, like Arabs I know. I work with and for Arabs.

One of them said: "Cap-tain, cigarette?"

"I'm sorry, I don't smoke. I'm a prisoner. It's forbidden for me to talk to you." I whispered this in English and again in Hebrew, but they didn't understand. So I made my hands as if bound together and pointed at myself and then put a hand over my mouth. One of them understood, and smiled, and explained to the others. They all smiled and nodded. I nodded and smiled and left them.

Jesus, there with them, and nothing but sign language, I felt human. And here with my own people, this hardness.

"What are you writing all the time?" asks Gadi the Lazy, looking down on me. Silence. They all want to hear.

"Philosophy."

"What is philosophy?" He asks this with his goofy grin.

I cast about. Most answers lead up a dry alley.

"A lake in Switzerland," says Shlomo. "Five words." He is doing the crossword puzzle.

"Lucerne," I say. That's right. Five letters in Hebrew.

I go across and ask him for the paper. I put it on my chest with the front page showing. Then suddenly I am embarrassed. Must I make a poster of myself?

"Philosophy is what you can say to this woman instead of taking her picture."

"Who's that?" asks Gadi the Lazy.

"Her son was kidnapped," I say, "and now the army has decided he's dead."

"Ilan Sa'adon," says Dubi.

Silence.

I say, "Somebody snapped that photo so that we could see her and not see her, both at the same time. The fact that somebody could stand in front of her and busy himself with a camera is also a fact. And this second fact neutralizes the force of what he is photographing."

"What can you say to her?" says Yoni.

Silence.

"I don't know. I doubt if anybody knows. That's what we're all looking for."

"So how can you write it?" he asks.

"Writing is a way of searching for it."

I give the paper back and return to my cot.

"He has answers to everything," says Shlomo. He is not being sarcastic. "You ask him a question and he says something that just stops you dead. You never thought of such a thing."

"Well, I don't have the answer to that one. That's what I just said."

"Writing is searching," muses Yoni.

"It's a way of communicating with the unconscious." But would they know about the unconscious? I say, "If you have a talk with someone, sometimes you say something bright that you didn't know you knew until you said it. Well, with writing philosophy, if you get on the right wavelength, things come out that you didn't even know you knew. You just have to be there with a question and a pencil and paper. And you have to be able to know when you've gotten onto a bad wavelength. There are people who spend entire lifetimes on a bad wavelength."

"How do you know you're not on a bad one?" asks Gadi the Lazy, grinning.

This stops me, and they laugh.

I say: "There are conversations which lead you away from that woman. But then a certain conversation starts leading you back toward her. That's the right wavelength."

"Kibbutz at the foot of the Carmel. Four words."

"Yagur," says Dror.

"Letters, asshole," says Ronnie.

"So what do you say to her?" says Dubi.

"I told you, I don't know."

"Here you are," he says. He sits up, shirt unbuttoned. Narrow brown chest. His brown eyes are flashing, hot. "You're not here like the rest of us. You're here because you refuse to go out and chase Arabs, and that's what the Arabs do. How do you explain to his mother the fact that you're sitting here?"

I always feel stumped when someone attacks me like this. Stumped and stunned. I am not a man for confrontations. But when I get over the initial paralysis, my first impulse is to quote figures: five hundred Palestinian dead, including one hundred children. How many thousands wounded I don't know. And have you been to the hospitals? Have you seen those mothers? But of course they haven't been, and haven't seen, and it's just arithmetic, and the Arabs do not value life, they think, the way they and their families and their friends and their fellow Jews do.

Silent, they await my recovery.

"I'll explain the fact that I'm sitting here by the fact that it's the most effective action I can take to stop the mess that we're all in that led them to do that to her son."

"You think you're being effective?"

"Oh, I know it's pitiful. But it's just the most effective thing I can do. I'm not alone, you know. There are two or three like me in Jail Six right now."

"Be glad you're not there," says Yigal.

"You wouldn't last a day in Jail Six," says Dubi.

"You've been there?" I ask him.

"I don't need to have been there."

"I've been there," says Yigal. "I've been in Jail Four and Jail Six."

"That's before he became Orthodox," says Ronnie, and they laugh. Yigal smiles and shakes his head.

"Jail Four is the worst," he says. "You don't get knives and forks. You get nothing but spoons."

"Did you have to work there?" I ask.

"Nope, but you're glad for any chance you get to work. You just sit and rot, except you're not allowed to sit on the bed. It has to stay unwrinkled. And every hour you have to stand up for inspection. And they're not inspections like ours. You have to stamp your foot a certain number of times depending on the rank of the officer. And if he doesn't like it he makes you run. Work! It's a gift when they let you work."

"They degrade you," says Gadi the Cheerful.

"Gadi knows too," says Yigal.

"Well, I don't think they'll send me to Jail Four. They send refusers to Jail Six."

"Ask them to let you come back here," says Yigal. "On the day you go free, tell Rafi not to give your place to anyone else. Tell him you'll be back before dark."

"Why should they send me back here?"

"They won't want to take you up to Six. It's a long drive."

"Who's your commander?" asks Dubi.

"Yosi."

"Yosi will send him to Six," says Dubi.

So Dubi knows Yosi.

Yigal: "Never mind about Yosi. You just tell the officer that gets on the phone that you've got a reservation here at Jericho."

"Do it," says Dubi. "Do whatever you can. One day of Six, you'll be down on your knees saying you're sorry and begging for a pardon."

This stings my pride.

"How do you know? Rami Hasson did one hundred and forty days in Jail Six."

Dubi considers for a moment, but then he says:

"I'll tell you something, I'm glad you're here. And I hope you always wind up here, for your sake and mine. For your sake, because this is the nicest little jail you can find. And for my sake, because you're the last son of a bitch I'd want to have as a partner in the Territories. You'd be standing over me all the time making reports on me. Worse than the officers."

"It's hard for me to imagine you being a beast in the Territories."

"What's being a beast?"

"Busting into their houses in the middle of the night. Hauling them out and beating them. Breaking their bones. Putting out cigarettes on their skin. Shooting at them when they're running away. Killing sometimes. Five hundred times."

"It depends on the unit," says Yoni. "We went to Gaza and there wasn't a single casualty. Then we left and Givati came in and right away it started on the radio, Gaza: so many killed, so many wounded. I've never beaten."

"I beat the ones who broke my foot," says Dror. "But I'd have beaten them if they'd been Jews too."

"You have no idea who the Arabs are," says Dubi to me.

"You can't just let them raise hell, you know," says Ronnie. "You can't let them get the feeling they can do whatever they want."

Me: "You sound like a man sitting on a cage of rats trying to hold the sides together."

Silence. Nobody is willing to say that they are rats.

Me: "Of course we're scared of them. We've kept them down so long. We have fantasies about what would they do to us if they could."

Dubi: "They'd cut our balls off."

Me: "They can't cut our balls off! I'm not talking about a Palestinian state with an army. State yes, army no. Let them have something to lose! Look at Jordan. Why hasn't Jordan made problems since 1970?"

And suddenly I have this uncanny feeling. They don't know. Some of them weren't even born in 1970. They're not readers. They lie around bored to death talking about airplanes that fly backward. Not one has brought a book. Abraham's seed. The seed of an ancient, literate people. "And you shall teach these words diligently to your sons. . . . And you shall write them upon the doorposts of your house and upon your gates."

"Jordan," I say, "lost its agricultural land in the Six-Day War. So King Hussein built an aqueduct leading the water of the Yarmuk down the Jordan Valley on the other side. He built farming settlements, and they all depend on that aqueduct. But he also let the PLO make raids from there. So one day Israel got the bright idea of blowing up the aqueduct. Hussein fixed it, but he got the message. There were a lot of other factors too, of course. The PLO had been threatening him. It finally got to be too much, so he did on the ground what Israel never dared to do from the air. He sent his army against the refugee camps. Thousands were killed, guerrillas and civilians—'Black September' the Palestinians call it. Syria tried to step in and topple him, but he beat them. If he hadn't, we were ready to go in against the Syrians.

Ever since then the border has been quiet—and not just because he owes us, but also because he's had all that agriculture to lose. You give the Palestinians something to lose . . ."

Dubi: "You want to trade territory for psychology."

Me: "It's not our territory to trade."

Yigal: "It is so."

"It is not."

He looks around, smiling and shaking his head.

Me: "The West Bank and Gaza are not part of the State of Israel."

Yigal: "What's this bullshit?"

Again something freezes inside me.

"Do you think Shechem is part of the State of Israel?"

"It sure the hell is."

"Holy God." I look at Dubi. Dubi is old enough to have seen a map of Israel before the Six-Day War. "Ronnie, is Shechem in the State of Israel?"

"It sure is."

"And Hebron?"

"It sure is."

"Ancient city in the Negev. Four words."

"Letters, asshole!" yells Dror.

"Avdat," I say.

"Is Avdat with an aleph or an ayin?"

"Aleph. No, ayin. Shlomo?"

He looks at me with satisfaction.

"Never mind. Yoni?"

"Shechem is not in the State of Israel. Neither is Hebron."

"Thank God."

"What's this bullshit?" Yigal feels betrayed.

"Well, it's not, you asshole," says Yoni.

"I don't believe it," I say. "You guys go and beat up on Arabs in those places and you think you're fighting in the State of Israel! I am in shock! I am in total shock! What the hell hope is there? I'm really . . ."

"It's your opinion," says Yigal.

"Opinion! Tell me something, you . . . opinion! Are Paris and New York in the State of Israel?"

"No."

"Is that a matter of opinion?"

He doesn't answer.

"Because I'll tell you something for your information next time you go chasing Arabs in Shechem or Hebron. Shechem and Hebron are no more in the State of Israel than New York and Paris are. And if Arik Sharon were here he would have to say the same."

"You're making a big thing out of it," says Dubi. "It doesn't really amount to a hell of a difference, does it?"

Stumped. Stunned.

"Let's drop it," says Yoni.

Me: "Yeah, but the fact is, you don't beat, and you know where the border is. It makes a difference when you know that the people who are throwing stones and gas bombs are trying to push us out of their own land, because we're occupying them. And wouldn't you do the same as they do, if you were in their position, and assuming you have guts?"

But they've shrunk back. I've made them feel ignorant. At last Dubi speaks, calmly now:

"What it comes down to, Stephen, is that they've got all those Arab countries to go to. We've got only our own little country and nowhere else to go. So don't make me cry for them. It's them or us. We've got to have our own state, you agree?"

"Yes."

"So how are we going to have it with them breathing down our necks nine miles from the sea? And don't give me the bullshit about demilitarization. Germany was demilitarized after World War One."

"I'll give you that bullshit because it's the only solution I can think of, and we'll just have to make sure that there's no repeat of Germany. You talk about the Arab countries," I go on. "You take a look at the map sometime. Not just the local map, the map of the whole Middle East. And you tell me how we're supposed to survive here ten years from now, twenty years from now, fifty years from now, if they don't accept us. Because technology doesn't know borders. And the Arabs are as smart as we are, believe it or not. And not to believe it is about the most dangerous thing you can do."

"Stephen," says Yoni, "you're not supposed to talk about this shit."

"Well, report me. They don't even know where the goddamned borders are. It's basic education."

"Cool it," says Dubi in English.

I cool it.

To Dubi: "I'll meet you when we're out of here. What's your favorite coffee shop in Jerusalem?"

He smiles. "None of the ones you go to."

8

Sometime in November. Kitchen.

THIS MORNING they did not send me to the regimental kitchen. The word is out that some top brass are coming (my consul, no doubt), and they have to finish the painting and get the place ready.

Ronnie has taken over as monitor. Yoni hates the job. So Ronnie ordered Shlomo and me to clean the big courtyard, and the first thing we had to do was empty the garbage can. This sits near the larger Arab cell on the south side, and it has to be emptied into a container near the regimental kitchen where I do the dishes. There are two ways of getting there. One is to cut through a gutted building which the reservists from our side are remodeling. That is the short way from our quarters, and it is the way I always took till this morning. The other leads out of the courtyard around behind the southern wing, which contains the bigger Arab cell. That is the acceptable way with the garbage, and as we turned the corner and walked out from between the buildings, the vista of the Great Rift opened before us. There were the dark mountains of Jordan stretching away on the left—I had always seen them as a single sheer cliff, but now the clouds deflected the early light so that it caught the rim of each, and I saw that they were in series, mountain surmounting mountain. On the right—the occupied side—was the steep drop down to the Dead Sea, with a beige hill like a step, the bottom step of the wilderness. In front of it the modern road goes up to Jerusalem and beyond it lies Qumran Cave Number One. I had seen it all so many times, but always in the position of a guide passing through. And there it was, and here was I. The hill like a step said to me:

"What are you doing here?"

"I'm a prisoner this time."

"The guard," said Shlomo.

Fifty yards to our left was the main gate of the camp, and the bored guard was watching us. We went to our right, and facing that way, I wanted to stop again. It was fantastic. The whole cliff face, and the opening of Wadi Qilt, were all lit up. I had never been down here so early.

"Cap-tain. Cigarette."

A small barred window. A dark face there, the fingers up to the lips making puffing motions. It was the back side of the large Arab cell.

"I don't smoke," I said to Shlomo.

"The guard," he said.

We kept going.

"You see that conical mountain? That's Kypros, a fortress of Herod the Great. Kypros was his mother. And just under it, you see the little bit of asphalt by the palm tree?"

Shlomo grunted.

"That's the Roman road going up to Jerusalem on the bank of Wadi Qilt. That's Wadi Qilt, that canyon. Jesus would have gone on that road."

"Would you do me a favor?" He stopped. We put down the can, still in view of the guard. He smiled at me sheepishly. A round, boyish face. "You see my uniform? I went to a lot of trouble to get it. It's American. But you see the hat doesn't fit it."

His uniform is indeed greenish and smart, but he has the same brown floppy pancake for a hat as the rest of us, except Yoni the paratrooper, who has a hat with a stiff front brim.

"Switch hats with me," he said.

A brilliance came into his eyes.

"My hat's the same."

"No, it's bigger. You see, we go around the corner, and there's the quartermaster's room. So you go in and say you want a different hat. It's too small. They'll think you're part of the regiment, because you work in the kitchen."

"They know who's in their regiment."

"It doesn't matter. You work in their kitchen, that's enough. Besides, what do they care? They have to have a certain number of hats, that's all. It doesn't matter what kind."

"So what do you want me to do?"

"Pick out an American hat."

"What if it's too small?"

"They won't check."

I began taking off my hat, but he said, "Not now. The guard. We'll start."

So we picked up the can and started, and as we neared the corner he said, "Now," and we switched hats.

"I'll really be grateful," he said.

The quartermaster's room was on our route, but it was closed. I felt relief. We went on and emptied the garbage into the bin. The flies were there, like a closely woven buzzing black net over the garbage. I shut my mouth tight and didn't breathe when we came near. Smell of rot.

I left him with the empty can and went into the kitchen. The cook named Mercy was alone.

"Mercy, I have to work with my colleagues today."

He is a short, handsome man. He has a lot of authority. Everybody wants to be friends with a good cook.

He squeezed my elbow. "Anything I can do for you?"

"No, it's all right. I'll be back tomorrow."

I didn't want to tell him about the consul. Not yet. Still savoring it.

"Your hat's shrunk."

"It's my head. It's gotten bigger."

"You can come here for lunch and dinner." He is always thinking of me.

"Thank you."

"I mean it. I'll be insulted if you don't."

I bummed a cigarette for Shlomo. This is called a "white cigarette." That means any cigarette other than the allegedly horrible-tasting brown-filtered cigarettes which they give the prisoners who are smokers. Shlomo lit up at once. He wanted to look for the quartermaster.

"Really, Shlomo!"

"It's my one chance."

So we headed back and stopped by the quartermaster's room, still locked. Then I left Shlomo by the can and went down the row, passing the cooks' room among others. All the doors were shut except one on the other side. I went up to it. Two officers sat there playing backgammon.

"Yes?"

"Is the quartermaster here?"

"Last room on the other side."

"It's locked."

"So it's locked."

I had the feeling one of them was the quartermaster. I started back.

"Maybe he's in the radio room," one said.

I knew where that was: at the end of the row between this one and the kitchen. I had noticed it, with the antenna, whenever I'd used their toilets. So I turned and started that way. Then it occured to me: What the hell am I doing? I went back to Shlomo.

"No deal. He's not around."

"You started going that way."

"The radio room. They said he might be there. Look, I'm not supposed to talk with them. I can't even go into the dining room when they're eating. If the colonel is there in the radio room, I could get a month added on."

Shlomo just looked down at the ground.

"Why is this damned hat so important to you?"

"I take the garbage every morning," he said. "It's always open. And now I have the chance to take it with you, and it's closed. That's my life, I swear it."

"I'm not going to the radio room. I have a wife and kids."

"Well, I don't. All I've got is a retarded sister and a grandmother in the hospital and a bad heart myself, and a mother who's going out of her mind, and half an American uniform."

"I shouldn't have given you the cigarette, with that heart."

"Well, what the hell does it matter? What the hell does my life amount to?"

"An American hat would make you happy?"

"Yes."

"Well, I'm not going to the radio room. He's probably not there, and I'll get a month added. He's probably in one of these rooms sleeping, and I'm not going to wake them all up for the sake of your goddamned hat. You should try with our quartermaster."

"You think I didn't?"

"Tell him about your family."

"I did."

I took a handle of the can.

"Let me finish this smoke." He was hoping the quartermaster would show up.

I thought of Carlyle's *Sartor Resartus*. I thought of Laurence Sterne writing *Tristram Shandy* in evening dress.

"Look," I said, "I'd be willing to do this: next time you bring the garbage and you see that it's open, you come to me in the kitchen and I'll get excused for five minutes and we'll do it."

"You mean it?"

"I promise. Or when you go to the doctor, if you see it's open."

He beamed. He was satisfied. His face shone bright as the cliff in the strong morning light. A touch of magic—and without a hat. He threw down the butt and stomped it out and picked up his side of the can.

"It's great to work with you, Steve."

After we had rounded the corner and switched hats again, I pointed to the highest mountain on the Jordanian side.

"That's supposed to be Mount Nebo, where Moses stood and saw the Promised Land."

WHEN WE got back, Ronnie showed me what they had in mind for me after inspection. It was a pile of rubble, mostly old cement and rusted iron, which half filled the tiny courtyard of the jailers' quarters. Apparently they had renovated some rooms and thrown everything here. I was to shovel it into the garbage can and cart it around back to the same bin. Seemed like hard work for an old man.

"I'll need a cart."

He said they would find one and I went back to picking up cigarette butts and candy wrappers in the big courtyard. I had one half, Shlomo the other.

"Cap-tain. Cigarette."

Maybe they wanted the butts. If I sneaked over and gave them the butts, they would never let us alone. They would call to us from the cells on both sides. A soft touch. American soap. I made the sign with my hands bound together and pointed at myself, mouth closed.

"Cap-tain. Cigarette."

He would refuse to understand. Where did they get the "captain"? Must be from the British period. Like this camp.

The top officer of the police station appeared in the doorway. He is above the jailers. In fact, he is a notch above another one who is above the jailers. To the jailers we have to say "commander," but whenever one of these guys even just appears we have to freeze where we are and wait till he says, "At ease!" I suppose it's instead of saluting, which is forbidden. This has been particularly difficult for me because I tend to take rules literally. An army seems pretty useless if the generals can't think logically about it. But they can't unless people are going to obey the rules. Or disobey them cleanly, clearly, purposefully, as I have. It's the fuzzy areas that are the great danger to an army. So when I finally figured out which guys I was supposed to freeze for, I would freeze whenever I saw them, even from down a dark corridor two hundred yards away. And of course they didn't see me. Or at least they didn't see that I was freezing. The first few times I stood and stood. What saved me, finally, was Tolstoy's *War and Peace*. For in the midst of one of these freezing sessions—while the reservists passed and stared—I remembered Tolstoy's opinion that the chain of command in any army is chimerical anyhow, in which case the orders are not to be taken too seriously. Allowing that he might be right, I let myself move, and when finally I was quite close to them, I froze again, and they graciously released me.

Now this fellow appeared in the doorway and I froze. Shlomo froze. He released Shlomo and came over to me. A tall awkward kid with brown hair in a crew cut.

"Stefan." (Thus.)

"Yes, commander."

"At ease. Do you have any personal connection with the American consul?"

Was that fear?

"No, commander. I'm a dual citizen, that's all. Commander."

"He's coming to visit you on Wednesday."

"I thought Thursday."

He looked puzzled.

"Wednesday. That's tomorrow. You're not to work tomorrow."

"Yes, commander."

"Get a change of uniform. Do you have a belt?"

"No, commander."

"Ami!"

Ami came out of the office and walked nervously over.

"Make sure Stefan gets a belt. And a change of clothes."

"Yessir."

A steely look down.

"Are those your shoes?"

My old Rockports.

"I have a note from the doctor. I have a thing inside my shoe."

I waved my right foot and he looked down at it. We stood like that. You could see his scalp through the brisk hair. My foot felt warm from his attention. It blushed perhaps. He had a gift, this young man, for arousing fear by silence. The army had not erred in him.

"Get him shoes for one day," he said. "You're just going to sit, Stefan. You're not going to work."

"I understand, commander. But I take size thirteen."

He looked up into my eyes. He appreciated the dimensions of the problem.

"I'll never find that," said Ami.

"Get him some red polish."

"I have brown polish," I said.

He nodded and started back toward the office. But then he turned around. I froze.

"I understand you are a professor."

"I was an assistant professor at the University of Houston in Texas, commander."

"What did you teach?"

"Literature. Philosophy. The Greek and Hebrew roots of Western civilization. Commander."

"Could you give lectures to my men?"

This stunned me.

"It would have to be carefully prepared."

"We'll talk about it."

He wheeled around and went back into the office. I unfroze.

"Let's go to the quartermaster's," Ami said.

So I put down my plastic wastebasket and we went—not to the regimental one this time but to our own.

Lectures! The military police in rows before me. These same guys who order me around. My jailers. "What is the fundamental unit of human life? Commanders. The individual, we tend to think. But is it really so, commanders? Of course, when you're alone in a room, you have no doubt that you exist. Commanders. But who is this you, commanders?" It would start by puzzling and end by boring. They would come out thinking, Is this what philosophy is? And want nothing of it.

A sign said the quartermaster's would open at nine.

"Come back here at nine," said Ami. "Tell them I sent you."

"Yes, commander. Did you find a cart?"

"There are no carts. You know what? Go to the kitchen."

"I haven't finished the courtyard yet, commander."

"Just go, Stephen."

So I went through the gutted building toward the kitchen.

I had noticed a policewoman named Orna. It occurred to me that she might be at the lectures. The first lecture only. It would bore her silly. But he had said, "My men."

"Commanders! Everybody write down the biggest question you can think of—a question that is important to you and other people."

"Is there a God?"

"Is life worth living?"

"What does anything matter?"

"Has the rain a father?"

Mercy and Uzi were in the kitchen. Uzi is short for Uziel, which means "God is my strength." He was at the sink doing the blue dishes.

"Is there a God?" they would ask, and here God was in their names and in the color of their dishes. Uzi had a cigarette dangling. He kept washing while half turned to me. Mercy glanced over from the burners, where he was stirring soup.

"I'm with you!" I said.

"What happened?" asked Uzi.

"Well, between us, the American consul is coming."

Uzi pursed his lips, and the cigarette rose in salute. Mercy gave a little bow of his head.

"Now you'll be all right," said Uzi. "They won't want to tangle with you."

"It's probably just routine. I think the consul visits all American prisoners, no matter what they're in for."

"Don't tell them that," said Mercy.

"I would never have thought of the consul. He asked if I have some personal connection."

"And what did you say?" asked Mercy.

"That I don't. I don't."

Uzi shook his head and clanged a pot. "You don't know how things work in this country."

"What good would it do? He's not going to get me out of here. He's not going to say, Pack your bags, we're going home. You guys don't seem to understand: if I didn't want to be here, I wouldn't be. I'd be in the gate of some settlement. Without the benefit of Mercy's cooking."

Mercy smiled. He had learned to cook from his mother. He can take the canned beef and do things with it such that the officers ask, "Where did you get fresh meat?"

I rolled up my sleeves and started rinsing. Tomorrow I'd have to stay clean for the consul, who wouldn't appear—Rafi had said Thursday, and he knew more than any of them—so I'd have to stay clean for the consul on Thursday too. Friday would be half a day because of Sabbath, and then there'd be Sabbath. Or they'd let me go home for Sabbath (the consul's influence), and I'd see the kids, and half of Sunday would be chewed up coming back, and then there'd be one more week.

So I too count days. For it is, after all, prison. I might put a bright face on it, and remind myself that I chose it, but it nibbles at one: this being constantly at the disposal of others in the matter of time.

Three days of rest, and then one more week, and then what? Reimprisonment. That's where the consul might help. Might let his interest be known. "From our point of view he is an American citizen, and you are hounding him arbitrarily. He has offered to serve within your borders, and you keep sentencing him." It might keep off a third term anyhow.

We finished the batch. More would be coming, but I was not allowed to go into the dining room to get them because the reservists were there. I sat down between the chopping tables and pulled out my notebook and started jotting down the notes for what you have been reading here.

"What are you writing?" asked Mercy.

"Philosophy."

He turned back to his magic. A more practical, more sustaining alchemy than mine. Yet it was Jesus, on the mountain just above us (says tradition), who replied to Satan: "Man does not live by bread alone, but by every word that proceeds from the mouth of God." Well, when you press God to the utmost of human capacity, as Job did, what is the word that proceeds from His mouth? "Has the rain a father?" In the Book of Deuteronomy the answer is Yes: "If you obey, He will give the rain for your land in its season." But in the Book of Job the question stuns and baffles. It belongs to a kind of questioning for which the ancient wisdom circles were famous: the wise man asks, and the seeker discovers his own confusion and ignorance. So God baffles Job with a barrage of questions, among them this, and Job winds up:

> *I have spoken without understanding*
> *About wonders that are beyond me. . . .*
> (JOB 42:3)

The word that here proceeds from the mouth of God comes to this: "My ways are too mysterious for you. You are in no position to judge me." But can this be, then, a God who enters into open, ongoing relation with human beings? It does not sound like the God of most of our Hebrew Bible. The latter makes Himself comprehensible. That is the whole point of revelation. In walking with Abraham toward Sodom, for example, God asks Himself: "Shall I conceal from Abraham what I am going to do?" And He does not conceal it.

Job ends in bafflement, in dust and ashes. (The tag-on at the end, where he gets his wealth back twofold, and new sons and daughters, is a kind of mocking lip service to the theology of Job's friends, even while God scolds them for that theology.) Abraham is also dust and ashes, but he can dare to reason with his Creator, because God has entered into a covenant with him. "Covenant" implies that God has made Himself to some extent understandable. When God does that, it is no longer possible to be reconciled to suffering by the statement that His ways are mysterious. To say so is to abandon biblical faith. A covenant which is incomprehensible is no covenant at all.

The God who asks, "Has the rain a father?" is not then the God of the covenant.

It is all right to read that baffling question in a book. But there is the basic principle I have mentioned (I read it in an essay by Rabbi Irving Greenberg): an explanation of suffering cannot count as serious unless you would be willing to give it while hearing the cries of the sufferer. Eliminates a lot of nonsense, that principle. Job lost his sons and daughters in the prologue, and during thirty-odd chapters of argument one has not heard of them again. By the time God questions him, his suffering comes across as a "suffering in general"—without the concrete detail of this son and this and this, that daughter and that and that. But to the mothers of the soldiers who disappeared, I would not want to say, "Has the rain a father?" Nor to that Palestinian father from Beit Jalla, west of Bethlehem (on the slope of Mount Gilo where they wanted to send me), who saw his son gunned down the other day. The police ordered the young man to stop his car, and at first he didn't, but a block later he changed his mind and did, and got out and waited, and one policeman came over and pistol-whipped him, and while he covered his face another policeman shot him in the neck and killed him. These were Israeli Arab policemen, who had replaced West Bank policemen at the start of the intifada after the latter, intimidated by their own people, had resigned en masse. The young man's father ran from the house and had gotten to within thirty yards of them when the shot was fired. Do you go to this father now and hold his hand and say, "Has the rain a father?"

You read about it in the papers, or in this book, and these are blank figures. A blank for father, a blank for son. Fill them in with anonymous faces, Arab. Journalism cannot reach reality. Journalism begins to dull our capacity to react—and thus it becomes dangerous—at the moment we assume it reaches reality.

Two batches of blue dishes have come in, and they are wondering when I'll leave this writing. Uzi is peeling potatoes. All right.

9

Morning break. Cooks' room.

So I DID the blue dishes. The rough black spots in the cups again. More each day. That is not journalism, for me I mean. The person who told me saw the boy who had the burns. Some nuance in the voice and expression of the witness conveyed a presence which to him was not anonymous and so is not to me either. One person transmits another. Even on the phone. I had never seen, for example, Helmut Tews, the director of a Lutheran school in Beit Jalla, but I had spoken with him a few times, arranging things for a tour leader whose group stays up there. The last time, after we had made the arrangements, I asked him:

"Well, how are you surviving all this?"

So he told me about his difficulties. They have pupils in Beit Sahur as well as Beit Jalla. Now Beit Sahur (with the YMCA where that kid showed his burns) has been carrying on a tax revolt. The army has shut the town down for sixty days, and the tax people have gone in and emptied houses of their furnishings and made arrests. The town's slogan has been, "No taxation without representation."

The men of Beit Sahur have been accepting twenty-month jail sentences rather than pay the fines. Twenty months away from the kids. And in these times. My twenty-one days might stretch to seventy, but I know that my kids are relatively safe in West Jerusalem. It's another world five miles away. These men go to jail, and God knows what may happen to their kids, or what their kids might try to do, having a father in jail. But they hardly have a choice. If they don't do the heroic thing, they are liable to lose their one great gain: that the kids look up to the fathers again in Beit Sahur.

Helmut Tews' school bus has been having difficulty getting the Beit Sahur pupils in and out through the army roadblock—that in addition to all the problems with strike days, when they can't hold school. And five pupils in jail. But the roadblock is the daily sore. He or one of his teachers from Germany rides on the bus in order to try to protect the pupils. But sometimes, he said, they have been taken off and beaten. *Geschlagen.* The word went right through me, from the telephone receiver right down to my feet. He said it so calmly. He was going on to other things.

"*Geschlagen? Sie sagten 'geschlagen'?*"

And he was surprised. Of course, *geschlagen.* Didn't I know? Didn't I watch the news, hear the radio . . . ? This sort of thing doesn't make the news, but if kids are getting shot in the neck, you can assume that many are *geschlagen.* Just today a fifteen-year-old was taken. (The German teacher was there but could not prevent it.) Later he turned up at school all bruised in the legs. The soldiers had made the pupils stand by the bus and had checked their papers, and they had recognized this one's family name. For weeks they had been searching for his uncle, who owes taxes. So they took him away, and the rest of the report comes from the kid. He thinks they beat him on the thighs for two to three hours, but he lost track of time. And one soldier kept pushing the barrel of a rifle into his belly and shouting, "Call me Popeye!"

"What?"

"Tell me my name is Popeye!"

"I don't understand."

Long silence.

"There's nothing to understand," said Tews.

"Popeye?"

"Say my name is Popeye."

Silence.

He continued: "And they beat him. He did not tell them where his uncle is."

Silence. I wanted to think they were Druze. Druze serve in our border guard. My racism there. It was still hard to believe that Jews could do such things. And I knew about Deir Yassin. And I was already living here when Jewish terrorists attacked the West Bank mayors. I had seen the few seconds that Israelis were allowed of a four-minute CBS film, in which our own Jewish soldiers, kibbutzniks, beat up two Palestinians whom they had just taken prisoner. But I could file away such things, if I wanted, as lunatic exceptions—a few baddies among us—whereas Tews was talking about routine.

"You're sure of this?" As if I could do something about it.

"I saw the bruises. All black and blue. I wasn't on the bus, of course. It was the German teacher who saw him taken away. But this sort of thing is nothing new."

Yes, but it's different to hear it from someone who has had to do with it personally and is speaking directly to you. A person transmits a person to a person.

Well, what in the world? Hemingway's Ernest Liberal's Lament. What in the world leads people to do such things? And us Jews too. I don't understand. I can't find the possibility in myself. But doubtless I too have possibilities which I cannot find in myself.

Afternoon. Cooks' room.

Orange dishes done.

The Great Escape.

It can start with the dishes. Most of the Orthodox—or what Israelis call "religious"—do serve in the army, and the kosher laws are kept. Among them is the separation of milk from meat. The dishes are blue or orange, and everything else has a blue or red dab of paint on it, blue for milk and red for meat: dishes, pots, knives, forks, spoons, sinks, chopping tables, refrigerators. I am not supposed to scour the breakfast pans with the same pad that I use for the meat pans at lunch. Some kind of contact taboo, one would think. It does not go back to biblical Israel. Abraham, hosting God and two angels, sets cream, milk, and a calf before them (Gen. 18:8). Those who told the story seem to have had no trouble with that.

There is, however, the verse: "You shall not boil a kid in its mother's milk" (Exod. 23:19 and twice later). God does not say why not. Some scholars think that the Canaanites had a ritual in which they did that and that the Israelites avoided it in order to distinguish themselves. If this was the reason, it was no longer relevant when the rabbis, more than fifteen hundred years ago, decided "to build a fence around the Torah." They established further laws separating milk from meat, so that no Jew would even come close to boiling a kid in its mother's milk.

Such is the usual explanation. I admit that it seems farfetched, especially in a good French restaurant. For why not say simply, "You shall not cook meat in milk." Wouldn't that be fence enough?

But whatever the reason, this and our other dietary laws (permitting meat only from cloven-hoofed animals that chew the cud, prohibiting it from an animal not slaughtered according to our ritual, prohibiting meat with blood left in it, prohibiting shellfish, and more) had the effect of keeping us apart from non-Jews. For it is basic to the forming of friendships that people eat together.

Such was the effect of the laws, but it may also have been part of their original purpose. The many curious, special ordinances—and not merely the dietary—kept Israel distinct: "a kingdom of priests, a holy nation" (Exod. 19:6). Just as actual priests had to observe special rules of purity, so the whole people had to keep itself purer than other peoples. The idea of Israel's distinction seems very ancient. We bless God that He "chose us from among all the nations" by giving us the Torah. Some Gentiles have held it against us that we consider ourselves chosen. And some among us have looked down on the Gentiles because they were not. On both sides the misunderstanding of the sources is abysmal.

Ancient Israel—at least the part that came to expression in the Bible—understood itself to be God's tool for the redemption of the Gentiles. It was a Christian scholar, Gerhard von Rad, who opened my eyes to this. He discovered a pattern in the first twelve chapters of Genesis: God creates, people sin, God punishes, but God then performs some redemptive act, so that all is not lost, after which people sin again, and the cycle is repeated. Thus man and woman eat of the fruit, God expels them from Eden, but He makes clothes for them. Cain slays Abel, God condemns him to wander, but He puts a protective sign on his forehead. Humanity becomes thoroughly corrupt, God sends the flood, but He saves Noah with his family and gives the rainbow sign. The last sin in this series is the attempt to build the Tower of Babel. God destroys the tower and scatters humankind, confusing them with different languages. And then what? This is the point where, according to the pattern, a redemptive act should follow. And what follows? The genealogy of Shem's descendants leading to Abraham, and the call of Abraham:

> *The Lord said to Abram, "Go forth from your country, the land of your birth, from your father's house, to the land that I will show you. And I will make you into a great nation. . . . And all the families of the earth will be blessed in you."* (GEN. 12:1−3)

Here is the redemptive act which the pattern requires: a man is called through whom the scattered nations will be able to return to a proper relation with God. At this point, therefore, the Bible shifts from primeval world history to the history of this particular people. Israel is presented not as the firstborn among the nations, but rather as the last, created especially in order to set right what went awry at Babel.

Of course, that may have been the opinion of just one person in ancient Israel—namely, the writer of the so-called J-document, who selected and composed these passages in Solomon's time or soon thereafter. Yet the vision must have been accepted in important places, or else it could not have attained such prominence. Four centuries later it found continuance:

Here is my servant, I shall support him;
My chosen, delight of my soul.
I have bestowed my spirit upon him;
he will bring law to the nations [goyim].
(ISA. 42:1)

The servant is Israel. (The prophet says so three times: 43:10; 44:21; 45:4.) Israel is sent to the *goyim*. Yet sometimes (in these chapters, 40–55, of the Book of Isaiah) the servant is rather a particular prophet who embodies the true Israel, and he is sent to the fallen, exiled Israel to restore them. Even then, however, he is not sent only to Israel:

It is too easy, since you are my servant,
to restore the tribes of Jacob
and bring back the survivors of Israel;
I shall give you as a light to the nations
to be my salvation to the ends of the earth.
(ISA. 49:6)

Israel, or the prophet incarnating Israel: a servant to God and the Gentiles. For *their* sake we were "chosen." That is what it means to be a kingdom of priests: Israel must keep itself distinct in order to be an example and a witness to the nations, just as the priests in the sanctuary must keep themselves distinct in order to serve God and the rest of the people. And as the priests observe special rules of purity which are not meant for the people as a whole, so Israel has special rules which keep it distinct, but which were never intended for the nations.

Where did this sense of mission come from? I shall not try to say now. For the moment this must remain a mere assertion: something is revealed, at the heart of ancient Israel's experience, which cannot be pent up within the original community. It insists on radiating outward to others. And if the community does not bear this revelation outward, it loses touch with its own center.

All that does not represent, of course, *the* biblical view of Israel's role. It is *a* view. We do not know how many people held it. We only know that it was important enough to dominate the account of Israel's origins and to reemerge in prophecy. It would also explain a phrase like "kingdom of priests." It would enable us to make sense of our special laws. There is also an inherent logic: if people experience one God, creator of the universe, but see that other members of the universe do not, they will conclude that something is awry, and they may easily understand that they were born to set it right.

This self-understanding was still at work in the early Christian mission to the Gentiles. For it was not only Christian; it was *Jewish*. When Paul spoke in the synagogues, the audiences included non-Jews, the so-called God fearers, who were welcome there. In baptizing Gentiles, Paul no doubt believed that he was fulfilling the call of Abraham, in whose seed (Christ) the nations were being blessed. And those God fearers were there to hear him because Jews had gone out to talk with them and bring them in—not as converts, rather as Gentiles who were to give up idolatry and worship the one God.

Even while that mission went on, however, Judaism was under strain, because of our wide dispersion. Then came the first catastrophic revolt against Rome and the destruction of the Temple in 70 C.E. ("of the Common Era," which Christians call A.D.). The old commandments began to take on a different function. They were no longer seen as the precondition for being a light to the nations. We had the problem of continuing to exist as Jews at all. The commandments became the means for preserving identity; our relation with God became an end in itself, to which the Gentiles seemed marginal. Indeed, there were some rabbis, a minority, who found no place at all for Gentiles in a redeemed world. The rabbinical task was a kind of holding action: to elaborate the commandments into ordinances which would shape a large part of daily life. Without the shaping we would no doubt have vanished into the nations. Because of things like the blue dishes and the orange dishes, I can be here today as a Jew.

The rabbinical "fence around the Torah" preserved us, but it confined the Torah. Then came the Scientific Revolution, and some among us broke the fence. There were those who burst upon the Gentile world with a sense of mission—the ancient sense of mission, secularized. Even the State of Israel, once upon a time, dreamed of being a light unto the nations.

Blue dishes at morning, orange dishes at noon. Blue dishes at evening. All that preserved us. We are a people grounded in memory, but after twenty centuries of just holding to each other, we have forgotten what for.

Cell. Evening.

Tomorrow I have free. Waiting for the consul.

The one notable thing that happened at dinner was that Taxi Driver came in and asked us to make sandwiches for the Arabs, meaning the Arab prisoners. "Palestinians," I should say, now that I'm a bona fide leftist. The word "Arab," as a noun, carries a certain taint in the mouth of an Israeli Jew, and maybe also in the mouths of others. When I talk to a tour group, for example, I can't bring myself to say, "the Arabs." I can't say, "The Arabs have a high birthrate." I'll say instead, "The Arab population has a high birthrate." The tour agent I work for has no difficulty saying, "I am an Arab." He says it proudly. But for me, even me, the word is tainted. Just so, a sensitive Gentile will not refer to "a Jew" or "the Jews." Rather he will say, "a Jewish man," "the Jewish people." I suppose the noun "Arab" in my mouth or the word "Jew" in a Gentile's carries the taint of something not quite human, but that taint is explicitly removed when you attach the word to another like "man" or "population."

So Taxi Driver came in and asked us to make sandwiches for the Palestinian prisoners. In the days before, he had brought them only vegetables from the storeroom. He would go in and fill two plastic bags with carrots, onions, turnips, whatever came to hand—not washing them—and these, I suppose, had to last them from evening to evening, for I never saw him do it but once a day. Like animals in the zoo.

I don't know what occasioned the change. But Kobi and I were assigned to make them twelve sandwiches with soft white cheese.

Kobi is a reservist from Jaffa. He is young by the standards of this regiment. He has dark skin—Moroccan? Yemenite?—and even a mustache. What I am getting at is . . . he looks like an Arab. (Even there, when I write the word, it leaves an acid trace in the mouth.) If he shaved off the mustache or grew a beard, it would be less of a problem. Or he could put on a yarmulke. There are dark-skinned Jews who do that, though they are not religious. I discovered this at the airport one Sabbath. I noticed that the porters were working with yarmulkes on. I asked the foreman: "How come they're working on Sabbath?" He said, "They're not religious. They just don't want to be taken for Arabs." I know a Palestinian who puts on a yarmulke and recites reams of Hebrew blessings. He used to bless tourists at the Western Wall, while taking orders for Hebrew name chains in silver and gold. And there are Jews, some of my guide colleagues included, who when driving in the West Bank put on a kaffiyeh—an Arab headdress.

Kobi does not want to shave his mustache or wear a yarmulke, and now his appearance has become a problem. His yearly reserve duty is usually in the kitchen, but this time they have me to help them, and since I *must* stay in the kitchen, Kobi has become redundant there. On the other hand, one of the dining-room workers is down with Herod's Revenge, so they want Kobi to serve food and clear tables. But after one meal he refused to go back. He would not explain why. He just kept disappearing. And curiously no one seemed to understand, so I went to Mercy and said, "They treat him like an Arab." Mercy considered for just a second, then turned to Uzi: "You'll do the dining room till Fetch Me comes back."

Uzi was silent. He is responsible for the dishwashing. Then he said:

"What's wrong with Kobi?"

Mercy was silent.

"He's uncomfortable there," I said.

Uzi mused long. Then he said OK. "Till Fetch Me gets better."

"Fetch me! Put me! Give me! Reach me! Shove me!" said Mercy.

"Stick me!" said Uzi. They went through this routine whenever they thought of Fetch Me, lying there pale in his bunk with the runs. The first day, when he was still on his feet, he tried to get control of me, ordering me around: "Fetch me! Bring me!" So that's where they got the name.

Mercy said to Uzi, "Find Kobi and tell him he's working in the kitchen."

So Kobi came back. He is right-wing, like many Oriental Jews. "Oriental" refers to those who came, or whose parents or grandparents came, from Arab countries. They make up about half the Jewish population now. There are leftists among them too—there is even a movement called East for Peace—but it's a pleasant surprise, nonetheless, whenever I encounter a leftist Oriental. Their tendency to the right is explained in various ways. They are supposed to harbor bad memories of what life was like under Arab rule. But more to the point is the fact that they have been discriminated against since their arrival in the early fifties. The pattern was established under Labor governments. By 1977, after the corruption in that party came to light as never before, they began to associate discrimination with Labor and vote Likud instead. On top of that there is the problem which Kobi represents: they look more like Arabs. So it is important to them to distinguish themselves—not just for display, but even for their own sakes—and what more effective way to remind others and oneself that one is not an Arab than to hate and mistrust Arabs?

Kobi spread the cheese very thin. "A prisoner is half a man," he said with a smile. He was teasing me.

"You aren't putting enough for half a man," I said.

"You don't have to load it on," he said. "These are not angels."

"Angels don't need to eat."

"These guys throw rocks. Gas bombs."

"In their land. Against an occupier."

I left to get another tub. When I came back he was finished. He watched me gob it on.

"There's something you don't understand," he said. "It's them or us."

"It's them *and* us. Either we live together or we die together."

"You give them a finger, they'll take the whole hand."

He recited the slogans calmly, quietly. A humble man, transmitting received wisdom.

And so it went, back and forth, slogan for slogan, until I ducked out.

I don't watch predictable TV programs either. These conversations always lead me around to one basic fact: we are a few million Jews on a small piece of land surrounded by nearly two hundred million Arabs, not to mention Iran. Sooner or later they will possess the same technology that we have and be able to use it about as well. So what's to keep them from wiping us out? Our nuclear arsenal. But they will have those weapons too. One need not be a prophet to see that. One need only think about the pace of technology in the last fifty years, then extrapolate to the next fifty. Mutual nuclear deterrence. Think of a Khaddafi or a Khomeini type with a button to push. Or an Abu Nidal with a portable.

It is a thought which we have only dared whisper till now, for fear that the enemy may be listening: we have no hope of surviving here in the long term unless the Arab countries accept us. But the main thing we have done, or rather failed to do—I mean the forty years of selective inattention in the matter of the Palestinians—has made *all* Arabs hate us the more. Now the Palestinians have stood up, and we find ourselves in the position of imprisoning, maiming, and killing them. We hone their hatred and the hatred of our neighbors. In killing their children we condemn our grandchildren.

Why then don't my countrymen see? I think because it is too bitter a pill, this notion that our survival depends upon their acceptance. It puts us in the position of the cringing, obsequious ghetto Jew, come to beg for a little piece of land. The whole point of the State of Israel has been that we should never have to be that again. Everything in us revolts against it. Hence the posturing, the militancy, the self-assuredness, the blindness to the longer view and the larger map. But the revolt against this image of the Jew is deeper than all posturing. We have a certain concept of ourselves. We are hard. We stand straight. The cringing, obsequious Jew has been expunged from our flesh. We cannot go back to that. And indeed we shall not. For if they do not accept us, then they shall die too. Samson has his hair back.

We are who we are, we modern Israelis, in reaction against that cringing, obsequious Jew. It is never very healthy to exist as a mere "reaction against." To choose life, in this historical moment, requires that we overcome both the ghost and the reaction against him, which makes us who we are. But this is difficult. Too many of us like the new image. Ben-Gurion, state builder, with his massive white hair rising: now there was a leader. Samson's hair.

SPEAKING OF CRINGING, obsequious: I have just filled out a form, a request for Sabbath leave. Four of the eight got to go last weekend, everybody who applied. Dubi, for example, came back smiling, having been properly trounced by his kids. It was his second Sabbath leave. Shlomo, Gadi the Lazy, and I had not applied. One does not apply for one's first Sabbath. Yoni had not applied either, since he had had it the week before. But now we're trying for this Sabbath, all four of us.

They tell me what to write: name, serial number, dates of entry and release, my offense.

"Do I have to write my offense?"

"Yeah, sure," says Ronnie. "He has to know you didn't stab anybody."

"He" is the chief of military police. He decides about all these.

I write: "Refusal to serve in the Territories."

"You'd better tell him why you refused."

"That'll just get me in deep."

"Tell him grounds of conscience."

"That's gonna be very hard for you to get," says Dubi. He has told me that before. He stands in front of his bunk, stripping his shirt off.

I write: "Grounds of conscience."

"You'll get it," says Ronnie. "If anyone will, you will. Write down how old you are. You've got kids. But you've got to pile it on thick. Everything you can think of, why you've absolutely got to be home this weekend. Your grandmother's dying. Your mother's having heart surgery. Your father's an alcoholic and has just had an accident and is lying in a coma. . . ."

"*My* father's an alcoholic," says Gadi the Lazy.

"It doesn't matter. They can both be alcoholics."

"They don't check," says Yigal.

"I have enough," I say. "I have enough with reality."

I write: "My father-in-law died before Rosh Hashanah. There is no other adult male member of the family here."

This is true, and I should have known, therefore, that the moon is waxing. We went up to his grave on the thirtieth day after the funeral, and the next morning I went to Schneller.

I write: "My mother-in-law and my wife are still in deep sorrow. My children need the presence of a male. We just went through the trauma of a fire. Cars were burned under our living-room floor three weeks ago, and I was too busy cleaning the ash from walls and closets, etc., to be able to spend time with the children."

A victim of the intifada! That should get to him!

I show my rough draft to Ronnie.

"You have to write the end," he says. "In suspenseful attention."

"You're kidding."

"In suspenseful attention. You have to write it."

I really would like that Sabbath leave. I write: "In suspenseful attention."

10

Evening. Cell.

NOGA VISITED last Sabbath. I have barely mentioned that. There is a great deal that I have said little or nothing of. This journal has a flow of its own. Much is passed over.

There is, for example, a sexual aspect. There are females here, the policewomen (but are they women at eighteen–nineteen?). They have no interest in me, of course. I am so obviously ineligible. Silver sideburns. I used to look young for my age, but apparently I do not look young enough anymore. They put me in the category of their fathers. While I was waiting at Schneller—while the base commander tried to find a prison for me—his clerk sat behind the desk. She had made a brown line around her lips. I found it repulsive and exciting. She tried to help me call home, and we talked about how hard it was to get through. I offered her pretzels. I asked her to use her influence to keep me at Schneller. There was just that little bit of contact. But when she heard I was going to Jericho, she said:

"Oh, I'm so glad. I served there. It's not like jail. You'll be all right there."

"Well, thank you for using your influence."

"Oh, it's nothing. I wouldn't want *my* daddy to go to jail."

Not that I am interested in them. Or it is a curious kind of interest, a subjunctive interest: how interested I would be, if . . . if I were younger, if she were older, if I weren't married, didn't have kids, if she weren't interested in getting married, having kids. There is, after all, a barrier from my side as well. They look too fresh and shiny. They are very much in the clutches of Nature, and I am not, have done my bit, have brought forth two children, have been released. The element is different. It is like the underwater observatory at Eilat. You are enclosed under the sea, and through a window you see the fishes swimming freely, living their lives. The mermaids swimming freely. They do not look at me, but I look and look. Even a subjunctive interest brings a purr.

One, however, has penetrated the glass. Has lodged straight in my medulla. Has pierced my age to some hidden vestigial root. It would take someone like this, with no subtlety at all, garishly narcissistic, heavily lipsticked, the second button carefully carelessly open, the walk deliberately slow, braking with the toes and slopping the heels so that the breasts bounce as if with a life of their own under coarse soldierly cloth. I can understand why old men make fools of themselves. Only Nature's extremest winks can still get through.

So there is that. I have left it out till now. But it would be a misrepresentation not to admit that it too is there. This girl-woman's name is Orna.

There is another named Miri. One pays special attention to the females, because there is so little love, after all, in army life—it is dry, sterile, mechanical—and then they come, bearing that whole dimension. Miri has long blond hair, and the lines of her face are so delicate and changing that one can find there all the ages of woman. She has blue sad laughing eyes . . . Well, you see how I go on. I doubt whether I would make such a study of her in civilian life. Here she is a flower in the desert.

We are not supposed to talk with them. The first Friday night both jailers were on leave, and one of the women was in charge. She left the cell door open till late, and we could wander out into the courtyard. I watched the *Weekly News Summary* in the police club room, and when I went out, I saw that it was just like college: girls and boys sitting talking together under the waxing Jericho moon.

Orna was interested in Yoni. But Yoni has subtler yearnings, as I had, too, thirty years ago. So he was more with Miri than with Orna. Shlomo, Gadi the Lazy, and I were new. No policewoman was interested in me, for the reasons stated. (There were a few Allenby Bridge reservists too, who watched the news with me, and no policewoman was interested in them either, I am glad to say.) But even Gadi the Lazy, so young and clumsy, with that goofy grin, had company. So did Shlomo. He told me that a certain female soldier, who also came to watch the news, invited him to her room. He feared getting caught and declined. I hardly know when to believe Shlomo. Nor does Shlomo.

After declining, he went, he said, in search of the doctor, in order to get the referral he is always seeking, for a checkup on his heart. No one was in the infirmary, so he poked around a little and looked through a window where there was light and discovered the whole Sabbath contingent of the regiment whose dishes I do watching what is called a blue movie. Here I believe him, because that morning there had been some murmuring in the kitchen and then Uzi had come up to me with a big tobacco-stained smile and asked, "Hey, Steve, do the police let you watch blue movies?"

I said, "Thank you very much, but I find them too exciting, and I can't go home like you guys."

"The blue movies are for the guys who are not going home," said Mercy.

"Well, I get too excited, and I wouldn't know what to do with it."

"There's always a bar of soap," said Uzi. He was going home. While fulfilling his conjugal obligations, he would doubtless like to think of me with a bar of soap.

"You have to clean the pipes once in a while," said Mercy. I let it end. Hard to explain. I was sure of this: that I did not want to undergo that degradation here. Even in me, this mild-mannered reporter, people cavorting on a screen can trigger a sexual force ten times greater than any that comes naturally. At the end of the holiday of Succoth, or Booths, one sees religious kids lying facedown on the plaza before the Western Wall and beating willow fronds upon the stones. They beat to exhaustion. They are beating out their sins, I am told. Twice in my life I have seen blue movies, and afterward I felt like a willow frond in the hands of that sexual force, which came from God knows where—or as if some fuse had been removed, and the wires directly joined, and then overloaded, and the house on fire—beaten and beaten to shreds against the stones. That was degradation. And not merely the result of a prudish upbringing. To be thus whipped, to be so mechanically controlled, to be so unfree, and again unfree, and again unfree, and not yet free, and still not free, is in itself degrading, regardless of how this or that particular culture copes with sex. I suppose that is why I turned them down. I still have a certain freedom with respect to my own body, and if I watched their blue movies I would lose it. Then at last they would have me. Cannot go home. Has to do it here. Cannot go home. Here he has spent himself. Here and not elsewhere. Now he is really here, in this toilet, in this prison, at the deepest point of his lower spine. Imagine that over and over, in the grip of that force. The spending of all that is in me, here.

Perhaps other people are not so suggestible as I. Or what is more likely, perhaps if I were to watch blue movies, my threshold of suggestibility would rise. The hand that whips me against the stones might weaken with use, and I might thus pass through the circle of sexuality and become free again. Yes, but it would be an anesthetized freedom. I like sex. Don't want to be anesthetized. Like freedom too.

Freedom consists to a large extent in the knowledge of what rooms not to go into. But one usually learns that the hard way, having gone into them. The forces are greater than we are. One gets caught, escapes, is caught again. Learns. In the interstices between known forces wends a way. Odysseus.

Shlomo did not go in. He stood at the window and was accidentally hooked. His eyes widened as he told me.

"Then they all turned around and looked at me and laughed."

"Did you run?"

"Yeah, sure I ran. But how am I going to go see that doctor now? He'll remember me."

"Well, you caught him watching a blue movie. On Sabbath, and he probably should have been on duty. He could wind up being a prisoner with us. I bet he'll give you whatever you want."

The brightness came into his eyes.

"You think I should go see him?"

"As soon as possible. Not tonight though. Tomorrow. Let him think about it tonight."

"You want to come watch?"

"No."

He was itchy. Hooked. I felt a little vicarious tingle. He would not dare to go back alone. Yoni was talking with Miri and Orna. Gadi the Lazy sat on the bench in front of the police office with two others. The moon played upon the mixtures, blending, forgiving all.

What did they find to talk about? Just a quick sidelong glance at Orna. The interstices.

There was a roar, and a jeep drove in, screeched, stopped. Dark commotion. Then it started again and turned toward us, flooding us with light, but kept turning, and stopped. Now there was a dark prisoner in the rightmost of the two circles of the lights, crouched on his haunches, face to the wall. So they had brought in a prisoner. The eyes of some others glistened from the opening where the corrugated strip did not quite cover their door.

They had not then been asleep. It is not that I had forgotten they were there, but rather that without really thinking about them I had thought of them as asleep. Convenient, to think and not think of them thus. No "Cap-tain, cigarette" to disturb the illusion. They too had their interstices. Had watched us flirting and smoking. Had watched each butt tossed. Where it was tossed. Did the longing for freedom and family, for any contact—any supportive contact—concentrate, perhaps, into the longing for a butt?

He remained on his haunches. They were not in a hurry to put him in with the others. A patient silhouette. That same nonfear. And how do they manage to sit so long on their haunches? I sometimes see the beduin sitting like that, waiting by the roadside for the bus up to Jerusalem. Whenever I sit like that for more than a minute and then stand, I get dizzy.

I stayed there, just to see if there would be any mistreatment. The conversations started up again. Shlomo went into the club; the reservists were watching a regular Friday night show called *Pretext for a Party*. Shlomo came out. Pale stuff, after a blue movie.

The soldiers from the jeep moved the truck tire and the corrugated tin strip, opened the bars, took the blindfold off the prisoner, nudged him in, and closed it all up again. That reminded the girl-woman in charge. *"Yalla,"* she said, which is Arabic for "Let's get on with it."

She marched toward our cell door jingling the keys. Then Orna too stood up and stretched, flexing her little fists. The coarse cloth lifted. So that was our evening out. Orna went to Gadi the Lazy in his group and, cocking her head, took him by the ear.

FOR US IT IS the lightest of prisons. My daughter cried when she first heard that I might be going to jail. I asked if she were ashamed, but she said no, it wasn't that. Her image of jail, she explained, came from Victor Hugo. Her father in a rat-ridden dungeon.

"Well, it is not like that."

"I know, but that's how I picture it."

"We'll be in tents." (I expected to be in Jail Six.) "On cots above the ground. And what's the choice? If I don't go, then conscience will be my jailer, and that's much worse."

She said angrily: "I don't know what that is, conscience!"

"Do you want to know?"

"No!"

So we sat in silence. Then she came into my arms and wept. The heat of her face against my chest was wonderful. She said: "You and your psychology."

"Well, I know you know what conscience is. I see your conscience when you try to lie to me and can't."

"How can you see it?"

"It's a flicker on your face."

Silence. Resting on my chest.

"If you ever lie to someone, then you'll see you'll go on making excuses to yourself, why you had to do that, but what you're really trying to do is throw conscience off. And if I go where they want to send me and become part of that, I don't see how I'll ever be able to throw conscience off. It's a bloodhound. Do you know what a bloodhound is?"

"Of course I know what a bloodhound is!"

"Well, I'm sorry. You grow up so fast, I can't keep track."

"I did a report on dogs."

"Of course."

"Then how come everybody else can go, and their conscience doesn't bother them."

"I don't know. I can't speak for them. I can only speak for me. I see that there are a million and a half Palestinians living in the Territories, and we are ruling them against their will, and when they show that they don't like it, we throw them in jail. What if we were a Palestinian family, and Israeli soldiers come in in the middle of the night while we're sleeping, and they see all these books and say, Oh, he must be a leader, and arrest me, throw me into a jail where it's really like in Victor Hugo, in some ways worse, and you don't even know where they've taken me, or if I'm still alive even, or what things they might be putting me through, it's all left to your imagination, and weeks go by, and when you do find out, it's hard or impossible to visit me—I wouldn't even let you visit me, I wouldn't want you to see me in those conditions—and none of us knows what they're accusing me of, and six months go by like that, without a trial, and they can renew it for another six months—and then they can rearrest me again the same way anytime. Because that's really happening. That's happening tonight and every night not very far from here. There are a thousand fathers and sons in jail under those conditions right now—it's called administrative detention—and thousands more who at least know what they are charged with and will get a trial—but a fair trail?—and then comes the sentence, twenty months, two years, who knows? And women too in jail. If it doesn't happen to them tonight, they will go through the night in fear of it. And what if I were one of the Israeli soldiers who goes in in the middle of the night to arrest them? Not to mention beating them or breaking their bones. It's the simplest thing in the world. I don't know why other people don't see it. And if I go, then my going itself says something. It says, Yes, OK, you can use me too to carry out the policy. I know there are people who go who don't believe in beating Palestinians, people who want to keep the violence to a minimum. That's great if you can do it. But suppose I'm there, and I'm ordered to go into a house and arrest somebody—somebody who might be accused of doing the same kind of thing that I would hope to have the courage to do, if I were in his circumstances. Suppose I arrest him, and I take him to the truck, and I make sure that nobody beats him. But then the truck drives away with him, and they beat him. Well, it was I who arrested him. So what should I have done? Should I have refused to arrest him? Then why not refuse to go there in the first place? I want to keep the violence to a minimum, but so what? Once I'm there, I'm part of the machine, and the machine didn't put me there to accomplish *my* purposes."

I know one should be wary of igniting a child's imagination. But my daughter has great strength and capacity. She is not given to bad dreams. She had stopped crying, and she nestled upon my chest.

"I can't go against myself," I said.

A few days later when I put her to bed she said: "About jail. I've thought about it." She nodded once. "It's all right."

WHEN I LIE BACK, I feel the imprints of the two kids on my chest. A month and a week ago their grandfather died. My father-in-law. And when Noga went to her mother's, I sat on the sofa and held the kids in my arms. We sat like that for an hour or so, and that was it. That was their mourning. But still I can feel, when I lie on my back before sleep, those two heads on my chest. Can smell them too, their different smells. If I get Sabbath leave, I shall sit with them like that again and renew the imprints. Of course that would be too easy. Sabbath leave would be all too easy. I won't get it, I think, though everyone except Dubi seems to be assuming I will. But if I don't get it, then on the day of my release—and before reimprisonment—I shall make a little detour on the way to the base, and hold them there again, renewing the imprints.

Sabbath leave would make the thing absurdly easy. Even without that, it is the lightest of prisons. Not Victor Hugo. And nevertheless it has, I believe, something of the essence of all imprisonment, which Dostoevsky caught in the title *The House of the Dead*. There is, first of all, a world outside, the world from which I came, and I cannot on my own power get in touch with it. In this lightest of prisons I can ask permission to telephone, but still, I can't simply decide to go and telephone. Someone else has to decide. I can of course send a letter, but the letter has to go through censorship. Or I can ask someone who is visiting, or a prisoner who is being freed, to take a letter for me—but again, it's in the hands of someone else. Or if someone wants to phone me or visit me, it's possible, but someone else has to decide. There is, in short, a screen of officialdom, like a hierarchy of archons, between us and the outside. Gadi the Cheerful has to some extent overcome it by charming the telephone operator, but even so, he must continue to charm, and it is for her to let herself be charmed.

I keep seeing, as I write this, a hole in a different ceiling, in the basement of a church called St. Peter in Gallicantu, St. Peter of the Cock's Crow. Some think that the House of Caiaphas may have been here, where Jesus (say the Gospels) was tried before the Sanhedrin, and where Peter thrice denied knowing him before the cock crowed twice. One goes down a staircase below the main chapel to bedrock, and carved out of the limestone are ancient chambers, which may have been merely a storage room and a cistern. But with a little imagination one can convert the storage room into a prison, and the cistern into the high-security cell, through the opening of which a man would have been lowered or pulled up by ropes.

So they took Jeremiah and cast him into the cistern of Malchiah, the king's son, which was in the court of the guard, and they let Jeremiah down by ropes, and there was no water in the cistern, but only mud, and Jeremiah sank in the mud. (JER. 38:6)

Nowadays there is a modern entrance from the side, and one can lead a group of tourists or pilgrims down in there. And there is a little window high up, from which a guard in the storage room or prison could peek in. One looks up at the hole in the ceiling, and one tries to imagine this place when that was the only entrance and exit. The idea is: if this was the House of Caiaphas, then Jesus might have been kept overnight here, before being handed over to Pilate next morning. How would it have been for him? For any prisoner? We would spend a few minutes thinking about that. But my imaginings were always forced. Now I am in the lightest of prisons, but I am thinking of that hole, and I know. One feels like a piece of flesh that can be shoved around at other people's bidding. And now I understand the meaning of their taking my watch. When I last wrote about that, I felt a kind of exultation: I was unburdened of the illusion that time is my own. I felt the giftlike character of those moments which I managed to steal. But now it has gnawed at me, this being-at-their-disposal-every-minute, this not-knowing-what-they-will-think-of-next-for-me-to-do. They have told me that I won't have to work while waiting for the consul, but the first rule is not to count on it, for they might think of something nice and clean, like collating forms. It is this constant being-at-disposal that gnaws. Even in the lightest of prisons. That is one thing.

And so Jesus. He was at disposal to be shoved around, crowned with thorns, whipped and crucified. Of course with him it was differ-ent, because just before his arrest, in the Garden of Gethsemane, he had put himself at God's disposal: "Not as I will, rather as You will." But there in the cistern of Gallicantu I am not concerned with doing theology; I am concerned with the feeling of what it is like, and now I know: it is like being a piece of meat which someone, some desultory eater, already full, is shoving about absentmindedly on a plate. The eater is up there on the other side of the hole. Occasionally one hears his voice. Is he thinking about me now? They are conversing. About me? About this piece of flesh? "Why don't you eat your meat?" In the police office, are they talking about me? One cannot quite make out the words. Hey, I am a man! I am the king of France!

Is my redeemer coming? Or am I forgotten? It feels quite forgotten under the hole. Good God, yes, that's what it is: a toilet. That's why I keep thinking of this hole in Gallicantu. A piece of flesh: that is a euphemism. A piece of shit, that's what it feels like. And what is more dead? What is more forgotten? A thing to be avoided. The voices: I am the last thing they will be talking about.

I know better, of course. Nobody here treats me like shit. And on the outside, people are thinking of me. Even in faraway America, even friends I had lost touch with. Every time I speak with Noga, there's something, some new word from someone I thought I had lost. The first time, the young soldier who was taking me from Schneller to Jericho let me call home from the Jerusalem bus station. I had already phoned her once with the news of my sentence, and she had called Rami Hasson of Yesh Gvul. They had my permission to publicize it. Since my arrest two days had passed.

"Stephen, you were in all the newspapers and on television!"

"By name?"

"By name!"

"Jesus, I didn't plan to become famous this way. Just for saying No."

"I've been getting calls from all over."

I felt a swelling of pride. She had thought I was just going up against windmills.

"Stephen, Paul Blanc! Do you remember him from Vermont?"

"No."

"I don't either. But he was at Goddard when we were there, and he remembered us. He's in San Francisco now. He's with the Friends of Yesh Gvul. He saw your name come in, and he called me."

"No kidding."

"He's called people in Philadelphia."

"Philadelphia? No one knows me in Philadelphia."

"You taught there. Listen, he also called Stewart."

"Stewart!"

Silence.

"Is Stewart alive?"

"Yes! He's having a meeting in his house with the Women in Black."

"There are Women in Black there too?"

"Yes. They've adopted you. Vermont's adopted you."

"So he knows." It filled me with pride. Once, on a visit to him—it was before the intifada, when we were bombing Beirut—he had said, "You probably weep every day." And of course I didn't weep every day. I didn't weep at all. But here I was going to jail, and he knew about it.

"That feels great," I said.

She was silent.

"Listen, I'm not going to Atlit. They're sending me to some jail in Jericho."

"We sent letters to Atlit!"

"You sent letters already?"

"The kids."

"I'll write them. I'll call you from Jericho and tell you the address."

"Why did they put you in Jericho?"

"I missed the car to Jail Six by five minutes. Anyway, the soldiers say it's a lot better in Jericho. And it's closer to you, too."

"Listen, NBC wants to interview you."

I felt myself turning red.

"I don't think I can. I'm a soldier."

"Well, there's a woman from a Tel Aviv paper wants to interview me."

"You'd better check with Rami."

"Listen, when were you a conscientious objector to Vietnam?"

This took me by surprise. I had forgotten all about it. It had never occurred to me to connect the two things. And that, of course, would be the interest for the papers here.

"How do they know about that?" I asked.

"I told them."

"Jesus, you know I'd forgotten about that."

My wife is a novelist. She has a novelist's mind. She remembers details. It must be a sign that she cares about people. With me everything gets vacuumed up into philosophy.

"In '61," I said, "but they stalled it six years. It wasn't just Vietnam. It was general. Yeah, you could say, In America he wasn't willing to fight, but when he came here he knew he'd have to serve in our army, and still he was willing. I should have said that at my trial, you know? You know, I did everything I could to stay out of jail."

"You did?"

That would surprise her. She did not say so, but I knew she knew that I was half looking forward to jail.

"I did. So Stewart knows."

There was silence.

"I've almost finished *Light in August*. It's great."

She laughed.

I said: "I remember when you were reading it. Eighteen years ago in the German Colony, in that room. You know I'm looking at the soldier. I think he's going to signal me in a minute. It's great to talk to you. It gives me a lift."

"They want to know what books you brought."

"Who?"

"The interviewers."

"Faulkner. Cheever's stories. A Bible. Ford Madox Ford, *The Good Soldier*." She laughed. "Two anthologies of poetry. All stuff I can read over and over. No philosophy. How did the neighbors react?"

"You remember Giora?"

He had lived in the apartment above us in our previous neighborhood, and he had gone to jail during the Lebanon war.

"He called to say he's proud of you and he supports you with all his heart."

Again the swelling of pride. It would have come as a revelation to him. I had never said anything.

"And what about the neighbors?"

"They're shocked. They had no idea."

"Yeah, I know."

"But they say . . . you know what they say? They say it's a different mentality."

"American," we said together.

"Yael said to me, 'Why is Steve making problems?' "

I winced. I sort of like Yael.

The soldier signaled.

"I have to go. I'll try to call you from Jericho."

I went to the bus. I felt very big walking over, as if my body stretched beyond its bounds. I didn't finish *Light in August*. I watched the wilderness flip by, and I thought about all she had said. It was already worth it. Just to know that Stewart was alive, and knew, made it already worth it.

> Then the king commanded Ebed-melech, the Ethiopian, "Take three of these men here with you, and lift Jeremiah the prophet out of the cistern before he dies." So Ebed-melech took the men with him and went to the house of the king, to the wardrobe storeroom, and there he found old rags and worn-out clothes, which he let down to Jeremiah in the cistern by ropes. Then Ebed-melech the Ethiopian said to Jeremiah, "Put the rags and cloths between your armpits and the ropes." Jeremiah did so. Then they pulled Jeremiah up with the ropes and lifted him out of the cistern. (JER. 38:10–13)

That is what it is like every time a message comes from outside. Like a rope. A little miracle. A little resurrection. And of course the effect lasts for a while, and even afterward I can summon the memory and bathe in it. But for the most part, during the times when it is not coming, when the phone is not pressed to the ear, there is again that hole above me, and the voices heard through it, of people whose words I cannot quite make out and whom I cannot quite reach. The House of the Dead indeed. The dead must feel like this if they can feel. Will anyone remember the death day to say Kaddish? Who can remind the living?

Let me not pity myself. In my case even the consul is coming. How many people have a consul riding in? What whisperings must have gone on and be going on about me? Perhaps he is bringing old rags and cloths and a good rope.

But still the hole is there.

I remind myself of the cell on the other side of the opposite wall. A white wall, the wall of our little courtyard, a few yards from my bed. "My bed," so easily said. One mattress, I saw. To fight over. No toilets. A bucket they have. The guard may come to empty it, may not. That's their contact with the outside world. Will he empty it, bring water, bring the bag of unwashed vegetables? Not to think about phone calls. Much less a galloping consul.

11

Waiting for the consul. Cell.

HE DID NOT come today. It took the authorities till noon to figure that out. He's coming tomorrow, as Rafi said.

Everything was spic-and-span. Boots and Rockports polished. I even got a belt—a white police belt, for there are no olive belts. Amazing what a difference a belt makes. What a lift in morale. I had felt, not realizing it, like a kid with his pants dropping.

Dubi was freed this morning after helping us clean, and a new guy named Danny has taken his bunk. This Danny is huge, a giant. He literally darkened the doorway. But he has kind gray eyes. These were amused, looking us over. It was perhaps nine in the morning, and all except me were flat out in their boots.

"Welcome," I said.

He nodded once. "Hello. We just lie here?"

"It's an exception. They think the American consul is coming today."

The force in those limbs. It would have to have action. Married and middle-aged, selling insurance, he would get fat.

"You can sleep," I said.

He shook his head.

"Read."

"I didn't bring books."

He went across to Dubi's bunk, the only empty one. He dropped his duffel bag and kicked it under and stretched out full length on his back. His boots were well over the edge. Brown boots. A paratrooper.

"Let it pass, O God!"

"Who's that?" said Yoni from the upper corner bunk.

"Danny," he said. "Sorry to wake you up."

So we introduced ourselves.

"Are you a paratrooper?" I asked.

"I'm Nachal." Fighting Pioneer Youth. These are soldiers who lay the foundation for a settlement. He named a place in the Jordan Valley. Then he arched back and shouted, "May it only pass!"

"Is it the consul?" asked Ronnie.

"No," said Yoni.

Ronnie groaned, turned over, groped back toward sleep.

"Why are you here?" I asked.

"Forgot my weapon." He propped his head on an elbow. Round head, crew cut, tanned. Long, sharp nose. Could almost make him ugly.

"Did you go back and get it?"

"Another soldier found it." He looked away.

"What did you get?" asked Yoni.

"Fourteen days."

"I got twenty-eight, because I left my weapon in the barracks when I went to dinner, which we'd always been allowed." Yoni sat with drooping shoulders. Frail. A kid with a build like that in the paratroopers. Sheer determination. "I took an antiterrorism course, and while I was gone they changed the rule. So this afternoon I'm on the phone to a buddy of mine and he says they might transfer me. A paratrooper with awards for distinction, with two courses on antiterrorism, with courses in reconnaissance, and they're gonna kick me out of the unit because nobody told me they changed the rule."

He had reddened. I had never heard him talk at such a stretch before. He did not like to talk about his unit. I had asked him once where they were stationed, and he had answered, quite properly, "I can't tell you."

"If they kick you out they don't deserve you," I said.

"Why are you here?" Danny asked me.

"I refused something."

"Territories," he said.

"The fucking Arabs can walk all over us, he don't give a shit," said Ronnie, half asleep.

Ronnie launched into a yarn that I couldn't quite make out. But it sounded like he had once peed in the water he had given the Arabs, and Ami had seen him. Then he got up and stalked out toward the toilets.

"Did he say he peed in the water?" I asked Yoni.

"No, he said he wanted to."

"He was dreaming," said Danny. "You've got a gal in the police here named Orna."

"That's right," said Yoni.

"And Miri."

"Yes."

"I know them. I was here on a Friday night about three months ago. Just visiting. I was with Miri, and this friend of mine was with Orna. You know what Orna has over her bed?"

We did not.

"A kaffiyeh, and on it is written, 'Death to the Arabs.' "

"No kidding," said Yoni.

" 'Death to the Arabs.' " He giggled and shook his head. "I saw it myself."

I felt her go out of my medulla.

"Over her bed," I said.

Danny nodded. "There's this kid in Kibbutz L—— who's got a PLO flag over his bed."

"That's a security risk," said Yoni.

"The thing is," said Danny, "this kid's mother, when he was eight years old, was hit by a Katyusha. They picked her up in plastic bags."

Silence.

"I asked him, 'How could you do that?' He said he started reading, wanted to understand."

He shook his head.

Ronnie came back and got into his bunk.

"Ronnie," I said, "what was that story you told before?"

"Nothing."

"About peeing in the water."

"I didn't pee in any water. You want to report me?"

He turned to the wall and closed his eyes.

I turned to my notebook, started noting this conversation down. Freed from Orna!

Danny and Yoni were talking quietly. Then he moaned again about the time.

I said, "If God offered to erase these fourteen days from your life," and so on, but he cut me off.

"I understand what you're saying. It's not that. I had a thing with a girl that was just starting."

"She can't wait two weeks?"

"She won't."

I had no answer to that.

"Do we lie here all day?"

"Until they make a phone call and find out the consul isn't coming."

"This is awful."

"I have books, if you read English."

"What are you writing?"

"Philosophy."

He went up on his elbow again.

"A philosopher."

"That's a big title."

"But you write it."

"Yes."

"So let's hear it."

"We've already asked him," said Yoni.

"It would pass the time."

I am not writing philosophy here. That's a front. I am writing, among other things, about these people who keep asking me what I am writing. I do have a philosophy, though, a message. Years ago I wrote a dissertation based on imaginary conversations with Heidegger, Buber, and Freud. A sprawling thing. It seemed too top-heavy on theory, too thin on experience (though there was experience). I awaited some confirming blast from above. During the whole period of adjustment to Israel, I damped the fire down, confining it to stops on the pilgrim route: Capernaum, the Mount of the Beatitudes, Gethsemane. And then, about a year ago, a woman who had toured with me sent me a tract which contained a quotation from Nicholas of Cusa's *Vision of God*. (Transcribed in freedom:)

> *When all my endeavor is turned toward Thee because all Thy endeavor is turned toward me; when I look unto Thee alone with all my attention, nor ever turn aside the eyes of my mind, because Thou dost enfold me with Thy constant regard; when I direct my love toward Thee alone because Thou, who art Love's self, hast turned Thee toward me alone. And what, Lord, is my life, save that embrace wherein Thy delightsome sweetness doth so lovingly enfold me?*

The idea, the very terms were the same as those in my dissertation. But I had talked about the endeavor, regard, and love between parent and infant, as well as between human lovers, whereas Nicholas meant himself and God. It was not the long-awaited confirmation from my own experience, but a remarkable correspondence. And here I was, middle-aged. I could go on, in silence, awaiting that confirmation. Or I could accept Nicholas as a witness. I felt that if I did not walk through the door now (a door which had opened even before my dissertation), I never would, and one day the guard would close it, saying, "This door was meant for you." By the time I went to Schneller I had been writing half a year on the theme of "I and Thou."

Danny continued about how bored he was, and how it was probably my fault because I was clearly, by my accent, an American, and the consul was no doubt coming to visit *me*. I caught a hint from Yoni that maybe I thought they weren't worthy of my pearls. So I shook off my laziness and searched for a beginning that might work, and I stumbled on this:

"When can you look another person in the eyes without talking about something and without feeling embarrassed?"

"That's interesting," said Danny, and he looked up at Yoni. "Isn't that interesting?"

Yoni nodded.

"Can you ever?" I asked.

"When you're in love," said Yoni.

"It's interesting," Danny said. "You can't really look people in the eyes. It sounds like psychology."

"You can look them in the eyes," I said, "as long as you're talking about something."

"So what's the point?" asked Yoni.

"Think about it," I said.

"You're gonna keep us hanging," said Yoni.

"It passes the time," I said.

They lay back and thought about it. Then Yoni propped himself on his elbows.

"If I look at you and talk," he said, "you have some idea of what's going on in my mind. But if I just look at you, I could be thinking anything. That's scary."

"Like staring someone down," said Danny.

"But in love it's allowed, you said," I said to Yoni.

"Well, then you know she's thinking good things."

"All right," I said.

"That's philosophy?" said Danny.

"All right, try this. I look at you and I talk about, say, sports, or politics, or the weather. Then the subject is exhausted and I look away. What's happened? We've known each other, say, for twenty years. You know I'm a friend, not thinking bad thoughts, not gonna rape you. Why do we look away?"

He shook his head. So did Yoni.

"All right," I said. "Just keep it as a question. I'm going to start on another tack, all right?"

They adjusted themselves.

"Imagine someone who's like a human being, but he doesn't have language—he can just make sounds—and he has no awareness of himself."

They lay back again. I asked if they were imagining such a creature, and they said "Yes." I asked:

"Now, how could he become aware of himself?"

"Is there an answer to this?" asked Yoni. "Or are you just gonna leave us hanging?"

"I think I have an answer," I said.

They thought. But then came a feminine "Ahem!" from outside. Miri appeared in the doorway. She told Danny he could make his phone call now. (We are officially allowed one call upon entering.) He said as he lumbered out:

"Don't go on without me."

There was a big, awkward space between me and Yoni.

He said: "I'm really interested in those things."

I remembered the long conversations at college when I was their age. But only *that* they had occurred. I couldn't remember substance. How did one philosophize—where did one begin—when one was eighteen or nineteen, illiterate in such matters, still slave to Nature? Philosophy requires leisure, Aristotle said.

Yoni lay back again. I did too. I pictured Bradford Jones' room at college. He refused to eat in the dining hall because his lost love was there with another. We brought him food. Out of all our conversations, I could only remember him reading from Henry Miller's essay on bread.

Danny stood in the doorway beaming.

"Twins!" he shouted and flapped his arms. "I've got twins!"

The slumberers moaned and groaned.

"Mazel tov," I said.

"Mazel tov," said Yoni.

Danny stepped into the middle of the room and kept flapping his arms.

"My first twins! And I'm not there!"

"How many do you have?" I asked.

"Five. Seven now!"

"Shut up!" said Yigal from sleep.

"He's had twins," I said.

"I can't believe it," said Danny. "And I can't see them!"

He got into his bunk, lay on his back, bounced up and down and rubbed his hands together.

"Do you know how beautiful they are!"

"Boys or girls?" I asked.

"Females," he said. "That's the beauty of it." He was smiling at me.

"Are these goats?" asked Yoni.

Danny whooped.

Yigal raised himself and looked over at him.

"Shut up!"

"This is a new guy," I said, "and he just had twins."

"*Mazel tov*," said Yigal. He settled down and closed his eyes.

Danny was smiling at me.

"The way you're carrying on," said Yoni.

"I've got two new little kiddies!"

"I was wondering what you were doing with twins," I said, "if you just met the girl."

"Don't remind me! Oh what a time to be cooped up here!"

He bounced on the bed cackling to himself and rubbing his hands.

"In fourteen days they won't be little anymore!"

"Sure they will," said Yoni.

"Not little enough! Maybe I could get Sabbath leave. What do you think?"

"Not your first Sabbath," Yoni said.

"Maybe your friends could bring them for a visit," I said.

"They'd have to bring the mother. Oh what a fucking thing to do!"

He raised his hands in frustration, as if the forgotten weapon were in them. Then he lay back. We were silent. But he cackled occasionally and kissed the air.

After a while Yoni said, "It's the hands, isn't it? The secret's in the hands." He edged up against the wall so I could see him and made motions in the air. "The guy sees his hands moving, and at the same time he feels it in his muscles. Always the same feelings in the muscles for the same hand movements."

"That's good," I said.

"Am I on track?"

"You might be."

He kept rotating his hands in the air. I lay on my back and tried it too. Volition. That could almost lead you to a sense of self. A "self-invariant," the psychologist Daniel Stern calls it.

Danny left off cackling and turned his face toward me.

"Does this guy see other people?"

"Yeah. I told you, there are only two limitations. No language, and no awareness of himself."

"Then how does he know that other people are people?"

"He just does," I said. "It's a given. But the ego isn't given."

"Oh," said Yoni, sitting upright. "If he sees other people, that makes it easy. He's made the connection between his hands and the feelings in his muscles, right?"

"Except he doesn't know they're his."

He thought for a moment.

"OK," he said. "Doesn't matter. He's made that connection. And he knows other people are people."

"Yes."

"OK. So one day he happens to stand in front of a mirror, or a pool of water, and he sees those same hands, but now he sees a body attached to them, and it's like the bodies of people, so he knows he's a person like them."

I said, "Your hands don't look the same in a mirror. And attached to this strange body, they won't look the same."

"Well, he notices that whenever he moves them, they move there in the mirror too."

I said, "He might just think there's someone in the mirror."

"You don't even need the mirror," said Danny. "All you need is other people with hands. You see their hands and their feet too, and you realize that your hands and feet must also be attached to a body, and then the mirror just confirms what you suspected."

"OK," I said. "Suppose you realize there's a person here, a person like them. But how do you know that it's you?"

Yoni: "What do you mean 'you'?"

"The one who's seeing and feeling these things."

That set them back to thinking. Yoni had a shiver.

"Strange question," he said.

"What's the question?" asked Gadi the Lazy.

Nobody answered him. I heard him shift around, and he was silent.

"All right," said Yoni. "Give us the answer."

I am no Socratic midwife. I burn too much with my message. I abandoned the dialogue and put the theory to them as directly as I could. I said that this wasn't just a brainteaser. I was talking about each one of us, starting from two months old. We can't remember what that was like, but we can imagine. The main thing is not that we compare our limbs with those of other people and make inferences. The main thing is that a person comes up to you (though you don't yet know it's you), and puts his face in front of you (her face, more often), and responds to you. He talks to you too, what people call baby talk. And this happens several times a day, day after day. It's clear that the person is focusing on someone, some one single being whom you don't see. In other words, by looking at him, you're becoming aware of yourself as the one he is looking at. You're doing things toward him, and you become aware of yourself as the one he's responding to. You experience his experiencing you. And the more attention you pay to him, the more vividly you become present to yourself. I mean in the one single ray of attention. It's not that you look at him and then think of yourself. The more you concentrate on him, the more you are there too, because he's responding to you.

"Can you imagine that?" I asked.

"But how do you know it's you?" Yoni said.

Danny made a pistol with his fingers toward me.

"Gotcha!"

"First of all, are you imagining it? A person above you. Do you see how you could become aware of yourself as the one he's responding to?"

Tentative grunts.

This notion seems so remarkable to me that I would have thought—if they really had it—that they would jump from their bunks. But they just lay there calmly.

Yoni: "So how do you know it's you?"

"It all takes place," I said, "in rhythmical games. He imitates you and varies it. He goes faster, you go faster. He makes it more or less intense, you do too. There's a matching up. His rhythm suggests the rhythm of the unseen person he's responding to, and that matches the rhythm you feel in your muscles."

"But you don't know they're *your* muscles," Yoni said.

"You know that the person he's responding to, the person who is exposed to him on the outside, is the same as what is being felt on the inside."

"You're still not answering him," said Danny.

"It's the same as what you asked me before," said Yoni.

"I know. All right. Some of the movements he's responding to, of the eyes, for example, or the hands, are not only part of the game but also acts of perception."

I paused. They didn't get it.

"Among the things he's responding to there are movements of the eyes, which you feel from inside. When the eyes move, appearances change, and you're used to this. In other words, the feeling of the eyes moving is already connected in your mind with seeing. So you know without having to think about it that the one whose eye movements he's responding to is this seeing. And the same with touching. And all without thinking about it. Just by concentrating on him. That's the origin of 'me.'"

I let it sit with them.

"Weird," said Yoni.

I felt a surge of pride.

"If it were true," said Danny, "then when I'm alone I wouldn't be aware of myself."

"Oh that's just the beginning," I said, ebullient. "That's Stage One. Then comes Stage Two." And I gave them the rest of the theory: how a moment arrives, along with the acquisition of language, when I can elaborate my experience of someone else—my mother or father, say—to the point where I can become that person in fantasy, can play him or her, as an actor plays a character. I can speak as if I were that person and listen as if I were I. Or the reverse. The self-bestowing event gets moved "inside." This is a structural change: I become a walking twosome, bumping into other twosomes. When I "talk with myself," I am conversing with an internalized Thou.

"Try not talking to yourself for ten seconds," I said. And I waited.

"That's more than ten seconds," said Danny.

"He's tricky," said Yoni.

"It doesn't matter how long it was," I said. "You heard a voice. Maybe you heard a voice saying, 'Hey, isn't that ten seconds already?' It doesn't matter what it said. The point is, you heard a voice. That was an internalized Thou. Or it was you talking to one. Each of us has Thous inside. People whose parts I play toward myself. They're the ones who still make me feel like a self when I seem to be alone. It's all a delusion, of course. None of them is really a Thou. It's just an image of a Thou, a character I've learned to play. An idol. Compared with a real Thou, it has a very limited repertoire, and the me it responds to is a very limited me. Once this system is set up, you see, life becomes more secure and predictable. But underneath there is still the longing for something really interesting, the longing for the Thou."

They considered this.

"It sounds like what you're talking about is thinking," said Danny.

"Yeah, people call it thinking. A philosopher wants to find a secure starting point to build on. He says, 'I think, therefore I am.' But this can't be a starting point, because a lot has already happened. His thinking is a conversation with an internalized Thou."

"Yeah, all right, but you *have* to do that," said Danny.

"Yeah, sure," I said.

"You can't be looking someone in the eyes all the time."

"What about blind people?" asked Yoni.

"Well, there are other senses."

"It would get pretty boring," said Danny.

"I don't know about boring. It'd be a very different world. But notice this. The babytalk in the beginning, all that poochie-moochie back and forth, is really a fundamental language, and what gets communicated is, 'You are! I am! You are! I am! I'm so happy that you are! And I'm happy that I am.' This thing—this relation—is good in itself. It affirms itself. It says that it is good. Of course it's not very comfortable, all the up and down. Up when the Thou is there and down when he isn't. We go into Stage Two as soon as we can. But the first stage, that I-Thou relation, continues to serve as the basis for the affirmation that life is good, that no matter what happens life is fundamentally good. I think this back-and-forth, even after we have forgotten it, continues to be the hidden standard. It is the most delicate connection, and later only a memory, the shade of a memory, but it is also the absolute good."

To which Danny repeated that it would get pretty boring looking someone else in the eyes all the time. That reminded me of the myth in Plato's *Symposium*, and I told it to the best of my recollection: how human beings started out double their present size, round, with two faces facing out, and four arms and four legs. They were so powerful in this form that the gods decided to split each of them down the middle and twist the face around, so that each would see the wound and remember. Then they sewed them up. But as soon as the mortals were let alone, each half went in search of the other, and if they were lucky enough to meet, they would cling together and wouldn't want to do anything else, not even eat or drink, until they died.

I had reached this point in the story when a disturbance entered Yoni's limbs.

Ami stood in the doorway smiling his bitter, I-knew-it smile and shaking his narrow dark head.

"What's this?"

I got up, put my hat on, checked my buttons, tucked in my shirt. Danny pulled his legs back inside the bunk post and stood up. Yoni was already there beside him.

Ami moved to the middle of the room.

"What the hell is this?" he snarled.

There were stirrings. He went to Ronnie and shook him. "You, monitor, get them the hell up! Where the hell do you think you are?"

"Get up, you guys," said Ronnie from deep fog.

" 'Get up, you guys,' Ami mimicked, and he went now to each one, shaking him.

"Is the consul here?" asked Yigal.

"The consul! Get on your feet." He went as if to kick him, but did not. "You think this is a nursing home?"

So the others shook the blessed sleep off and took their positions, Ronnie to my left by the door.

"Get this place ready," said Ami, and went out.

"Five minutes!" he yelled from outside.

"Mmbaaah!" said Danny, and he belched.

We smoothed the beds and set the blankets right, each a compact bundle with sixteen folds. Then we checked ourselves again. Yoni counted his folds as he always did. He was most punctilious. He turned to Gadi the Lazy:

"Put your hat on straight. I'll break up."

"Anybody laughs at this inspection," said Ronnie, "goes to Jail Four."

"He'll probably think I'm the American," said Shlomo across from me.

"You can ask him for a hat," said Gadi the Cheerful. He wrenched his Hebrew into a drawl. " 'This is a disgrace to the American uniform. Get rid of that Israeli pancake and give this man an American hat.' "

Yigal swiped Shlomo's hat and threw it to Gadi the Cheerful, who stood next to Danny. Gadi the Cheerful threw it up high, and it caught on a nail in a beam that runs the length of the room down the middle of the ceiling. Then they started throwing hats up to try to knock it down.

"We'll all go to Jail Four," said Ronnie.

"If he comes," said Yoni, "everybody put your hat under the mattress. He doesn't know about the hat rule. Ami won't say anything."

They kept throwing their hats up, while Ronnie watched at the door.

"You guys are too desperate," said Danny. "Somebody get on my shoulders."

"Who are you?" asked Dror.

"This is Danny," said Yoni.

"The one with the twins," said Yigal. *Mazel tov.*"

"*Mazel tov,*" said the others vaguely.

"Thank you," said Danny. "They're just goats really."

Gadi the Cheerful climbed onto his bunk and launched himself into sitting position on Danny's shoulders. Danny carried him near the hat.

"Now try throwing," said Danny.

They gave Gadi hats, and he threw them and sometimes hit, but he couldn't knock it off the nail.

"You'll have to stand on him," I said.

"Hold my legs," said Gadi. "And you guys stand around to catch me."

He grabbed Danny's head and used it to balance himself as he got his feet up onto the shoulders. But now he was going to have to let go and stand.

"Is he coming?" he asked.

"Not yet," said Ronnie.

"Shlomo," said Gadi, still not standing, "why don't you just go to the bathroom?"

"That's an idea," said Yoni. "Like you had a case of the runs."

"I do have the runs," said Shlomo.

"Then go," said Gadi, "and we'll do this later."

"Oh that's just fine," said Shlomo. "You guys swipe my hat and land it on a nail, and then I'm the one who gets screwed because I'm absent at inspection."

"I didn't purposely land it on a nail," said Gadi.

"You can't argue with him," said Yigal.

Gadi began to stand, but his legs quivered and he grabbed back for Danny's head.

"Why is your head so smooth?" he said.

"He's coming," said Ronnie.

Gadi slid down Danny's back and everybody ran to his place.

"Under the mattress!" said Yoni. He put his under, so we all put ours under.

"Detainees will prepare to receive the commander! Detainees will come to attention. Two, three . . . !"

"Kshev!"

Ami loped in. He loped through the room and then back toward the door, tapping his antenna into his palm. He stopped with his back to us. Then he went out.

Ronnie looked outside and said, "Detainees will prepare to receive the commander! Detainees will come to attention. Two, three . . . !"

"Kshev!"

He came in and stood near me. Someone laughed. Then Yoni bent over from the waist and laughed.

"Is this the way you receive an American consul?"

"He looked at me," said Gadi the Lazy.

"We should do it outside," said Yoni, "where we won't be facing each other."

"You expect to receive the consul outside? He wants to see you where you live. Your living conditions."

"Is he here?"

"Not yet, not yet." He tapped. "Your good luck and mine. He could be here any minute. And not only him. Where are your hats?"

Silence.

"Under the mattresses, commander," said Yoni, looking straight ahead and blushing.

Ami strolled about smiling sourly, beating the antenna and shaking his head. Then he stuck the antenna under Yoni's mattress and lifted it until he saw the hat.

"What is this, you guys?"

"One hat is up there, commander," said Yoni, lifting his face.

Ami looked up at it.

"How did it get there?"

"By mistake," said Gadi the Cheerful.

"It got there by mistake," said Ami. He tapped.

"We tried to get it down and couldn't," said Yoni. "So we figured—I figured—the consul wouldn't know about the hat rule."

"And what about the chief of military police?"

There was general swallowing.

"You think the consul comes alone?" he burst out. "Do you know what'll happen to me and you, each one of you, you too, Stephen, if he sees this? You guys!"

He hurried out.

"Give me your hat!" said Shlomo to Gadi the Cheerful. "That'll be yours up there. *You* can have the runs!"

"It's not my fault!" said Gadi.

"He's right," said Yoni. "You threw it."

But Ami came back.

"Miri's going to try to hold them if they get here. Ronnie, you and someone, Yigal, get the ladder."

"We don't need a ladder," said Danny. "We can do it with that." He pointed to the antenna.

Gadi climbed onto the bunk again, and onto Danny's shoulders, and Ami opened out the antenna and handed it up to him, and he got the hat down.

Ami received the antenna back, telescoped it, and tapped it into his palm.

"Now let's do it right," he said.

"Can we do it outside?" asked Yoni.

"No. When they come you'll have to do it inside."

"We won't laugh in front of them," said Yoni.

Ami paused, tapped his palm and looked around at us.

"Outside," he said.

We took our hats and stood in the small rectangular court between our cell and the toilets. We stood in a single line so that we would not have to see each other. Ami did the inspection, and it worked on the first try. Then he brought a roll of paper towels and two cans, a can of black shoe polish for most of them and a can of brown for Yoni, Danny, and me. We sat on the cement floor of the courtyard and polished or repolished.

"Finish the story," said Danny.

"They were all clinging together, clinging until they died."

They nodded.

"The human race was dying off. Dying from love. And the gods didn't want that, because then they wouldn't get sacrifices. So what do you think they did this time?"

"Pried them apart," said Danny. "Blindfolded them."

"Something cleverer. They gave them genitals and arranged for sexual release. That way they could let go of each other, and in some cases it also led to reproduction. So the human race was saved. Anyhow, that's why we are the way we are."

"That's a great myth," said Yoni.

"It's a description," I said.

"It's a good story anyway," said Danny. He left his boots, lay back, and propped himself on an elbow on the cement floor. He sneaked a look into my eyes.

"You might think we're kidding, but we're not."

Bright gray.

"What do you mean?"

"When we say we're interested."

I gave a little nod.

"It's a good story," he said, "but you'd really get sick of looking at each other."

"All that poochie-moochie," I said.

"Right."

"Yeah, well, it doesn't stay like that, obviously. But Plato asks, What if the blacksmith god were to come along and offer to weld the lovers together again? *After* they have genitals, I mean. Would they accept? And he answers that true lovers would."

"What's it a description of?" asked Yoni.

"Of the pain of loneliness. As if someone had cut half of me away and I'm running around looking for it. Except the description would be better if the gods hadn't sewn us up, if they had just left the open wound. That's the way it was for me anyhow before I was married. Marriage can heal the wound, and the work of the blacksmith god is done when you have children. A child is two welded into one again."

Ami came back to announce that the consul would be visiting tomorrow after all. He told us to change our uniforms and go to work.

"You won't go to the kitchen today," he said to me. "You'll be our gardener."

He set me to clearing paint scrapings from a long trough of dirt in front of the police station in the main courtyard. Then he brought a box of narcissus bulbs, and I tucked them into the dirt in rows of three.

12

Still dark outside . . .

. . . and sleep has lifted. The moon is not to be seen, has passed the thatch of barbed wire and the wall. It could be two o'clock, it could be close to five and wake-up time, I've no idea.

Must be because of the consul. Expectations.

At first I got up and walked in the small courtyard where we polished our shoes. The floodlight, above the toilets, above the thatch, is like the eye of a god. And now I have come back to our cell, to our tamer bulb. Not knowing how much of the night is left, I cannot return to sleep.

They did not ask me this evening to continue my philosophy. All those loose ends. So be it.

When he raised his eyes from the boot polishing and said that they were interested, and meant it, I could have guessed that they had had enough.

Philosophy is a tiring business. You break your head. So they sleep now, more blissfully perhaps, dreaming of poochie-moochie and Platonic myth.

Hard to imagine them beating Palestinians. Yoni never has. He said so. Danny tends his goats in the Nachal, is not put in the position of having to beat Arabs. Would not, I trust.

Yigal would like to. Ronnie probably has. Dror did, but only the ones who broke his foot, he says, and he would have beaten Jews for the same reason. Gadi the Lazy just finished his training. Gadi the Cheerful, perhaps. Shlomo? Perhaps. Who knows? Who knows anymore? I have a friend whose brother just finished the army. This brother says it's "in" to beat. And there's the four-minute CBS film. Kibbutzniks. Who would believe? How can someone raise a club and beat someone tied up on the ground?

The kids from Beit Sahur: the one with the cigarette burns on his back, the other who was supposed to say Popeye. Jews did that. Jews, not Druze. And here I have lived a good part of my life in the illusion that we Jews wouldn't do such things, that we were somehow better, not by nature, rather because of our history. I've built up a whole theory about that too. And I still cling to this notion of us. I cling to the demonstration of the four hundred thousand, after Sabra and Shatila. A remnant of us remembers our history. A remnant is what I think of as "Jewish." But is Yigal not Jewish? Is Ronnie not Jewish? Soldiers whacking tied-up prisoners—not Jewish? A good part of my life, and much of my academic work included, is washed away in this flood.

Someone like Hermann Cohen, for example, a great Kant scholar, was drawn to Judaism because of its ethical character. What would he say today?

I cannot help being astonished. Is this us? If I had known this was us, I doubt that I would ever have come here. I would still have made my connection to the Jewish people on that Christmassy day when I discovered Rosenzweig, but if I had known—if I had known that the Jewish people in power would be, oh, just a nation like the nations—then Israel would have seemed the last place in the world to seek the distinctive truth of Judaism. The fact is, I believed all the good things, and if bad things were said, I somehow did not even hear them. I believed that the communal ideal of ancient Israel permeated the new state, making it unique.

To show how far this went: in the States, as Noga reminded me, I was a conscientious objector. How then could I move to Israel? For a man my age moving to Israel knows he will have to go into the army.

In the early sixties I defended my stand before the U.S. draft

board, beginning with this simple truth: the next person's life is
as important to him as mine is to me. I wanted to live by that
principle. I refused, therefore, to put myself in a position where
someone could order me to kill someone else. They used to ask,
What if someone attacks you? Attacks your sister? Your family? That
was a standard question. And I had to admit I would defend them.
So they asked, What if another country attacks your country? And I
answered: "That's not the situation! But you have people out there
killing other people!" In those days there was the domino theory: if
South Vietnam falls to communism, then one country after another
would fall, until it got to us. I said to them, "I don't buy your
domino theory."

In 1966, after an FBI investigation and a three-hour interview, the
U.S. recognized me as a conscientious objector. I was twenty-five by
that time, so they never called me to alternative service. Then came
that snow-white day, Rosenzweig, the connection with the Jewish
people, and half a year later the Six-Day War.

"What if another country attacks your country?" In America I
could answer, That isn't the situation. For Israel it *was* the situation.
No dominoes.

As so often for me, a book was decisive. A book called *The Seventh
Day*, about the agonies of Israeli soldiers in that war. About their
unwillingness to kill, the hesitation before pulling the trigger, even in
the midst of battle. How proud I was of them! And of course these
things were true. There were such agonies. But sitting in the States, I
did not hear, for example—I only heard recently—about soldiers
coming home on leave a year later, who found the skeleton of an
Egyptian soldier and strapped one of his bones to the front of the bus as
a trophy. The friend who told me about it got off the bus. She alone got
off. *She* reminds me of the Israelis who were interviewed for *The
Seventh Day.*

So I believed that Israel was different. And when I came here—
first as a student in '71, then as an immigrant eight years later—
Israel still sat on those whom it had conquered in the Six-Day
War, and still, for want of dominoes, I justified this as the least evil
among existing choices. I kept on thinking of us as a country under

attack. It never occurred to me that time was passing—all those years—and that we were doing nothing to shape a new alternative, or worse than nothing, erecting obstacles. Then the intifada knocked me on the head.

AND THAT LITTLE confession has not helped me get back to sleep either. The thoughts do not stop flooding in. Things left undone.

Again, for example, the whitewashed wall, four yards from this bed. It means to me something like "the wall of our little courtyard." It does not mean to me, unless I push myself, "the back wall of their cell." I am here for their sake, but if I really cared—if my Palestinian tour agent were there, for example—then every time I looked at that wall I would think of him and them.

So there is more between us than just this wall. There is whatever there is that keeps me from really caring.

And what is that?

I went on about how redeeming it is to get a phone call. Like a lifeline down through the hole. Rope and rags. And that time I brought them water, wasn't it the same thing—but me doing it for them? I could go over now, for example, and tap on the wall. But I won't. I've forgotten Morse code.

Or I could bring them cigarette butts tomorrow. That would be rope and rags. What was it I thought? "If we bring them butts, they'll never let us alone." That's a certain way of thinking about them. Like Kobi: "If you give them a finger . . ." *Them.* For me too they are "them."

I will tell you how I know them. I know them principally not in the person of the tour agent, or in the persons of the tour bus drivers. I know them principally in the way that most Israeli Jews know them. These are strange creatures who appear in our neighborhoods wearing sweaters even in summer (they get up at four to commute from the Territories) and handed-down slacks. Nameless, addressless muscle power, thick-tongued, grunting out the few words of our Hebrew which they have had to learn, jabbering with each other in strange sounds— scarce on consonants they seem—a language formed by modulations of the cheeks. A language only half formed, and they too seem half formed: the features mindless—the mind has not penetrated, or so it appears. Amid their laughter we think we hear "jihad," "jihad," "jihad," the cry to holy war. They work—cleaning the soot from our building, for example, after the cars were burned—as long as the contractor is near. He goes, has an errand, another job somewhere— and everything slows down. I keep bringing coffee in the hope of winning them over. ("You see, I like Arabs," this gesture is supposed to convey. "I see Arabs as human beings.") But inevitably there is sloppiness, a paintbrush laid on a table, paint on a rug, something dropped. I wash the coffee cups two or three times over. I will not use them for a few days. I wonder about the toilet, the towels. Subhumanity is a communicable disease.

When I go down to the bottom, I find the same racist image in me that I imagine exists in Kobi or Yigal or Ronnie. Arabs don't need toilets. Arabs can make do with one bag of unwashed vegetables per day. The fact that they suffer on the other side of the wall—that's nothing, that's to be expected, these people are used to suffering, ordained for it. They don't expect any better.

If my tour agent were there, asking for cigarettes, then of course I would bring him. He is my friend. I feel close to him. But that doesn't nullify or even qualify the racism. He went to a prestigious university in the States, has an advanced degree in engineering which he cannot use here. Because I can talk with him on an equal footing, toward him go all those feelings of natural human warmth which I deny the rest.

So I too am a racist. Even I. I do not want to be, and that helps—I am here because I don't want to be—but still, I am. How then did I ever catch this bug? I did not grow up here. No one indoctrinated me. The media, perhaps, a little—the image of Arafat—but that could hardly account for something so deep-seated. How then? Where does it come from?

AND NOW a number of things flow together.

Guilt is at the heart of racism.

When you violate someone's rights, or even just benefit from that, guilt is there. Ineluctably. Like air filling a vacuum.

This may seem just a declaration, but it follows from what I said to Yoni and Danny. In the I-Thou relation—before it's distorted—I receive selfhood from the other person. So that person matters to me as much as I do. This is the foundation of the moral law, which says just that: each other person matters as much as I do. So the moral law is established in the course of becoming a self. We are stuck with it.

But then I learn to play the two sides at once. I bring the poochie-moochie "inside"—and get the feeling of selfhood there, without need for a Thou. Other people no longer seem to matter as much, and with all that going on inside, they don't appear in their fullness. For the first time I can act in disregard of another person's humanity. Whenever I do so, however, the neglected fullness would make itself known as the feeling of guilt.

Would make itself known. Because of course one can avoid the feeling. There are ways.

So here, the needs of part of the Jewish people brought it into conflict with part of the Arab people. In 1948 we won, and with due respect to the qualifications and complexities, the fact remains that we took over homes and lands. After 1967 the dispossessed and their children became visible to us. We occupied them. We absorbed their men into our labor force at the lowest levels. We see them now in the jobs which I have mentioned. And not only do we see them, but we benefit materially from the fact that they are stuck in these jobs. And because we benefit, the neglected fullness of their humanity would make itself known.

When it is a whole, distinct people whose rights are violated, there is an age-old technique to avoid feeling guilt. The moral law applies chiefly to human beings. What we can do, therefore, is try to convince ourselves that "they" are less than human, rather "two-legged animals," as Menachem Begin said, venting his anger at Arab guerrillas. Or here is Rafael Eitan, once chief of staff, a Knesset member today: all that the Arabs would be able to do, if we could put a hundred settlements between Nablus and Jerusalem, would be "to scurry around like drugged cockroaches in a bottle." When the leaders speak thus, what may one expect from the followers? In fact, one hears such expressions all the time. "The dirtiest people in the world." Or simply "animals." "Animals, animals." These are just so many exercises in the avoidance of guilt.

When we attempt to dehumanize a whole people, the guilt comes in by the back door; it appears not as guilt, however, but rather as dread of their ultimate revenge. We *should* dread them; we have in fact awakened rage. (And some of them—"the extremists, the terrorists"—may do things which make our dread seem quite realistic.) Because we have pushed their humanity underground, the dread takes on a mythic dimension. They are not thought of merely as subhuman— as vermin, for example—but as subhuman with demonic properties. Where the natural feeling of guilt would have led us to repair the relation, the dread of them leads us to violate it even more. Thus begins a spiral in which evil multiples itself. The more guilty we become, the more we must dehumanize them in order not to feel it; then guilt appears as dread, and the more we dehumanize, the more we dread; the greater the dread, the more we beat; the more we beat, the greater the guilt . . . and so on, round and round, ever deeper. By a kind of inversion, the force of our guilt determines the force by which we break and kill. And so one can get to the point where one lifts a lit cigarette to dehumanized human flesh, or beats, simply beats, beats them down on the ground and keeps beating.

No invidious comparisons. I have defined a process which is set in motion whenever one people violates the rights of another. The evasion of guilt is the beginning of racism. My people was the victim of a technologically equipped pagan revival far worse than racism. We have no part in such a revival, but to common racism we are not immune. In our state of high tension, the spiral can lead—and now has led—to atrocity.

Racism derives its force from the constant moral law within. No use, then, to preach to a racist. The more forcefully you expose the guilt, the more deeply entrenched the racism becomes.

Racism is not chiefly the cause, but rather the symptom and result, of the violation of human rights. Its cure is to stop violating them.

For eight years—until the intifada—I justified the occupation as the least of evils. I benefited from it and accepted the violation. That was time enough to get infected. Nowadays I still benefit from it. Indeed, the intifada woke me up, and I have started seeking a cure, but the infection remains. That is why I don't really think about them on the other side of the wall.

The bleeding hearts or do-gooders like me are not necessarily people who fulfill the moral law. They are more often people who realize that it is there, at the foundation of their being, and that they are failing to fulfill it. But this realization is enough to stop one from crossing the line, the real "green line." It runs between those who struggle against the temptation to dehumanize the Arabs and those who do not. That, then, is what it comes to: I am overcome by the temptation, yet I fight it. I am part of it, yet I cry out, I will not be part of it! I refuse!

AND NOW I close my eyes. But soon comes the scuffling of the sleepy jailer. The key grinds in the lock. Five already? I sense him as he passes into the center of the room. He shouts—he shouts it as if he were in the middle of a crowded theater—"Wake up!"

13

Thursday afternoon. Cooks' room.

THE CONSUL HAS COME and gone. A pale thin man with thinning hair, and he did me the honor of wearing a suit, light blue, and a narrow red-and-blue-striped tie, a dignitary in Jericho. A man in a fix, I guessed, because of the expectations he would have to disappoint. His briefcase would contain no rope, no rags. But he did bring a United States military attaché, a trim crew-cut redhead with prominent cheekbones. The attaché exuded wholesomeness. A jogger, I guessed. He wore a white short-sleeved shirt and gray slacks but he looked military anyhow. And because he came, his uniformed Israeli counterpart had to come too. And of course the chief of military police. So that made four. The spectacle of all that authority in the doorway was awesome enough to banish any worry about breaking up. We looked aside, a little down.

"This is where they live," said Rafi. He had come back that morning.

They entered hesitantly, almost shyly. Just a few steps. It was perhaps their first honor guard. Or they felt that they were intruding. It is, after all, where we live. They looked around, even up into the corners, as if inspecting.

Rafi stood in front of me.

"This is Stephen."

The consul took a step forward.

"I'm Bill Walker, consular secretary."

We shook hands.

"Stephen Langfur."

"And this is Richard Heard," he said, "our"—and he named a service—"attaché."

Our.

We nodded.

"And this"—he indicated the younger officer—"is Yoram Levine, Richard's liaison on the Israeli side." Lightly: "He's our tour guide today."

"Aha," I said. I held back from saying that I am a real guide, would gladly lead them over interesting, unbeaten trails to little-known vistas if only they would take me away.

He did not introduce the police chief. Perhaps he thought I knew him.

"Quite a delegation," I said.

"We'd like to spend a few minutes with you, if you don't mind."

So we went out, much to the relief of all. We went back to the police station. I noted with satisfaction that a narcissus bulb had already projected green.

The whole staff was huddled in the office. The women too.

"Let them talk alone," said the police chief in Hebrew.

A door was opened into a back room with a table. I had been in the police office to make phone calls, but I had never noticed this back room. It was newly plastered, whitewashed and air-conditioned. The chairs and the table were of a smooth fresh pine. We Americans went in.

"This is very nice," said the consul.

Miri closed the door. Her Renaissance smile. Or was it the hair, the long blond hair? Venus surfing on a seashell. How did she ever get that hair?

"First of all," said the consul, "this is who we are."

The two whipped out their cards and presented them. I read them. Full formal names. Consular secretary. Attaché.

"So you are not the consul?"

"It's the same thing," he said.

"Well, thank you for coming. You have no idea how you've helped me already." (I left a pause, on the chance that he might say, "Oh, that's nothing. Stevie, we mean to get you out of here." But he merely looked surprised.) "You've saved me two days of work," I said, sitting down. They sat down.

"Two?"

"Yes. They thought you were coming yesterday. So all day yesterday I was kept on the shelf." I did not mention the gardening. "I was able to sit and read and write. And today all morning."

He looked amused.

"You know that this is a routine visit," said the consul. "Whenever a U.S. citizen is jailed in a foreign country, we try to visit him."

No rope, no rags.

"I know," I said, "but they don't know."

"Oh I think they do," he said.

"Since it also involves the military, I have come along," said Richard Heard.

"Well, I thank you both. You have them shaking in their boots."

The consul raised an eyebrow, but he was again amused.

I said: "Just the announcement that you were coming had a big effect. They've been very careful about me."

"And how were they treating you before?"

"Oh fine. Don't get me wrong. As if I were their father."

"And the other prisoners?"

"Fine."

"I ask because once I sat with someone who was sentenced for murder, and he told me his big worry wasn't the jailers but the other prisoners."

"No, they're fine. Of course I don't know what it'll be like next round."

The thin eyebrow arched again, but this time in a question. Maybe he was used to bugged rooms. If you're a diplomat, you have to know how to talk with your eyebrows.

"The day I get out," I said, "I have to report straight to my unit, and they could give me another order for the same place. So then there'll be another round, I don't know where. If you would visit me wherever it is, it would be a big help. Or even just make an appointment to visit me. Make an appointment and cancel it. Just so they know you're paying attention."

"We'll try to visit you," said the consul. "But I don't think there'll be another round."

That may have been the most significant thing said at this meeting, or it may have been just an off-the-cuff attempt to relieve me. I can imagine the conversation on the way down here: "Please try to understand our position, Mr. Walker," says the police chief. Or perhaps it is the liaison, who would have better English. "We don't like putting a man like this in jail. We'll bend over backward not to, and we'll get it over as soon as we can. But when he comes on frontally and announces that there are certain areas in which he refuses to serve, we don't have much choice. If we let him have his way, we have to let others have their way too. An army cannot operate—I'm sure you understand—if its soldiers have the final say about where they're going to serve."

It's true. There's little that can be said to that. That's why this phenomenon is a threat to the army. A blanket conscientious objection would be tolerable, because the army would know in advance how many forces it has, who is in and who is out. But selective refusal is dangerous. It breaks the chain of command. Yet I am only number ninety-one, a small tremor still on the scale.

I could have asked the consul whether he had any firm reason to think I would not get another round. Was this the rope after all? But it might have spoiled some delicate understanding.

So I asked, "How did you find out about me?"

"As a matter of fact I think there was an article in one of the Hebrew papers. An interview with your wife. Somebody in my office read it."

There was a knock, and Miri came in with blue dishes full of cheese sandwiches, sliced tomatoes, sliced cucumbers and cookies.

"Aah!" said the consul.

She went out but left the door open. Then she came back with a bottle of Sprite and three plastic cups.

"Aha!" said Richard Heard.

"This isn't necessary," said the consul.

"You see the kind of treatment I get," I said.

Still gently smiling, she closed the door softly behind her. One could fall asleep thinking of that smile. No slogan above her bed.

I took my hat off. We helped ourselves.

"*B'teavon*," I said. "That's Hebrew for *bon appetit*."

"*B'teavon*," said the consul. He already knew it.

"*Bon appetit*," said Richard Heard.

We munched.

"So if it hadn't been for that article," I said, "you wouldn't be here."

"We wouldn't know."

"I bet if you scratched around among Palestinian prisoners you'd find lots of American citizens. The treatment they get is something else. There are Palestinians here, did you notice?"

Munching, he shook his head.

"When you go out, there's a cell on the left and a bigger one on the right. That's what the tin sheets are covering. The one on the left has no water and no bathroom. One mattress on the floor. There are usually three or four guys there. They call out for water sometimes."

The consul hesitated, then laid his sandwich down on the plate. Richard Heard did likewise.

"Of course they get water," I said. "Not always when they call out for it, but they get it. They get water and food. Mostly vegetables. It's very little, though."

I picked up my sandwich and ate. I was glad to have remembered. Apart from my basic indifference toward them, I have been feeling so sorry for myself, so anxious for myself, so mystified, perhaps even traumatized—that I of all people should find myself in this situation— that now before the consul, my parent surrogate, I might easily have forgotten them.

I resumed talking, and they returned to their sandwiches. Considering that they were here to inquire about my treatment, I thought I could talk about my trial. Let them judge whether it was fair or not. But in that context I would have to repeat what I had said there. And since I was talking in English for the first time in two weeks, I could also include a great deal of what I would have liked to say there. And in order not to confuse them by distinguishing pedantically between what I had actually said and what I would have liked to say, I simply lumped it all together, as if I had said it. My dream trial.

There was a time, I said, when we could justify the occupation as the least evil of the alternatives, but no more. We have had twenty-two years in which to work toward a new alternative, one which would guarantee freedom and security to both peoples. That might be a Palestinian state, for example, without heavy arms, and with guarantees on the ground and in the air that they would not get them. We could have achieved that after the Six-Day War, or in the early seventies, or even in the late seventies, after they elected their own mayors—before we expelled them. But now, now we have the Jewish settlements. Now it will be much harder. So instead of working toward a better alternative, we set up obstacles.

And the rest of the world knows it, I said. The rest of the world has plenty of blind and callous spots, but it has an eye and a heart for unarmed Palestinians going up against soldiers, for a hundred killed children, for the mothers and fathers of the children. My judge told me that negotiations are proceeding under the table, and that we mustn't rush, must play our cards close to our chest. "Are you making all this trouble," he said, "because you're not satisfied with the *pace* of the negotiations?" And I answered, I said (though I did not, rather would like to have), that we do not have time. The rest of the world is turning against us, including the United States. The extremists among the Palestinians are gaining over the pragmatists. Our army, sent against a civil uprising, splits along political lines—witness me. If we wait for circumstances to force our hand, the final arrangement will leave us much less secure than what we can still get today. And while we sit with our cards close to our chest, time is running out on the chance to stop nuclear proliferation.

I talked about the five minutes he gave me to think. The Drobles Committee. I did not mention that high-ranking officer with his "Nuremberg trial." No comparisons.

The consul and the attaché heard me out. They gave no sign. I assumed, of course, that they secretly agreed with me. How could they not? How could anyone not who is not blind and callous? At a certain point, though, midway through my speech, I remembered that you can never really tell about other people, at least not until they open their mouths. But these two were so silent. How did I know, for example, that Richard Heard was not an Armageddonist? And suddenly the planes of those prominent cheekbones seemed to tilt differently in the light, rearrange themselves. An Armageddonist? And for a moment I feared. I had seen that self-made wholesomeness before. "Armageddonist" is the name I give to a certain minor species of Christian fundamentalist. Those of this species whom I have guided believe that the great battle of the end time is at hand and that it will occur between the Arabs, Sons of Darkness (with mighty Russia behind them), and those Jews (Sons of Light) who have accepted Christ; that its focal point will be by Tel Megiddo in our Plain of Jezreel (Har Megiddo in Hebrew, hence "Armageddon" in the Book of Revelation 16:16); that there will be great carnage, but that at the crucial moment God will intervene for the Sons of Light, who will then be victorious, and after certain further developments, including something called the "Rapture," God's Kingdom will be established forever. They watch the escalating hatred in our area with breaking hearts, they say, but I think it is rather with relish and satisfaction—how neatly God is working out His plan! Just as He said in the Prophets! Well, no doubt I do them an injustice. As befits the damned, I cannot listen to an Armageddonist for more than a minute. After that I do not run away or explode, but quietly switch to the channel for the insane. Was Richard Heard one of these? His lines and planes had a general resemblance to those of a certain ex-army man whom I had guided. One has to watch out for the clean-living military.

He would not quote the Book of Daniel to me here. He was representing the United States, not his church. Nor would he say anything during the drive back in the presence of the consul. But perhaps sometime later, a little slip to the Israeli liaison: "Nice little quisling you got cooped up down there in Jericho." "What do you mean?" "Don't you teach them not to spill their political guts to foreign officials?"

I was steeped so far in my speech, however, that there was no return. But at least I wanted to know. I did not want more suspense. I gazed at him as I spoke. He would not betray his leanings by the flicker of a jowl. "Time is against us," I repeated—and then thought of a way. "We do not have seventy weeks, and we are acting as if we had seventy weeks of years." That is a reference to Daniel. In the eye of an Armageddonist it would have caused a glint. It did not appear to register upon Richard Heard.

So I felt relieved. I finished the story of my trial.

Let him say what he might, I could not allow the ear of a U.S. consul to pass me by. I quoted the psalm, "From where shall my help come?" No reaction. "I doubt that it will come from within," I said. "We are a house divided against itself." No reaction to Lincoln either. "We are trapped in our own slogans. We are trapped in fear and mistrust. We are like the monkey in the Indian monkey trick. Do you know what that is?" They shook their heads. (At last, something.) I explained. You take a jar with an opening of such a size that a monkey can stick its hand in but cannot pull its closed fist out. You tie the jar to a stake in the ground and put a banana in it. The monkey comes along, sticks its hand in, grabs the banana, and is trapped. All it has to do of course is open its fist and let the banana go. But it cannot bring itself to do that. Boys taunt it, throw stones at it. It runs this way and that, jerking at the jar. But it cannot bring itself to let the banana go.

"We need the United States," I said, "to make us let the banana go. We cannot do it on our own. We are paralyzed. I don't know if you know how stuck we are in old ways of thinking, in the old slogans about the Arabs. Or how insulated we are from the intifada, and how we go reeling nonetheless from crisis to crisis, unable to take the long view. But you have more distance on our situation than we do, and you can see the long-term danger better than we can. And you have the means to force us to let the banana go."

So there it was, out naked. Richard Heard could—can—crucify me.

"That was my trial," I said as a fig leaf. "I hope I won't have to go through it again."

"I hope not," said the consul. Then he produced from his briefcase a wad of paper printed with names and addresses. "This is a list of lawyers who have agreed to work for U.S. citizens in trouble."

He gave me the list and my heart sank, for it showed that my consul was rather out of touch. It was their standard list of Israeli lawyers. A lawyer is irrelevant to an army disciplinary hearing.

"We won't pay for the lawyer," he said with a little laugh, "but just showing that list can make a big difference."

I stroked it like a talisman.

"Thank you," I said. "But I think your show of interest can also make a difference. For example, you could call my commander on the day of my release."

"That might backfire. What do you think, Dick?"

Richard Heard nodded slightly like a military expert: "Might certainly backfire."

"I mean just to ask what is happening with me. So you can visit me. That might help me not to get a *third* term, you see."

"Well, we'll try," he said, standing up. "And we will come and visit you, though I don't think it'll be necessary. I don't think you'll get another round."

"Thank you. If I'm freed I'll call you."

"Please do."

That was it. That was my consular visit. I went back to the cell, where the others were still lying. They asked me about it. I passed it off as the routine that it was. I lay down. After a while Ami came in and told us that we would be going to lunch and then to work.

"Stephen," he said, not looking at me, "don't be upset. He didn't approve your Sabbath leave."

It was charitable of Ami to be so embarrassed.

Someone groaned. Yoni.

"That means he didn't approve any of us, right?"

"That's right. Everybody stays here."

Groans.

"I knew it!" said Shlomo.

"I know why," said Yoni.

"He's a tough one," said Ami.

"He's tough and he's new," said Yoni. "Right?"

"Yeah, he's a new one."

"Our luck," said Yoni.

Ami went out.

"We'll have a good time," said Danny. "We'll have a party with Orna and Miri."

14

Thursday evening. Friday.

THAT THE TRAUMA of imprisonment should fill all these pages! I had thought to use them as ways of escape, but somehow I got to talking about this dry, dusty camp—perhaps out of a sense of duty to the present.

A true present would extend to include past and future. Organically they would inform it. It would include places too: Gibeon, Shechem, and Yoknapatawpha County. But I am far from being as present as that.

I was pretty down about not getting Sabbath leave. Ridiculous. Dubi was right, I should never have expected it.

What made it worse was the fact that he said No while I was in there talking with the consul. Not afraid of the U.S.A.

I went to lunch in the regimental kitchen and worked there. I dislike the work, but I know that all I have to do is throw myself into it and the time goes by. Thursday is delivery day. We unloaded a truck. There's this little quartermaster who comes with it and the moment he hits the ground starts shouting, so that everybody goes into a rush just to get rid of him. We bump into each other, cartons spill, and he gets madder and half grabs cartons out of our hands, shoving us around with them—"No, this one goes to the checkpoint, you idiot! No, don't put that there! How many times—don't cross me! Don't talk back to me! That goes to the Hilton!" We are, it seems, the food supply depot for the lower Jordan Valley. The "Hilton," for example, is an ex-Arab hotel on the north shore of the Dead Sea which was really called the Lido. The sheikhs of Araby used to bathe there. Today an outpost.

We finished. The red-faced phenomenon left. We did the orange dishes and savored the quiet. Even the radio seemed soothing.

Then Mercy told me to go, so I went to the cooks' room and wrote about the consular visit. We did the blue dishes, and then I crossed through the gutted building and found Ami outside his little office, which is near our cell.

"Commander," I said, "may I call my wife and tell her I didn't get Sabbath leave?"

He agreed and started to take me toward the police station, but Gadi the Cheerful passed by. Ami told him to put me on the kitchen phone, where I could talk as long as I wanted. So Gadi took me into the storeroom of the kitchen on this side. There is a phone on the table there.

"Hello, sweetie," he said into it, "can you give me a line?"

He winked at me.

"I know I did, but it's not for me. Hey, you gonna be here this weekend? We're all cooped up here. We're gonna have a party. Oh that's too bad. Good for you, I mean, bad for me. Oh I'll be good. No, I promise. I'll just stay in my bed and read. Thank you, sweetie."

And he gave me the phone. I thanked him and he left.

Noga was there.

"I'm not getting Sabbath leave."

"You're not getting Sabbath leave?"

I used to think she's hard of hearing. But it's not that. It's her way of stalling while her response forms.

"No Sabbath leave."

"I'll come visit you . . . !" And she called me by a pet name which I shall not divulge.

On the phone she could sound immensely happy. There was a spring in her voice. In fact, these are not happy days for her. Her father died six weeks ago. Her husband is in jail. Her novel barely inches forward at the publisher's.

"Do you want me to bring the kids?"

"Oh I don't know. You saw what it's like here."

"They loved your letters."

"Could they read them?"

"Yes. I helped a little. They're beautiful."

"I wrote Talya not to show her letter to anybody, not even you. She was supposed to work it out by herself."

"Well, I was curious. And now it's even in the paper."

"What do you mean?"

"In the interview in the Tel Aviv paper. They quoted part of it."

"That was meant as a private letter."

"Well, you made it very quotable."

"What did they quote?"

"That about you being one of the freest men in the Israeli army."

"Oh, that." Damned dualism!

"And that you're serving better than many who think you're not serving at all."

"Sounds good. Sounds awfully noble. Like Sidney Carton."

"Who's that?"

"'It is a far, far better thing that I do, than I have ever done . . .'"

Her laughter warmed my heart.

"How long can you talk?" she asked.

"I think as long as I like."

"If you didn't want me to read their letters, you should have written me one."

It took me a moment.

"Well, I knew you were coming to visit. And they weren't."

"Stewart called again," she said.

"No kidding."

"He asked if we need money. I told him No. He wants to do something. He's had a meeting of Women in Black at his house."

"There are really Women in Black in Vermont?"

"I know. It's strange. He's talked about you to the governor, and she's going to talk to Shamir."

"Who?"

"The governor. She's coming here. Maybe she'll meet with you."

A woman governor, I dimly remembered. But what could she say to which Shamir wouldn't have some ready wooden answer?

"I had the meeting with the consul today."

"Oh!"

"Routine really. I asked him to visit me at my next prison. He said he didn't think there'd be one."

Silence.

"Darling," she said, "are you there?"

"Yes."

"You know, Stewart had his leg amputated."

She always says "you know" when it's something I don't and couldn't know.

"He had his leg amputated," I said.

"His right leg."

He had been having trouble with his legs. He has had diabetes for twenty-five years. He has been almost totally blind for the last ten.

"I didn't know whether to tell you."

"Oh, Noga. I'm just glad he's alive."

But I felt my heart swell up.

"He sounded cheerful. He sounded really wonderful. He said he'd been depressed, but this business of yours has given him something to do."

Again I felt the pride. And then I pictured him blind and without a leg now. Sitting at the dining-room table.

"He wants you to call him as soon as you get home."

"Yeah, sure, I'll call him."

I dread calling him. Always have. I have always had to pluck up courage. A part of this is, I've never known whether I'd find him alive. My fear is not so much of the diabetes, though I guess it could kill him too. My fear is of him. Of what he might do in the dark. I don't only mean the blindness but another dark, which I can see is enshrouding him when it enshrouds him, but which I myself do not know firsthand and cannot understand. The people whom I have most loved in this world have known it and assure me that I am better off in ignorance, standing helpless and befuddled before their mystery.

"Is Janet with him?"

"Yes, of course. He says she's fine. He says thank you for giving him something to do."

"It's funny, he was always the political one."

He was always the great one. A great soul. When we first met at college he was already so social and political that I could not imagine when he had ever had time to read. He seemed to have gotten the gist of a whole range of poets and philosophers during some immense "before." He could feel about distant things. We were in awe of him. He sat and cried in front of the TV in the college rec room because a black girl was kept out of a white school. And I froze. How could somebody cry at the news? "Politics," he said to me once, "is everything," meaning that to be is to be political, something that I could never be—I always had to force myself to get involved. All those philosophers and poets, the enthusiasms, the immense care came to a burning focus when he listened to you, answered you. In his presence you felt, I felt—feel—suddenly significant in a significant world. When I look back at the beginning of this entry about the ideal of a true present—I suppose I wrote it under the influence of this conversation with Noga about him. He is the closest I have known.

If it is, say, 1:00 A.M. here, then Janet will have been home there about an hour. But it must be a long stretch while she is at work. I imagine he sits at the dining-room table. With us that was always *the* table, and it was still so with them when I visited. But he cannot walk now. He sits there in the dark in a wheelchair. And what does he do in all that long darkness? For the time being I have gone to jail, and he has stretched himself to encompass me. I am here, but my being here includes my being in his mind. That's it. I have to realize that. The cell feels different then. My fellow jailbirds in the sleep of youth feel different. (So old were we, and so slept we.) The thatch of barbed wire, in his mind. The moon-deserted black. And he in mine, and between us this roaring space.

Friday, at wake-up. Cell.

MENE, MENE . . .

Friday evening. Cell.

The Berlin Wall has crumbled.

I took part in the Sabbath evening service, and then I violated the Sabbath by watching the *Weekly News Summary* on the TV in the club. The others are partying. No relation to Berlin. Much like last week. Our keepers are gone, the moon even fuller. Ronnie went free this morning. Gadi the Lazy moved down and took his bunk, the impossible half-springless one—but they are all like that, it seems, except mine. A paratrooper was brought in and took Gadi's place above. He got twenty-eight days for not shaving and arguing about it. The military police conducted what they call Operation Dress in Jerusalem today, descending on any soldier who didn't have his uniform and appearance just right and handing out thousands of tickets, which for the accused meant having to stand in long lines to be tried, warned, and fined. But this guy Barak, meaning lightning, argued with Rafi, who then ticketed him, and so he finds himself here. Orna is interested. Miri is with Danny and Yoni. The others are with others. I sat alone for a while and looked at the moon, which is overwhelming.

And now I have returned to the cell and found my journal entry for this morning. He had just awakened us. I had lingered in bed a minute, and then it had come to me: MENE, MENE . . .

MENE, MENE, TEKEL, UPHARSIN. It is from the Book of Daniel, so the consular visit must have played in. Belshazzar, king of Babylon, is feasting; a human hand comes and writes these words on the wall; Daniel is brought to interpret. MENE, God has numbered the days of your kingship and brought it to an end. That could relate (prophetically, this morning) to the Berlin Wall. The days of the Soviet Empire, numbered and over. TEKEL, You have been weighed in the balance and found wanting. UPHARSIN, Your kingdom is divided and given to the Persians.

MENE, MENE . . . Freud would ask, Why just MENE, MENE? Why not the whole saying? A dream, he wrote, is the fulfillment of a wish. The emphasis is on numbering. The wish is that the days of my imprisonment be numbered and over, and it could also be a wish that the days of Israel's occupation were numbered and over.

But it dawns on me: I played Hamm in Beckett's *Endgame* in college. Hamm is blind and confined to a wheelchair. His servant Clov says to him, "I'm going to my kitchen to stare at the wall," and Hamm says, "What do you see on your wall? MENE, MENE . . . ?"

Thus the main thing has to do with the news about Stewart, as if he, blind and in a wheelchair now, were comforting me, assuring me, "The days of your imprisonment are numbered."

But it's a question to Clov, and that complicates the interpretation, because the one who played Clov was another close friend. I said a light word to him in his hour of need and lost him. I doubt whether he even condemned me. But it was a critical moment, a friendship lost in a word.

I hadn't yet learned to recognize that strange darkness, much less navigate it. No one from the college ever saw him again until Sid Manning spotted him on a movie screen and told me about it. I went to see the film and there he was for about five seconds, somewhat fatter. My tourist-pilgrims often mistakenly call me by his name.

There was also a brown mouse that lived in our room that he christened Master Fennel. This creature used to take flying leaps from the dressers over our bedded heads. I couldn't sleep and poisoned it. Maybe it was that, as well as the light word.

Later I betrayed Sid Manning too. Again stupidly, unintentionally. When I start on this theme, they begin to swarm in, the ghosts of betrayed friends, dangling a poisoned mouse by the tail, or a letter I wrote. The letters they never answered all come back to me. And some they did answer too. And a student I overpraised to his own harm. And on and on, the ego-stripping parade. At night or in the early morning, upon waking up. MENE, MENE . . . but what I really think of is what comes next, where the three dots are: TEKEL!

A prisoner of conscience indeed.

"I understand the issue of conscience," my commander said. He probably thinks of it as a banner which I want to hold above the mud. "A clean conscience." My conscience is middling soiled. Could I have taken this step if it weren't? That's how I know to fear it. Am already its prisoner, don't want to circumscribe myself more. It is already a Hound of the Baskervilles, eating my body at dawn.

WE HAD A TALK about conscience when Dubi was here. It was after he told me that Sabbath leave was an act of mercy.

"If you need mercy so much," he said, "you didn't need to come here."

"Tell them you're sorry," said Yigal. "They'll give you a pardon."

"But I'm not sorry."

"You don't understand," said Dubi to Yigal. "What he's doing is a political act. If he says he's sorry, that ruins it."

"I'm sending a message to the government," I said.

"You know that's bullshit," said Dubi.

I said, "Yeah, sure, as long as it's just a few of us. But if more guys do it—a hundred at once, say—that's something else. The army wobbled in Lebanon, remember, and we got out of there."

"Sounds like treason to me," said Ronnie.

"At this moment I am serving the people of Israel and the State of Israel in the best way I know how."

"You are undermining the State of Israel," said Dubi. "You're not just violating the law. You're openly proclaiming yourself to be above the law. The message you're sending is: the law shouldn't apply when a man doesn't agree with it."

"That's not what I'm saying."

"That's the message we hear. And if your dream comes true, and more people put themselves above the law the way you do—I mean guys like me too, not just the left—then this country will come apart. It's not America here, Stephen. This country is very fragile, internally. It's very nervous. We're all on a short fuse—and what you're doing is more dangerous than you can know. That's why they have to apply the law straight down the line with you."

I considered this. It is true, about the fragility. Volatility. The grenade that killed Emil Grunzweig during a peace demonstration in 1983: thrown by a Jew against Jews. If that could happen, why not again? Any movement toward a peace agreement will push our people to extremes. The law is a delicate fabric here. It must be strengthened, but I am ripping it.

Ronnie chimed in: "We're a democracy. You don't like what we're doing? You can vote, you can demonstrate, you can say whatever you want."

"But once the decision is made, I have to do what the majority says."

"That's right."

"Then your concept of democracy is missing something."

I turned back to Dubi.

"This is how I would answer you too. Maybe there are luxuries which Israel can't afford, but freedom of conscience is no luxury. It's as basic as the freedom to vote, or free speech, or whatever. If the majority decides to do a certain thing, and your conscience tells you it's wrong, you have a right to disobey the majority even if it means breaking the law."

Dubi shook his great curly mane. Ronnie whistled in mock disbelief.

"It all has to do with conscience," I said.

"So anybody does what he likes," said Ronnie, "and he says his conscience made him do it."

"Conscience is not what you like. Suppose the bank machine goes berserk and keeps shoving out money to you, thousands of shekels that you didn't ask for, and nobody sees you, and you really need the money. So what you like is to take the money. All your needs and desires say, 'Take.' Only your conscience doesn't go along. So it's not a need or desire like the rest."

"You wouldn't take the money?" asked Yigal.

"The fucking banks," said Dubi. And he started in about a bank president who had recently retired and run off to America with a pension of five million dollars.

TREPPENGEDANKEN: If a nation-state enacts an evil policy, it can then turn around and change its leaders or its constitution. But if you take part in enacting that policy, you cannot later change the mind and body that did those things. You are condemned to be a prisoner of your conscience. Therefore it is a human right to place one's own conscience above the requirements of the state. This must hold even when the conscience is odd, as long as it doesn't interfere with other equally basic rights. Of course a state must seek to determine whether a given act of disobedience is really a matter of conscience. That can be expensive. But if we can't afford it, then we should stop pretending. For this is no luxury.

Once, perhaps, that was a sufficient argument. But there is an even deeper problem today: conscience has lost its former status. It is considered on the same level as a matter of taste.

There are lots of reasons for this: the rise of natural science and the decline of religion, which for centuries had been bound up with conscience in people's minds; cultural anthropology; Freud.

Freud explained conscience as the result of early identifications with authority figures, who represent the culture. Their values get incorporated along with them. And since cultures vary in ideas of right and wrong, there seems to be no final tribunal, no absolute good and bad. "Everything is relative," as my students of ten years ago used to say. Conscience too. In that case there is no basis for setting its claims above those of the state.

Freud's discoveries concerning identification are vital to me. They account for the transition from the truth of mutuality to the illusion of an independent ego.

But Freud never saw how deep, how far back, mutuality goes. He emphasized all a child's dependencies except one: that even for its sense of itself as an entity, a child is dependent. He spoke of a "primary narcissism." But mutuality, I say, is first, and in mutuality conscience is grounded. Self-love comes later. It is the counterfeit of love, the result of playing parent toward oneself.

Conscience speaks in particulars: the light word, Master Fennel in the pangs of poison, a student overpraised. It speaks about my doing, but it discloses something about my being—namely, that I lack full presence. And my being is divided because an act of identification, performed long ago, altered the structure of self and world.

I imagine a time before that act. I am alone, say, not fully aware of myself, longing for the one who has previously brought me into focus. At this moment the Thou is an image in the mind. But what is that—an image in the mind? It is just as good to say, the Thou is present to me— to my longing—in the particular mode which we call "absence." (What is not present at all cannot be absent, just as one who never speaks cannot be silent.) And now the Thou comes back into the room and plays with me. Now it is vividly there, and I vividly here.

But suppose that I get to Stage Two, where I take the role of the Thou toward myself. This is a basic structural change. When the parent who was Thou comes back into the room, the Thou does not. The father (or mother) who stands before me seems less important than before. I do not get the feeling of selfhood from him. The counterfeit, internalized Thous provide this feeling now, and so there is inter- ference, and my real parent is less intensely in focus. What then has become of the true Thou? The spaces in which I consciously live—my "inner" space as well as the "outside world"—no longer contain such a being. Where then? The Thou is absent. Yes, but where? This is a new kind of absence, from which a Thou cannot (except by a kind of miracle) return. The new kind of absence requires a new kind of space, which in some contexts is called heaven or paradise.

Here is the origin of one of the meanings of God in human experi- ence. At first my parent is an all-important Other, who brings me into focus for myself as a being, who may be said to *know* me, therefore, through and through—until the day comes when I make part of myself over in his image. But the banished Thou does not then become nothing. It remains a reality, absent in a special way. The lost Thou is not a "supreme fiction" either, for it is nothing made up, and though it exists only "in the mind," it works on me—it is the secret object of my longing.

The longing for the absent Thou may take the conscious form of a longing for God. The unconscious dread of that same Thou (dread, because I was so dependent, and because I have erected a substitute) may take the conscious form of the fear of God.

This is not to deny the existence of God or gods. We know little about them. But I admit: this theory reduces a great swath of religious experience to human relations. Only not to the kinds of human relations we normally know! It "reduces" much religious experience to a possibility of human relations which is all but lost to us. It is all but lost because *we* have reduced *our* human relations.

The banished, longed-for and dreaded Thou is real, is not mere, is to be taken seriously, affects our lives.

Each actual person I meet is a potential Thou. If I behave toward someone in disregard of her being as human as I, then her humanity comes back to trouble me. It is she as a Thou who haunts me, the Thou whom I should have seen and did not. In the silent protest of her humanity, I hear again the accusation of the unconsciously longed-for and dreaded Thou. I am accused of the particular thing I did, but at the same time conscience says: you are leading a life which banishes the possible Thou.

It is easy to confuse the Thou with its images. The internalized "parent" can also warn or scold. When it does so, it may seem to be of one cloth with the longed-for, the dreaded, the heavenly absent. In this way conscience receives superimpositions. Freud liberated us from the latter, but he mistook them for conscience itself.

The original bestowal of selfhood was good. It included its own "Yes!" It was the creation of goodness. The first act of identification cut it off, and therefore this act may be evaluated as evil. A necessary evil in an evil world perhaps, but evil still. And this evil is absolute—not culturally relative—because the I-Thou relation is fundamental to each person's being a self.

Conscience is the memory of the truth of mutuality in us. The living memory. It is a unique phenomenon, not reducible to our own or society's needs and desires. People may differ about it; what seems basic to one may seem a superimposition or distortion to another. One may persuade another. But until persuasion occurs, the mere fact that something is a matter of conscience suffices to lend it a certain integrity and priority: integrity, despite the partial truth of the Freudian analysis, and priority, even above the requirements of the democratic state.

15

Sabbath morning. Cell.

NO CALL TO SHUL. They needed me last night because their tenth man was sick. The Orthodox are sometimes caught short here on Sabbath, since many soldiers get leave to go home. Without the quorum of ten, which we call a minyan, they cannot do the public Torah reading and they cannot say Kaddish.

Kaddish is an ancient prayer in Aramaic which praises God, asks that the Messiah come in our time, and seeks peace upon Israel. It is said often during a service—sometimes by the leader of prayer and sometimes only by mourners. Males who have lost a close relative are supposed to say it at each of the three daily services for eleven months after the death.

I do not follow Jewish law. Or not much. (I am writing this on Sabbath, for example—a thing forbidden: it is considered to be work.) But my father, who did not much follow the law either, asked me on our last day together to say Kaddish sometimes. In Israel it is easy to find a minyan, so I resolved to say it once a day.

Early in the endeavor I overnighted with a group in Tiberias. There is—or was then—a synagogue in a lone stucco house by the lake near the big hotels. We barely got ten. We did the afternoon service, and in the break the leader asked me, "For whom do you say Kaddish?"

"My father."

The leader's beard was black, and he wore a long black coat and a black fedora, from the tradition of the Vilna Gaon. A different world from mine. A life devoted to the sober study of the sources—to the assumption that God's will was in them in a special sense, that Torah was holy in a way that Kafka could never be. Yet there was something sharp and practical in the face. He had noted of course my guide's clothes, canteen and pouches, the crumpled yarmulke, but now he looked past the differences. It was, at first, just a flicker.

"A son."

The lips pursed, and then he looked up and explored my eyes.

"Once a day," he said. "Don't get anyone to do it for you. There are people who do that, but don't you do it. There is nothing like a son."

I nodded and said, "I thought once a day."

We performed the evening service, and as I was leaving, he looked at me again.

"There is nothing like a son."

He knew his business. He did not ask for three times.

Kaddish once a day became a need, a balm, a sweetness, a way of making peace with my father. "Peace upon us," goes its last line, "and upon all Israel. And say: Amen." If the day went by and I had not yet said it, and the sun was going down—the time for the last service dwindling, and still no tenth man—I would get into suspense, there would be a welling up. Somehow we always managed, hauling teenagers off the street. Once I said Kaddish in the presence of nine kibbutzniks. I put Labor party beanies on their heads.

It is four years since my father died. My difficulties with Judaism have grown. On the basis of the Orthodox attitude toward women, for example, I could refuse the call to a minyan. Women are not allowed to say Kaddish. So when called, I could answer, "Call a woman!" But I do not. I remember the eleven months of mourning, that welling need. I rise and follow, though the question follows too: and women? Don't they need to mourn?

So yesterday in the late afternoon when the tall young police-side cook, Moroccan, Orthodox, asked me to the minyan, I hesitated briefly only as a token to self-respect. I was not inclined. We prisoners have so little time of our own. The week's work was done, our jailers had gone, had left us to an underling named Udi who did not much care what we did. I had been sitting in front of the club, enjoying the last of the light in the big yard. The shadow of the police wing was up to the metal barricades, which stood set off against the brighter planes behind. Each thing at this hour appears in itself. The rest of the day it is merely functional—it is most itself when we do not pick it out for attention. But at this idle hour the light picks it out, lifts it out. The barricades glowed, admirable in the blue precision of vertical bars and spaces—sufficient, burgeoning with being barricades. A truck tire held the corrugated tin sheet against the bad cell (the one with no water or toilet). The tire was large, gray, heavy, and round. Its ridges were laced with golden down. Its furrows were deep and black. The tin sheet had ridges and furrows too, Doric, admirable. Everything was admirable. In the aperture between the tin sheet and the jamb showed a little of the bars of the cell. Palestinians there. Quiet. On this side too, in the larger, better cell, they were quiet. The far wall to the right, at any other hour a muddy hue, blinked brightly back.

I sat in a wooden chair on one side of the doorway to the club. The guard sat on the other side, his wooden chair back-tilted, a sub-machine gun on his lap. We did not know each other and did not speak. I pulled from my thigh pocket, which is commodious, the thick red volume of John Cheever's stories. With a delicious sense of ease, and a tacit blessing for the coming day of rest, I found one and sank in.

That is when he appeared, my messenger. He towered lean and dark, blocking the golden yard. The guard could not, of course.

"Only for tonight," he said. "One guy's sick."

We passed the larger cell heading east. His small black knitted yarmulke, centered in the great round burst of Moroccan curls, was a radiating planet touched by the sun. (I had none. My pancake would have to do.) I followed it into shadow around the corner southward—out of the compound. The hill was there—the one that steps down. Dull now, but across the Dead Sea the eastern cliff was touched. Mount Nebo. Often I had passed through at this hour, had seen it brilliant thus.

My planet had turned westward and disappeared. I found a lit doorway. On the nearer jamb was a cardboard sign with the word "synagogue" scrawled in crayon.

So here it was. Strange. I had somehow missed it on the garbage run with Shlomo. A mere room in the compound. Shabby. Yellowed peeling walls. Beyond the nine, who noted me, on a table in the middle of the wall they turned to face (the west wall of the room, for they faced Jerusalem) was a cabinet for the Torah. A blue felt curtain covered its front. It showed an outline of the tablets from Sinai embroidered in gold, with the first words of the Ten Commandments. In line with this, toward the middle of the room, was a second table, a high one. The bearded leader stood there, his back to me. He was draped in the long shawl called tallit. Along with the others he had checked me off as I came in, and his eye had predominated—one cold eye—and then he had turned and launched into the *ashrei*, first prayer of the afternoon service.

> *Happy are they who dwell in Your House.*
> *They will yet praise You. Selah.*

I crossed the back of the room to the far corner, where there were table and chair. I could say the first verses of the *ashrei* by heart, so it was impossible not to—like a tune one catches from another.

> *Happy the people for whom it is so!*
> *Happy the people whose God is the Lord!*
> *A psalm of David:*
> *I will exalt you, O Lord, O King . . .*

The other long-bearded officer (for there were only two—the rest looked less distinguished) broke ranks and brought me a book, his lips going rapidly. (He would know it by heart, would probably know the whole service by heart.) Smiled at me while speaking to God. He held the book open to the prayer and kept on praying as he showed me the place. I took it, swept into the part I did not know by heart, started moving in rhythm. We rock back and forth when we pray. With me it is involuntary, as if the mere utterance starts a motor between hips and spine. His smile dispatched wrinkles. Warm eyes. A Sabbath light there. The candles which he knew his wife had lit were reflected there. He did not, thank

God, beckon me up front. He understood. He nodded, still praying, turned, returned.

I feel somewhat more at home in synagogue than I used to. At this service I could relax: one does not read the Torah on Friday night. I am still uncomfortable with that. The Torah is read in sections—there is a new portion each week, and that in turn is divided—and people are called up to say the blessings before and after each division. One dare not refuse—it is supposed to be an honor. But I almost always make a mistake, even when I bring my prayerbook with me and read the blessings. I stumble over the steps going up, or over the words, my knees shake, my voice shakes, I lose my place for want of breath, or pause in the wrong place—so that someone says *"Nu?"* or someone butts in to instruct me. And while I pretend to follow the pointer—for the reader reads on my behalf—I am immersed in my terror, waiting for the moment when I shall have to bless again. Then it comes— ". . . Who gave us the Torah of truth, and planted eternal life in our midst"—and if by some miracle I manage to squeeze through without a slip, then I wind up dazed, like one who has just been hurled off a spinning top, and I forget to kiss the last word with the corner of my tallit, or forget to roll the Torah shut, and do not know when to shake hands, or I give my Hebrew name wrong or my father's wrong, and am never sure exactly when to step away to make room for the next. But God forbid that they should assign me some nonverbal honor, like lifting the Torah—I might drop it!—or dressing and binding it—I would get it all wrong.

Once, a few weeks after my father's death, it happened for the first time that I was the only mourner in shul. I discovered this when I alone stood up to say Kaddish. Everything shook. My voice went out ahead of me somewhere, careening into impossible tremolos, uncatchable. Suddenly my throat narrowed—there was no voice at all—and sweat welled out under my clothes. The others sat and waited. Cat got his tongue. I pushed inward, desperately hoping to find something automatic in me that could read and get it out, the rest of it, strange Aramaic word by strange Aramaic word—and something in me did do this. The others uttered the amens quietly. I took three steps backward out of the throne room of God—"Peace upon us and upon all Israel"— and, as they said amen to that, collapsed on the bench. The service went on. My disgrace was passed over, as if forgotten. No one talked to me about it afterward.

The critical mass of them, nine at least, their eyes upon me, empty me of being. I am mortified, neutralized. Something strange, which is my body, knows rudiments of the prescribed behavior and pushes golemlike through them. I suppose this resembles stage fright. But it does not happen in front of tour groups. Only here.

Even when I am simply part of the minyan, swaying and praying, I feel eyes upon me sometimes. Not those of the actual men. Colder eyes, behind me, above me. It is these, I suppose, which get incarnated, when I am called to the Torah, in the eyes of the actual men. They know when I skip, when I have lost the place, when my phylacteries are unraveling. The presence of ten conjures up these others, haughty, forbidding. "*He* isn't doing it right."

I wrote that I am not so uncomfortable now. This is true, as long as I remain inconspicuous. I have learned the ropes, can do it right. I am proud of knowing when to stand or sit, or when to bow and how much, or when and when not to interject, "Bless and be blessed His Name." I do these things with a certain aplomb. But that isn't me either. It is someone playing Jew.

I am not an impostor thrust into circumcised flesh. I am a Jew. Only in synagogue do I become an impostor.

Perhaps because I do not believe it. Cannot affirm with them. But this does not seem to matter to the nine. They do not ask what I believe, do not need me to testify. They need me because circumcised, Bar Mitzvahed, I am—as Rosenzweig said—a testimony. They call me to the Torah because I am the son of Hershel son of Jacob, who was the son of Hershel son of God knows whom, going back to Abraham our Father, testimonies all, those who could testify and those who could not.

It is the custom, during a certain moment in the *ashrei*, to open the hands in a gesture of receiving.

You open Your hands and give each living thing what it wants.

I took satisfaction in opening my hands at the right time. Then came a Kaddish and the official start of the service. We bowed toward

Jerusalem, blessing God. I had never—it occurred to me—prayed
west before. We did the eighteen blessings, in which each takes three
steps into God's throne room and blesses Him. Standing, praying in
silence, swaying. It was satisfying to be linked up. Even if all the
words were false—even if we had it all wrong—a streaming force
came up from my feet and flicked my body, linking me. That force was
not in the content of the words. But at least in the mere pumping I was
not an impostor. I did not feel unkindly looked at. It was as if they—
whoever my unseen examiners were—had found in me a channel and
themselves linked up.

This terrible unworthiness. That is the source of my dread when I
become conspicuous in shul.

Unworthy to be the link that I am called upon there to be.

No need to believe in ancestral spirits in order to feel the link.
Rosenzweig's point is enough: like it or not, one *is* a testimony.

My sense of unworthiness is not merely the result of bad education.
It has an element of *tremendum* before the numinous, a feeling of
smallness and ineptness in the presence of the holy.

The holy—is it the community of elders, or is it God? Or the two
together?

When I was seven, they took me to an Orthodox shul on the Day of
Atonement in Far Rockaway, New York. It was my first time. They had
put up a tent for the overflow, and that is where we went. It was strange
to see all the men there, gathered as a tribe apart from Woman, all
draped in white shawls, all pumping, imploring—whom? no one
visible—and in a strange language, and my father and grandfather
joining them. The service went on and on. I was dumbfounded,
bewildered, hot, half suffocated, and bored to the depth of my being.
But there came a moment when I ceased looking for the hundred
thousandth time at this or that silken back or edge of beard or my
father's oddly serious eyes and open mouth. Suddenly it seemed as if
the crowd of silken men had become a single person, invisible,
composed of all, and the fact that he was possible made the other one
possible, the one to whom they were—"he" was—talking. That unseen presence frightened the daylights out of me.

And now nine backs in a desolate army shul. I finished those of the
blessings which I can bring myself to say.

He who makes peace upon the heights,
May He make peace upon us and upon all Israel.
And say: Amen.

I backed away three steps and sat down. The leader began to repeat the blessings. I looked out the doorway toward that step of a hill. Just a wisp now.

The leader said Kaddish. We stood to praise the Master of everything. The time came for the mourners' Kaddish, but there were no mourners. A young crowd, this.

Darkness upon the threshold, we went at once into the psalms that receive the Sabbath. Then:

Come, my love, to greet the bride . . .

The bride is the Sabbath. But it is a Kabbalistic song, and God's bride is also the Shekinah, God in female aspect, sometimes called the Community of Israel. We sang it in booming voices, as befits an epithalamium. The brokenness of the world, in this mystical teaching, is a brokenness within God. The exile of the Community of Israel is an exile of God from Himself—or Herself, a state of divorce between God and His Shekinah. We are the children of divorced parents, trying to bring them together again. And so we sang loudly, gladly, because at least for the Sabbath we were ushering them together again: God and His Shekinah, God and the Community of Israel. Like boisterous boys outside the nuptial chamber, we made the yellowed wall before us shake.

I am learning to look differently at walls. And suddenly I realized what was on the other side. By leaving the compound and coming in from the perimeter, we had erased the consciousness of proximities, but in fact our synagogue was the next room to the larger cell. Beyond the vibrating wall they sat or lay on the floor, enduring our fervor.

Their enemies at prayer. They would joke about it on the cool cement floor of the cell and then fall silent. They would dismiss it, but at a deeper level than dismissal would remain perhaps an unacknowledged fear: that this league, of which they heard the ebullient human side, was for real; that it was the secret which had put them here and which would keep them forever down.

And I—now part of the hubbub. The potent mumbo jumbo of the conquerors.

Stone throwers there. Or worse, Molotov cocktails they threw. They have killed and maimed, or if not, they might have. I have seen the maimed, the burned, window-shopping afterward like normal people in the streets of Jerusalem. And these men, lying on the cement floor, listening to us, were wrong to have thrown what they threw. Were criminal. Instead they should have learned from Mahatma Gandhi. They should have withheld taxes, burned their ID cards, done without jobs and licenses, grown their own food—although the army might have uprooted the gardens—well then, they should have done without food until the world paid attention, should have let their household belongings be confiscated, let their cars be confiscated, and filled our prisons, filled them beyond capacity. In all these ways and more, they should have nonviolently cut the thousand strings that tie them to the occupation. Oh it is easy to preach to them. They would have needed a mahatma. They would have had to be willing to swallow their rage and endure even greater suffering. But who am I to tell them to suffer— when I myself do not suffer? Let the one who preaches nonviolence come here first and practice it. Let him lie down in front of the army bulldozer when it goes to destroy a house. Even that is not enough. The army will arrest him and send him back where he came from, for he is not a Palestinian. There is no way that an outsider can suffer in the way that *they* would have to suffer, if they were to practice nonviolence.

Criminals. But who is the greater criminal, those who lie there or those who sing here? I cannot get over this basic fact: we have been occupying them, telling them what they can and cannot do, for twenty-two years. I keep coming back to that. I cannot get over or under or around it. It stares me in the face, as plain as the yellowed, peeling wall.

I shall imagine a face, Arab. A thin body sprawled there. He threw something. "Oh you should not have thrown that." "Yes, well, what was I supposed to do? Sit back and take it forever?" And because I have no right to preach nonviolence, there is nothing I can answer. "I am not a saint," he says. "I am a man in a situation, and there are no saints in sight. It's you, you Israelis, who put me in this position. If I want clean hands, I have to choose between sainthood and submission. And now you stand there loudly singing your song to God. Your hands are dirtier, but I'm the prisoner. How can you sing so loudly? It's obscene."

You have had enough of sitting in the valley of weeping,
And He will pour forth His compassion upon you.

It sounded like a war chant. It would have made their blood alternately curdle and boil. "Oh sing now!" I imagined them saying. "Oh sing while you can, you! But a day is coming!"

I have heard that the Kabbalists of Safed, four hundred years ago, used to sing this song while marching into the fields to greet the oncoming darkness, and at a certain point they would turn around to usher the Sabbath back into town. This is said to explain the custom of turning around on the verse "Come in peace." The nine began to turn around toward me, and I turned around, even a little before them. And why did I do this, and why did I go on mouthing the boisterous song? My body took part, still rocked even, apart from me. It all happened too fast. But if there had been time to think, would I have stopped singing and refused to turn and endured their stares—and the stares of our ancestors staring through them? Of course the nine would not have understood. They would have assumed I didn't know the custom. One would have signaled me to turn around. Should I have cried out, "God is not with His Shekinah! Not this Sabbath!"

No, even if there had been time to think, I would not have cried out, would not have disturbed the prayer. My turning was instinctual cowardice—I had forgotten that this verse was coming—but if there had been time, I still would have turned. Not singing boisterously. Perhaps not singing at all. But still, I would have granted my body this minimal participation. Because I am a Jew. If I needed that connection when my father died, how should I not honor it now? And it is not undeserving of honor. This tradition had a part, after all, in teaching human beings to look through walls.

So yes, even with dirty hands. But softly, while the nine voices, suddenly louder, penetrated the khaki shirt, raising the hairs of my back:

Come in peace, crown of your master,
in joy and exultation . . .

She will not come. She will not come today.

Come, bride. Come, bride.

This is sung bowing first to one side, then to the other. I always forget whether to bow first to the left or first to the right, or in which direction to turn around again. In the normal, large Friday-night congregation I can take my cue from those in front of me, but here I was quite alone in the rear. I bowed very slightly first to the left, then to the right, then turned slowly around to the right. They had already turned around. I had no doubt turned too slowly. Perhaps someone would come up afterward to instruct me. "*Shabbat shalom.* By the way, we bow first to the right." "Thank you." In this manner I had been taught to keep my feet together during Kaddish and at what angle to wear the head phylactery. "Thank you. I am happy for instruction." But in my heart, walking home, I used to dismiss them. A men's club with an obsessional neurosis.

We entered the evening service. We shielded our eyes, proclaiming:

Hear, O Israel . . .

This God, with this particular name, is our God, one and only. And you shall love Him with all your heart and soul and might. And you shall bind these words upon your heart, and speak of them, and teach them to your children, and write them upon the doorposts. A people created and bound by words.

Then came the verses about how God will reward us if we keep His commandments and punish us if we don't. I don't believe this, and I no longer say them.

Then came the memory of the delivery from Pharaoh. As you rescued us then, so shelter us now. Spread the tent of peace over us. And over them. We shall have no peace until they have peace. What kind of peace is it if we have to throttle their need to become human beings, and that need pushes upward ever again, giving them no peace?

We stepped toward Jerusalem, the Temple, God's throne room—and toward them. For the world is one, it is not divided into a physical realm and a spiritual. The fact that they lie on the cement floor in the next room between us and Jerusalem is no more or less incidental than a bone in the throat.

We said the blessings without voice—it is the custom. How God rested on the seventh day and set it aside as a day of rest. Delight of days, souvenir of Creation. O God and God of our fathers, desire our rest. Gladden our souls with Your salvation. Purify our hearts to do Your work in truth. Bequeath us Your holy Sabbath.

I LOOKED TOWARD the cell as we went back through the yard to dinner. It was quiet in the dark interstices.

16

Saturday night. Cell.

NOGA VISITED TODAY with a friend of ours named Saul. Udi led us to the club. We sat at right angles to the blank TV. But Saul looked above and behind me, shuddered and laughed. "Could you sit somewhere else?"

I twisted around and looked. A mural takes up the wall. Helmeted skeletons feast at a table laden with bleeding human body parts, the whole thing in motion, borne along by skeleton horses, panting, smiling triumphantly. The blood is in purple. The rest is in blues and grays. There is no signature, but rather a title, in the lower right: *The Banquet*. I had seen the mural before, I suppose, but it had never really registered.

"That's awful," said Noga.

"I don't like seeing you against that," said Saul.

I moved across between them, so that they, in looking at me, would not be looking at it. They realigned their chairs.

"Can't you find us another room?" asked Noga.

"We're lucky we don't have a guard standing over us with a stopwatch."

"What kind of weird person would paint a thing like that?" she said.

"Some kid," said Saul. "He has nothing to say, because he's too young. He thinks the purpose of art is to arouse strong feelings.

180

He knows that *Guernica*'s a famous painting, so he's infected by that."

"Reminds me of me," I said to Noga, "before I met you."

"Where's the bathroom?" asked Saul.

I sent him to the normal toilet (ours are holes) down past the police kitchen.

We greeted each other again.

"So how are you, Stevanovich?"

"Happy most of the time."

"You monk."

She brought out dried apricots and almonds, and laid them on a bench before me.

"To your health, my monk."

I still had the ones from last week, but I did not say so.

"Thank you."

I ate a few nuts, and then I asked:

"How are you bearing up?"

"Fine. The people from Yesh Gvul are calling all the time, giving me courage. One named Hanoch from Tel Aviv."

"I don't even know these people."

She was silent.

"You're kind of reserved."

"It's strange seeing you here."

"You sat right here last week. That painting was here too."

"The light wasn't on."

"Maybe not."

I went over and turned it off.

AFTER A WHILE she said, "Here comes Saul."

She stretched back and took an apricot.

"The kids?" I asked.

"Benny made kiddush last night."

"No kidding."

"He did it from memory, the whole thing, perfectly, exactly the way you do it, the intonation, everything."

Kiddush is the blessing of God as Creator of wine. We have this little ceremony in our apartment on Friday night at the start of the first Sabbath meal.

"And the bread?"

"Everything."

"Did you bless them?"

"They wouldn't let me."

"That's wrong. Tell them they should let you. Are they getting any trouble from their friends about me?"

"I don't think their friends even know."

Saul came in and sat down. I offered him almonds, and he took some.

"It turns out he likes it here," said Noga. "Doesn't want to come home."

"I'll come home," I said, "if I don't have to wash dishes."

She said, "If he has to wash dishes, he'd rather stay here, you see?"

"I want two months off from washing dishes!"

She drew herself back and looked at me from a distance. Brown eyes sparkling. "You like it," she said in English. "You secretly like it. Come on, man."

That "man," so unexpected, has always attracted me. It discloses another side. I envision her, suddenly, in loose jazz dens. The kind of girl that I in high school dreamed about. None of the Long Island inhibitions. She picked it up perhaps, along with smoking, in the late sixties in London, to which she went straight from the army—from two years in a tent in the Sinai. In the pubs, she told me, if you got drunk quickly, they said, "You're cheap, man!" I find her delicate and noble, but I like the punctuating "man."

"He's got a monk in him," she said to Saul.

"It's true," I said. " 'I could be bounded in a nutshell, and count myself a king of infinite space, were it not that' they shove me around."

"That's the army," he said.

"Now dishes, now inspection, now sleep, now get up . . ."

"The army. It's not prison especially. The guy who washes dishes next to you—he's doing his reserve duty. What's the difference between him and you?"

"He doesn't have to wear a hat outdoors. He doesn't get locked up at night. He can go to the *shekem* and buy a Coke. He gets paid. He gets Sabbath leave."

"Yeah, but you get to be a hero of the left."

"A philosopher in jail," said Noga.

I gave her a look.

"He doesn't want to admit it," she said.

I kept my mouth shut. (My gob, she would call it.) She wants to think of me as a philosopher? Let her.

"He's as much of a philosopher as Sartre or Camus," she said.

Why choose these gods of the left? Is this how she thinks of me now? Does this image of me help her to get through the twenty-one days? And should I disturb it?

"I once knew a faculty wife," I said, "who never said, 'my husband.' She said, 'my husband the philosopher.' 'My husband the philosopher is down with the flu.' "

"My husband the philosopher is in prison," she said.

"Not qua philosopher."

"Oh qua qua qua. Him and his qua's."

"You want a philosopher," I said, "you got to take the qua's."

Suddenly came a clattering from across the yard. Someone shouted: "Where are you?"

We fell silent. Noga alert, listening. Saul and I—eyes meeting, escaping.

Clanging and clattering.

"Where are you?"

Fierce, deliberate clanging and clattering.

"No water! No toilets! No food!"

She shuddered and paled.

A thud. That would be the truck tire going down. Louder clattering.

I said: "Good thing you didn't bring the kids."

And now even louder, much closer. The shouts now in Arabic, closer.

"There's a cell on this side," I said.

That shudder of hers. I would store it up. She had felt the reality.

We are so jaded. There is so much processed misery launched at us. Wonderful, that someone can still directly feel.

Now Udi's voice: "What do you think you're doing?"

"We're not human beings?"

"You stop throwing stones, we'll treat you like human beings."

"No water! No toilets! This is a zoo, this."

"They'll come and give you."

"Nobody comes."

Udi stuck his head in the doorway. A boy trying not to look bewildered.

"Where's the guard?"

I shook my head and he left.

Again, the voices:

"How can you keep human beings like this?!"

Clattering on both sides.

"You just remember why you're here!"

"You think I know why I'm here?"

And he laughed. Someone from the cell on our side laughed. So more than one knew Hebrew.

The guard appeared from the direction of the barracks, in fast stride, limping. The fat, bearded one. Udi did not reprimand him. That guard could have been his father.

It calmed down. They were being taken care of. We returned to talking. We talked about the difficulties of the Sabbath in an army prison—the lack of officers, of personnel. Then we speculated about whether I would get another round. Noga was thinking of calling Schneller, talking with my commander. I told her to consult first with Yesh Gvul. Udi stuck his head in again and announced that it was time.

I gave her letters and my notebooks.

"So many! You're so prolific, Stephen!"

Once she called me "spontaneous." I knew then that I would try to marry her. She had the gift of seeing in me what I was not, but wanted to become.

"I've only brought you four," she said. "I didn't think you'd fill so many."

"I'll write small."

Outside, it was the hour of planes and shadows, of peace upon the heights. As we walked by the tin sheet of the larger cell, someone was in the aperture.

"Where are you from?" he asked. He had almost no accent—unlike the one who had yelled from the other side.

"Jerusalem," said Saul.

We kept on walking. He said to our backs:

"Call the contractor Smilansky and tell him his worker's in jail. It starts with 2-4-6."

We kept on.

"OK?"

Noga hesitated, stopped. We stopped, but we did not turn around. It was as if we were talking together near the tin sheet.

"Smilansky. 2-4-6 something," said Saul.

There were voices from the cell in Arabic.

"And the boss at Hadassah, Beit Hakerem," said the same one. He was translating. "Tell him Suleiman is in jail."

"Hadassah's in Ein Kerem," I said. "Next to Beit Hakerem."

Again a heated discussion there. But then he said out to us:

"Beit Hakerem."

"There's no such thing," I said quietly.

Saul asked: "What's his name?"

"Suleiman."

"The boss's name."

Discussion.

"He thinks Ya'akov. And the contractor Rubin from Jebel el Mukkaber. Mahmoud is in jail. OK? Tell him where."

"Rubin," said Saul.

"Jebel el Mukkaber. And Smilansky. 2-4-6."

We went toward the opening of the compound. Mercy appeared from the other side, smoking, pacing before the expanse of the wilderness.

I introduced Noga and Saul. "Mercy," I said, "is the best cook."

Just then they descended upon us from behind, the cavalry, or a posse coming to get me—but they rounded the corner, already ten, and funneled into the synagogue.

We kissed good-bye. Mercy walked me back. At the outer cell gate he said, "Come to dinner. You don't have to work. Come eat."

I thanked him and said that maybe I would.

THE SABBATH'S-END pickings were so slim in the police mess—and the synagogue group so long in coming—that I walked out and felt my way through the gutted building to Mercy's kitchen. He loaded spaghetti with tomato sauce onto my blue plate, and I went into the serving room, which has an opening to the dining room. To this the reservists of the regiment come to get their portions. I always eat here. They see me, of course, when they come. What strange disease does this man have that he sits apart? Sometimes they ask me for something. I sit next to the dairy fridge with the juice, and they ask me to renew the juice, which I do. Nothing contagious.

There were more than I would have expected tonight. Small groups kept drifting in and out, talking about the day's soccer games (for they had no doubt done nothing but sleep and listen to the games all day), at last leaving their dishes in tubs at the far end near the door. Sticky. There was the tomato sauce and a semiliquid white cheese and the sesame sauce called *tehina* and the ineluctable fly-ridden plum jam. A small gray-haired kitchen man named Obadiah went for the tubs when they were full and carried them briskly back the length of the hall. He would go out of my sight, and a second later I'd hear them crash into the sink. So the water would have all that in it. I thought I'd have another plateful and then perhaps help him.

Mercy was by the stove stirring soup for the morrow.

"*Bendicos manos,*" I said.

He smiled and shook his head.

"It's Ladino," I said. " 'Blessed be the hands.' Spaghetti sauce is the only thing I cook, and yours is better."

He took my plate. We went back to the serving room together, and he dished me out a big helping.

"Too much," I said.

But he insisted.

After eating, I helped Obadiah with the dishes while Mercy peeled avocados. Then I wet down the floor and pushed the water into the drain with a squeegee. Mercy waited for me and locked up.

"You've had two Sabbaths in a row here," I said.

"It's because I'm the only cook. They sent that other son of a bitch down to the Dead Sea. Let him give them the runs down there."

There had indeed been another. Uzi had kept warning me what not to eat.

"We're finished on Monday," he said. "Did you know?"

"No."

"A new bunch is coming in. I'll talk with their commander for you."

So the kitchen work would be over.

"Don't bother," I said. "Might as well find out what jail is like."

"Anyway you only have a few days."

"Who knows."

"No, they won't want to monkey with you."

"Don't raise my hopes."

"Listen, before I leave I'll give you my address. When you're in Haifa, you have to come visit."

"Thank you, but watch out. I'll show up with a whole tour group. They always want to meet Israelis."

"Do it. Just phone first."

"Fifty people for dinner."

"I manage it here, don't I?"

"And I'll do the dishes. We can open a restaurant."

Between the long buildings, in the moonlight, I saw Kypros, the Herodian fortress on the south side of the opening of Wadi Qilt.

"You see that mountain?"

"Kypros," he said.

"How do you know that?"

He shrugged. "We know our motherland."

He laughed and waved good-night and left. I stayed to look at her.

KING HEROD'S MOTHER. An upthrusting white cone with two eyes—they would be the cisterns. They had received water from an aqueduct which was linked to the springs farther up the wadi.

I have hiked the Qilt, oh, thirty times, in all seasons, with American church groups or German pastors or German youth groups behind me. The way is lined with caves in the canyon sides, and often one sees the remains of stone walls at the mouths. In them lived monks fourteen hundred years ago. The water of the aqueduct is to be heard, as one walks the trail across from it on the north face; birdsong is to be heard (of swallow, pigeon, partridge, grackle); and the squeals of coneys—copulating, or wanting to, or running away from other coneys that want to. The spectacle of fat, lusty coneys must have strengthened the chastity of dualistic monks. But one does not hear today what a pilgrim of that day reported: how toward evening the monks in their neighbor caves would sing the prayers, tuning to one another, so that the canyon quavered with holy song.

Kypros. From my perspective, at roughly 7:00 P.M. (Mercy time), her left side plunges white and armless into the Qilt's dark canyon. It is a rare natural break in the cliff—the only local wadi that always has water. Two thousand years ago people used to take this way from Jerusalem down to the Jordan, where John was baptizing. He would have raised his eyes past Kypros, seeing no mother figure.

A voice calls in the wilderness:
"Clear the way of the Lord,
Level a road in the desert for
our God."

Isaiah 40. The Gospels associate this verse with the Baptist. The voice was his. From the east bank of the Jordan he pictures Kypros toppled, the wadi filled: a straight broad path to Zion, and the Lord going up in power to establish His Kingdom.

Jesus, whom John baptized, wandered forty days in that wilderness. Satan tempted him there. Then he went up to Galilee, and healed and taught, and at last came by way of Jericho, taking this road on which our camp is set, and climbed the untoppled shoulder of Kypros toward Jerusalem and his passion, solution, goal.

But each time I hike in Wadi Qilt I have to make an effort to think of any of this. The canyon walls are beige and gray and clean of history. They give forth long white squill, and winter anemones, and out of the crevices new generations of coney. But stories, none. It takes a guide to return the stories to their places, resisting the natural immediacy of the surface. To history our earth is immune.

As for Wadi Qilt, it is, strictly speaking, Palestinian earth. But its freshness and virginity contradict ownership. That which endures all negates all. No event makes an impression. Hence it seems important to find in a rock a footprint of Jesus, a footprint of Muhammad, or to dig into a hill and find ruins and connect them with an ancient text. As if by uncovering our history engraved in the rock, we could claim a right to the rock—and through *its* firm existence a right to our own. We have no claim. "The land is Mine," says the Lord. "You are but strangers and sojourners with Me."

At night the earth withdraws a little, ceasing to mock our pretensions. So Kypros in moonlight. She gathers history like a white shawl around head and shoulders. She thinks of her royal son. His destruction began and ended just there across the wadi beneath her.

Then daylight comes and it is a hill. These things never happened. Kypros, Herod, his beloved Mariamne . . . these people never were. What is and was and will be are the dark-ribbed slope, the sudden white thrust of the cone.

17

Sunday afternoon. Cooks' room.

THE WHOLE VERSE goes, "And the land shall not be sold in perpetuity, for the land is Mine, for you are strangers and sojourners with Me" (Lev. 25:23). The idea is that the land has to remain within the family. If it is sold, then it must return to the family at a specified time, called the Jubilee. The family has the land from God. They are His tenants, so they cannot permanently sell it.

The farmer transforms the land by his labor. No mortal has a greater claim to possession. With respect to other human beings he has the right to it. With respect to God he does not.

The West Bank has been heavily worked for three thousand years. The first to settle it thickly were various tribes, loosely bound into a league called Israel. Their descendants dug cisterns. They cut down forests and replaced them with olive and fruit trees, the thickets with vines, the grasses with wheat and barley. They followed the lines of layered limestone and scooped out terraces in the slopes, brought up red soil from the valleys and walled it in. An enormous labor. Some of these terraces were renewed through the ages, but many are today just lines on eroded hillsides. "After the Israelites," we are accustomed to say, "came the Assyrians, the Samaritans, the Babylonians, the Persians, the returning Jews, the Greeks, the Romans, the Byzantines, the Arabs, the Crusaders, the Mamluks, the Turks, the British, the

Jordanians and again the returning Jews." That is the history of the rulers, but it has little relation to those who were actually working the land. The Palestinians include among their ancestors all the groups that ever struck root here. They are descended not only from Arabs but also from our old enemies, the Canaanites and Philistines; and from our old allies, the Phoenicians; and from Israelites: those whom the conquering Assyrians did not force out, who joined transplanted exiles to form a new mixture, the Samaritans. The latter were once the main population in the northern half of the central range. They revolted against the Christians and were massacred. Many descendants of the survivors converted, under compulsion, to Islam. Barely five hundred Samaritans remain today, but "e Samara"—the Samaritan—is still a common family name among Palestinian Muslims. These are also our brothers, throwing stones.

The changes have run deep, but even deeper down the old stock abides. After three thousand years of monotheism, the fields that receive their water from nature only—without irrigation—are still called, by the Palestinians, "Baal earth."

Rulers came and went, but the families remained to the extent that they could on their terraced plots and mixed with new arrivals. We, the most recent, huddled with our teacher in the guide course, maps in hand, relearning the country which our particular ancestors, stubbornly holding to Judaism, had left. The words which had bound them together in exile were largely about this land, recorded how God had promised and given it, taken it away, given it again; described its borders, encampments, battles, graves; prescribed the rules for living on it; and expressed three times a day the longing to return. Now here we were, relearning the land in order to guide still stranger strangers through it. One day, for example, seven years before the intifada, we huddled in a wadi at a village called Katana. But we, incarnate fulfillment of those ancient binding words, did not—most of us— believe them, did not feel ourselves to be bound by them. The serried lines of a page of Talmud were as strange to us as the terraces on the hillside opposite which we were next going to have to climb. We sat, renewing a kind of possession through knowledge, while the women at the spring, a poor stone's throw away, chatted and laundered, and their boys (the girls in school at this hour—they would switch at noon) played and shouted around them. They cast hardly a glance at the intruder: this compact group, and the guide-teacher facing us, spewing forth. We looked to them, perhaps, like an elephant talking to itself through its trunk. Here were two worlds in one place. We did not graze. But we had two old rifles just in case. An Israeli group in the West Bank must by law be armed.

My concept then was that it was all right to carry rifles, as it was all right to be there. The rifles were not against the women at the spring. They were against hypothetical terrorists. The women at the spring, their kids, their husbands working no doubt in our cities at that hour—so ran my concept—accepted our occupation. We (the forty particular members of that year's course) were not forcing ourselves upon them. We could in good conscience, therefore, politely, distantly observe. They would accept our nongrazing visit, because King Hussein had been much harsher, and because they had electricity now, and plumbing now (although they continued to use the spring—for free water and the local news), and schooling for their children, and improved health care. They were worse off than we, of course, but better off than the Egyptians, Syrians, Lebanese, Iraqis, or Jordanians. The oil states treated their relatives like dirt. So all they lacked with us, really, was self-determination. Most Arabs in other lands didn't have that either. And what would that be, practically speaking? It would be a voice in the conditions imposed on them when they wanted, for example, to go and come, to marry someone from outside, to build a house. But the want of a voice seemed no great price, considering that "they" had started the wars, and considering how benevolent we were in the conditions we imposed, how understanding, respectful. We were only occupying them because of the damned terrorists. They were no doubt secretly happy that we shielded them from them. Nor would they need to fear alteration in us. We were the Jewish people. Had suffered. Knew what it was.

Women passed all the while, and the elephant talked to itself. Plastic tubs of bright laundry and plastic buckets of water glided by upon their heads, perfect fixtures, plumb to the center of the earth. Beneath them the softer, liquid bodies of the bearers adjusted to the hill, advancing as they had a thousand or ten thousand times before unwatched. They stopped chatting as they neared, and the teacher, hearing them stop, moved in to clear the path but did not stop. He was himself a great apparently unstoppable spring—of history local and far, of birds and bees and the earth, of humor and passion, a fund of the piquant. One of our women interrupted: "How do they do that?" "You start practicing at three years old," he said, "you'll be able to do it too," and went on about the village, why it was down here by the spring and not up above as the villages usually are. History natural and unnatural. He seemed always to have the whole story, no matter how insignificant, how unbiblical the place. As if he had sat long evenings with the village chiefs. Perhaps he had.

A tall, beautiful woman came toward us, a plastic bucket on her head.

"Watch this beauty," the teacher said, "how she lowers her eyes."

Someone started to speak in Arabic.

"No Arabic," the teacher said.

He stepped in. The spring stopped for a moment. That could stop it. A tension in us. A kind of acknowledgment. She lowered her eyes.

And was past. Adjusted herself for the hill. The heat subsided. The color of her cheeks. Infinite.

And he went on. Mongols and minarets.

Then we crossed the wadi and single file began climbing. The teacher found the farmer's way from terrace to terrace. No destruction. It would be as if the farmer had passed forty times. They would of course be watching us, to see what we might uproot, undo. But we glided upward unpausing, effortless as ghosts. They would perhaps approve, that the teacher knew how not to destroy. He found the diagonal ways that surmount the gray pocked slope, at each stone wall (unmortared, for the rain to trickle through) its curving ramp. Unpausing, for he knew the farmer's mind. We followed him up through the farmer's mind. This was earth, but it was the farmer's mind. The surface of the earth in the West Bank is all mind. The red soil brought up from the wadi is mind. The scarps cut back for breadth, the fig trees, olive trees, pomegranates, the distance from one tree to another, the height above sea level, mind. Or the grape vines, sleeping with a stone for a pillow like Jacob, or crucified on a wire, to spread out the ripening, to lengthen the time on the market. All mind. Even where the terraces have long been neglected, the soil washed back down, the hard beds repillowed with thorns, it is mind, ancient, dead, waiting. If one loves this landscape, one loves the mind.

The current mind had brought up this soil, still untrammeled, red and fresh, had rebuilt the walls, had fit stone to angular stone. Watched now perhaps from below. Wife and children watched him watch, as we mounted through his mind and body, taking care to humiliate as little as possible. He had not had us in mind, when he had built these curving ramps from terrace to terrace. We were not him forty times. Did he appreciate that we took such care? His land, yes and no. The surface, form, finer shape are his, but not the stuff. He has a right to it in the face of his fellow man. My life, yes and no. God does not owe it to me. A lion in the jungle does not owe it to me. Yet I have a right to it in the face of my fellow man.

So he would feel perhaps a little raped. Freud's father's hat. The next rain would wipe out the lines of our sneakers. It was, after all, like many other little things that happened in those days.

The top of the hill is Tell Kfira. A Gibeonite city. Standing upon it, knowing what it had been, we could renew an ancient claim. We too had a right to be here. Why not? We had a treaty with the Gibeonites.

So we stood there and looked around and identified places, imagined the present away and the ancient back. Argued about the Gibeonites. Got into our bus. And visited Nebi Samwil, and Gibeon itself (El Gib), and some megaliths which the Arabs call "the graves of the children of Israel," an older traditional version perhaps of Rachel's tomb. And drove back to Jerusalem. That night it rained.

In this way we "plowed" the West Bank, as a Hebrew expression has it. And they were always also there, quaintly laundering at a spring, harvesting, threshing, binding, riding on asses, baking bread, except of course for the basic breadwinners, who while we were there were mostly not there. Thus I learned to look down on them. I did not then admit it to myself. I found out later, when the uprising started, that I had looked down on them. They too must have despised themselves. How could they let us glide over them like that? Let forty members of another people just bus in with rifles, tramp around however delicately, observe, discuss, bus away. By what right? By what allowance? Because they did not have whatever it took to unite and be a people. If they had what it took, they would rise up. But we could make do with two old rifles, because we knew they would not rise up. So how not to look down on them? How should they not despise themselves? It seemed a lower form of humanity, that softened by electricity, plumbing, schools, health care, and drivers' licenses would not rise up, would not say No, would not demand to be as free.

Sunday night. Cell.

There were times, going through the West Bank, when I felt exalted. As a student in the States I had looked forward to this landscape. It was not disappointing. Something had occurred here which my ancestors had described in terms of God and people. I wanted to ferret it out.

I arrived, "plowed" the land, began to guide. And these hills, precisely because they remained (in their surging, their rough gray limestone mottled with darkish green) so indefatigably innocent of history (despite the surface transformations, deforesting, erosion, quarrying, new roads, auto junkyards, Jewish settlements, Arab villages spilling down the slopes), rose in such a way that sensing their masses, I could feel linked up to my ancestors who had had, among the same masses, that core experience, whatever it was. I sought here a way to the long lost, the inherently meaningful. I had understood my task to be: to penetrate beyond the old terms, to retrieve a new-old possibility.

The biblical Shechem, for example, in Nablus today (but it is more than an example, it is for me the center), straddles the narrow place on the east end of the pass between the mountains Ebal and Gerizim. I used to stand on the ruin of the temple there, at the edge of the tell looking toward the pass, and imagine the tribes on the slopes of the mountains, as ordained in Deuteronomy (27:11–17):

On that day Moses commanded the people:

When you have crossed the Jordan, the following will stand on Mount Gerizim to bless the people: Simeon, Levi, Judah, Issachar, Joseph, and Benjamin. And these will stand to curse on Mount Ebal: Reuben, Gad, Asher, Zebulun, Dan, and Naphtali.

The Levites shall respond, pronouncing loudly to every man in Israel:

"Cursed, the man who makes a statue or idol . . . and sets it up in secret."

And the whole people shall respond and say, "Amen!"

"Cursed, who curses his father and mother."

"Amen!"

"Cursed, who moves his neighbor's boundary."

"Amen!"

It goes on in this vein. Here is a people being welded together by words. The picture is doubtless idealized, reimagined, like that at the end of the Book of Joshua, where Joshua renews the covenant with God at this same place. But these are idealizations *of something.*

I have a theory about this "something." Rosenzweig gave me the first hint on that winter day. Now this theory grounds my understanding of Judaism. It turns on the question: What unified the tribes into "Israel"?

Normally the earth plays a crucial role in forming a people. But here the landscape does not promote unity. It is so varied, what with the single bulky range of Judah, the clustered mountains and valley passes of Manasseh, the broad swath of the Jezreel Plain, the rugged highland of Naphtali, the steep rise to the plateau across the Jordan, that the natural tendency has always been toward smaller units.

If not as landscape, however, the earth in its function as farmland can form a people. When families depend on the soil, it is easy for a strongman to find them again and again, to tax their crops, thus to maintain a standing army and bureaucracy, and by means of all that, to *force* the smaller groups into a unity. The first major strongman in Israel was David. Yet the tribes called themselves "Israel" and fought together under that name at least one hundred and fifty years before him.

This earliest Israel was not a stable unit, rather a loose association. In a crisis a leader would try to muster the tribes to fight. Deborah did so, for example, against the Canaanites, and Gideon against the Midianites. According to the archeological surveys, the Israelites were newly settled in the mountains and valleys; traces of their hamlets show up by the hundreds, in regions which had been almost empty of towns during the century before. The new iron tools may have helped: they could clear land, fell trees, dig cisterns.

They were farmers, but without long-established roots in the soil (or they were shepherds in the process of becoming farmers). Each tribe still sought to guard its independence, but now they had fixed property to lose. They needed to protect their fields and unwalled towns against the Canaanites, Midianites, Ammonites, and finally the Philistines. They had to be able to unite, therefore, in a crisis. At the least, they had to unite in order to *keep* the land. But if the biblical story of the wilderness wandering is accurate, they had to unite in order to *take* the land as well as keep it.

From what source then, if not the earth, could this "Israel" get its unity?

From the divine. They had to experience the divine as One in order to be one people. If instead they had allowed themselves to worship many gods, while lacking deep roots in the earth, they would have had nothing at all to unify them. They would have been easy prey.

That is one leg of the theory. But the question arises: what does it mean—in terms that we, today, can understand—to "experience the divine as One"?

Suppose that in a crisis a leader arises from nowhere and by sheer magnetism unites the people. The ancient way of experiencing such an event was different from the modern. We witness a Gandhi, a Martin Luther King—or to take a negative example, the extremest negative— a Hitler, and we speak of the person's "charisma." We mean a kind of mysterious power, an aura or radiance which makes that person seem bigger than life to his or her followers. At the same time it is a magnetism which draws the followers and binds them. They experience this power when the leader speaks and acts.

The word "charisma" is ancient Greek. It means "divine gift." (The Greek gods were not necessarily good; the divine could be demonic.) But we moderns speak of charisma in the above, narrower sense as if it were a characteristic belonging to the person, an inherent power. This one has it, that one doesn't. In the presence of such a leader, what we primarily experience is him or her—we may even make a cult of him or her. And this is part of our overall modern approach to things. I do not—except by reflection—find much to wonder at when an insight "occurs to me," "dawns on me," and there seems little *theo* left in en*thus*iasm, nor do I feel the presence of the giver on hearing the "gifted" pianist. My first impulse, anyhow, is to praise Van Cliburn, not some god. Bread rises, grape juice turns to wine, I have an insight, and Lech Walesa has charisma.

The ancients found mystery in growth from the soil, the rising of bread, the fermenting of wine, as well as in the way song occurs to a poet, insight to a thinker, the extra burst of energy to an athlete or soldier. And when they stood in the presence of a charismatic leader, they did not primarily experience the leader. They experienced a god, speaking the word through the leader, determining the act, bestowing the magnetic power.

That is the point of all the biblical stories which tell how God calls a leader. Moses stutters, Gideon is from the weakest clan, Samuel is a child, and so on. The person is dust and ashes; it is God Who empowers. This is also the basic assumption later, when the mouth of the prophet moves and people hear the word "I"—and it is not the "I" of the prophet.

Because the earth could not unify them, the early Israelites had to experience the divine as One. But to put this in terms that *we* can understand, although at a distance: in the words and acts of successive leaders they had to experience the signature of one same God.

Faith was whatever it took to recognize in the radiant, magnetic power of the present leader—say, Samuel—the gift of the same singular God who had earlier cared for the community through Gideon, Deborah, Joshua, and Moses. Each time a crisis arose they depended on this God to become manifest again. He became manifest not by appearing in heaven, nor even, primarily, by parting the sea or shaking the mountain, but by granting to some human being the power to muster and bind.

Such was the *source* of this people. Not earth—though earth was essential, promised and desired—not directly earth, but rather words. "Hear, O Israel! The Lord is One!" And yet today, what do they cry out—the settlers, who think they are renewing the ancient source? They cry: "The land of Israel! The land, the land, the land!"

In the Bible itself the relation to the land is paradoxical. God promises it to Israel indeed, but fulfillment includes a hidden danger: once people sink roots into the promised land, it will become an alternative source of unity. The land will replace God as unifier. And that is precisely what happened.

There are signs of the struggle against this—against the inevitable. The promised land must never fully belong to Israel: "The land is mine," says the Lord. So the family may not sell it in perpetuity, as said. To mark their independence of the earth, it is to lie uncultivated every seventh year.

Or the pilgrimage festivals: they are earth rites, harvest rites: barley (Passover), wheat (Weeks—Shavuot), and fruit (Booths—Succoth). But in two cases out of the three, the emphasis is on a historical event before the taking of the land. In Passover it is the exodus from Egypt. In Succoth—having gathered the grapes, olives, figs, pomegranates, and dates—the Israelite does not simply go home like a typical farmer. Rather he and his family live in a booth for seven days:

> . . . so that your descendants will know that I had the Israelites live in booths when I brought them out of Egypt. (LEV. 23:43)

The biblical writers preserved the wilderness tradition not because they were fond of the desert. They were fighting the power which farmland had as an alternative basis for unity. Against that enormous given (the earth into which generations could sink their roots) they wanted somehow to preserve the intensity and intimacy of the early relation, when God alone could unify.

The earth won out—but only with the help of the Philistines.

HERE IS a corollary: in the early situation the principle of divine retribution quite literally *worked.* If the people had faith—if they discerned the same, one and only God acting through their leaders, and if they obeyed Him—then they would be one, and in the strength of that unity they would prevail.

The principle worked for the group—not for the individual. But in that time group feeling—the sense of family and community—seems to have been quite strong.

The principle worked, moreover, only in the special situation of those years, while Egypt was weak, and no Mesopotamian empire loomed, and before the Philistine threat became constant.

It did become constant. The people, with roots in the earth by this time, went to Samuel and asked for a human king, to be "like all the nations" (I Sam. 8:20). No longer needing God for their unity, they began to worship the gods of the land.

The prophets—God through the prophets—kept calling Israel back, as if the intense love of old could be restored. God said that He would make Israel like a desert, as bare as on the day she was born; that He would take away her grain, new wine, and oil; ruin her vines and her fig trees, make them a thicket, punish her for running after the Baals. But having uprooted her, He would renew the ancient source:

> *"Therefore I am now going to allure her;*
> *I will lead her into the desert*
> *and speak tenderly to her. . . .*
> *There she will respond as in the days of*
> *her youth,*
> *As in the day she came up out of Egypt."*
> (HOS. 2:16−17)

The God Whom the people needed for unity, once upon a time, here tries to reassert His power. But given their crops and their strongman, the plain fact is: they do not need Him for that anymore. And so He says: I am the God of your new situation too. I control the rain. Thus arise the verses which I no longer say in shul. They come from the Book of Deuteronomy (which appeared not in the time of Moses, rather centuries later):

And if you obey these commandments which I command you to-
day, to love the Lord your God and to serve Him with all your heart

and with all your soul, then I will provide the rain of your land in
its season, the former rain and the latter rain, and you will gather
in your grain, your new wine, and your oil. . . . Keep alert, so that
your heart will not be tempted to turn away and worship other
gods and bow down to them. For then the anger of the Lord will
burn against you, and He will shut up the heavens, and it will not
rain, and the ground will not yield its plenty, and you will quickly
perish from the good land which the Lord is giving you.

(DEUT. 11:13−17)

The writer has received the tradition of the formative experience, from a time when the principle of divine retribution quite literally worked, and here he tries to translate it into the agricultural terms of his own day. But nothing clicks anymore. The special conditions no longer obtain. Land and king provide unity now; the individual seems more important than the group; great empires have arisen again in the north and south. But still, the writer of these verses stubbornly proclaims the old divine justice! He proclaims it in flat contradiction to common experience, where it rains on good and evil alike. Thus he drives a wedge between faith and experience (to be precise, between faith and the rest of experience). Faith, from now on, will be other than what it was—no longer a particular way of experiencing events, but rather something that one holds *in spite of* experience. And experience too will be something else. Godless. It is as if we human beings once had an organ for sensing the divine *in* experience, and at this moment—for us in the West at least—the organ ceases to function, begins to atrophy.

There is, then, at the source of Judaism and Christianity, a colossal mistake in translation: the old, intense relation with God could not be carried over into agricultural terms. For centuries the guardians of faith managed to find excuses. We were exiled to Babylon, but that was because of our idolatry. We suffered under the Greeks, our own Hasmoneans, and the Romans, but those were the birth pangs of the end time, when God would set things right. The end time was delayed, but innocent sufferers would be compensated in the afterlife. The afterlife! It was the last and seemingly unassailable redoubt of a faith that had long been cut off from experience. But even this great fortress has been undermined of late. How could God compensate, in the afterlife, a parent who was forced to choose between his children? In all of eternity, what could possibly console the parent for having made that choice then, in time?

Deprived of the old excuses, and faced with the horrors of the Holocaust, our theologians manufacture new ones. But none fits the God of our Bible.

One says: "The question is not, 'Where was God then?' Rather, where was man?"

Is God then irrelevant in history?

One says: "If God interfered all the time, our free will would be meaningless."

But if He could intervene against Pharaoh, why not against Hitler?

One says (I have heard it said here in Israel): "The Jews of Europe were assimilated. They were not obeying the commandments."

The Hasidim of Eastern Europe? Eighty percent of our people's rabbis and Torah students?

One says (I have heard it said here): "The Holocaust was like the four hundred years in Egypt, and the State of Israel is the modern equivalent of God's bringing His people into the Promised Land."

One person's gain does not make up for another's suffering. See Ezekiel, Chapter 18.

One says: "There are times when God hides His face."

Indeed, but not from the innocent, according to the biblical covenant.

One says: "His ways are mysterious."

An incomprehensible covenant is meaningless.

No, none of this new theological clothing fits, and the old is all in tatters. There is no justifying God's ways to man. There are no excuses. But that God need not apologize; He never existed. The God Who was our source, the biblical God Who *did* exist (and Who may appear again) encountered our ancestors and saved them only in special historical circumstances.

BUT IF THE CIRCUMSTANCES were so special, what good does that core experience do us?

Here is another corollary: when the earth does not unify a people, and yet they need unity, it is vital that their relations with each other be right.

We, the heirs of this tradition, take for granted the link between divinity and morality. But this link was forged in ancient Israel. That one only God demanded less for Himself than for their relations with each other:

Do not steal.
Do not lie.
Do not deceive one another.
Do not swear falsely by my name. . . .
Do not cheat your neighbor or rob him.
Do not hold back the wages of a hired man overnight. . . .
Do not take revenge or bear a grudge against one of your people,
but love your neighbor as yourself. I am the Lord.

(LEV. 19:11–18)

The formative experience revealed a possible way of hearing, seeing, tasting the divine. Just one way among others. But this way is bound up with the possibility of community. That was ancient Israel's great discovery.

The earth is the basis of the nation-state—of unity enforced—but it is anticommunal. The farmer's family is essential to him indeed, but between extended families, each on its plot, the soil intervenes. Crops, so easily taxable, support the state, the institutionalized means of succession, the system of foreign alliances, all of which promote an illusion of human self-sufficiency. Against that came the Israelite discovery: of a divine force, *here in experience*, which binds people to itself and to each other. This force could only be discovered in the want of earth. It could only be discovered, in other words, by people who lacked the ordinary means for building a national illusion of self-sufficiency. The discovery had such impact that it has echoed down through twenty-seven hundred years of faith without experience and experience without faith. Despite the empirical falsity of the verses about the rain, the memory of the discovery—or not the memory, rather merely the impulse from the forgotten, an impulse embodied in words upon words upon words—held us Jews together, without earth of our own, for two thousand years. It rocks us back and forth in the synagogues still.

When the discovery is not yet distorted and betrayed, it impels its bearer outward. The binding force was born of particular circumstances, but it was found to be good in itself. So its discoverers thought of themselves as a "nation of priests," "chosen" to bear it outward—not primarily to teach or proclaim, but rather to *be*—to be the core of a community which would include more and more: to be a blessing to the families of the earth, a "light to the nations."

STANDING IN THE RUIN of the temple at Shechem, looking toward Ebal and Gerizim, imagining the tribes on the slopes, then turning and calling out the curses over the noise of the power station—and my Gentile pilgrim-tourists answering "Amen"—I felt, therefore, exalted.

It was a mystical attraction to the place. For the tough-minded I have to concede: perhaps no such words rang out between temple and mountainsides. Even so, the biblical accounts epitomize this core experience: words of story, words of law, shaped tribes into a people. Let this landscape be mere symbol, but the symbol is of something that occurred.

Words, often about the earth, had priority over the earth. Such was our beginning. And so it was possible during two thousand earthless years to remain one people on the basis of words. Words of story, law, and prayer served for us as the native ground did for others. The Bible, the Mishnah, the Talmud, the Shulkhan Arukh, the prayerbooks—the portable ground of our being. As our foundation, so our continuity. I, a Jew, could stand between Ebal and Gerizim because of words which my ancestors had spoken thirty-two hundred years before, and which had perhaps echoed between these mountains, and after that (without "perhaps") for centuries in the heart.

The mountains come down like sections of a theater; the layers of weathered limestone, rows of seats. Arab houses of whiter limestone perch upon them now, haphazardly it seems from here. The mound of ancient Shechem crouches in between, the small temple thrust more toward Ebal than Gerizim. This asymmetry bothers me. Gerizim has pines above the houses. Ebal is just stark gray; pocked and jagged. The houses of course, but then it rises above them—arrogant, oblivious. So grandly forgetful: of Joshua, the Levites. The tribes of Israel, forgotten. Or not forgotten. Never noticed to be forgotten. No impressions upon the rough gray rock. Does not notice, will not need to forget, the stone cubes strewn now upon its lower parts. A gray whale plunging through history. A blank slate for the imagination, despite the cubes, despite, in the pass toward Gerizim, the roaring power station, above which I have to shout:

"Cursed, the man who makes a statue or idol and sets it up in secret!"

"Amen!" answer the Christian pilgrim-tourists.

We do this in Hebrew. "Amen" is Hebrew too.

Words that long ago smacked the air here (perhaps) smack it again, with an American accent, and weakly now. But *again*—because they were retained in the flesh of generations to be returned to this mountain now, to lick again the porous rock, though no tribes stand there now and perhaps never did. It is not essential. The words are essential. Brought back, a rearrangement of the air, stronger than the rock:

"Cursed, who curses his father and mother!"

"Amen!"

The holy found shape here. The fact that a Deborah or a Gideon rose to speak the needed word was for them no psychological event—it was the holy, and insofar as they found in such an event something to wonder at, they were better attuned than we are. The two mountains gathered the people so that the words they spoke and heard could bind them, give them shape. Or if not really, then the mountains are a metaphor for the words that really did bind them and give them shape.

"Cursed, who moves his neighbor's boundary!"

"Amen!"

The holy appeared in the limbs and the voice of that human figure who called them together. They were dependent on this in a way that people rooted in the earth could never be. Hence the intensity of the relation, its high seriousness. The truth of monotheism is not only or chiefly a truth about the divine. When people are delivered over to one God to be one people, this God refers them back to each other:

"Cursed, who leads the blind man astray on the road!"

"Amen!"

"Cursed, who withholds justice from the alien, the orphan, or the widow!"

"Amen!"

They are, as Rosenzweig put it, "rooted in one another."

The two mountains coming down like this mean to me the ancient community of my people. And mean to me also the ideal of a community, the object of my longing. The I-Thou relation of two persons, without wider community, befits a baby, to whom its mother and father are practically all there is. The equivalent of mother or father for an adult would be the world. Two cannot, therefore, rest satisfied with being true to one another, when ignorant armies clash by night. The I-Thou relation, beginning with two, can endure at all only insofar as it extends beyond itself, including more and more. This is to long for the impossible, just as Jesus, on another mountain, demanded the impossible, also for the sake of a true community, which he called "the kingdom of heaven." A longing for the impossible—but it is there, in our midst, to guide us, and it is true, at root the only true longing.

I have not been able to go to Shechem for two years now. I cannot bring pilgrim-tourists there. The intifada has made it too dangerous. And how else shall I go? Like a Jewish settler, armed to the teeth? That would be invasion. The earth is the Lord's, but they live here. Nor did they enter by force. If anyone has a right to a patch of ground in the eyes of mortals, they do to this.

When I used to go with the multitude, leading the procession to the temple at Shechem, I would carry a small hidden pistol, just to make a noise if attacked, so that the soldiers at Joseph's tomb, or in the Balata refugee camp across the street, would hear. I did not think of it then as invasion. My concept was the same as in the guide course. Most of them accepted occupation. The pistol was against extremists.

We would file down to the tell past a row of auto repair and stone-cutting places, and that was the part that made me nervous. Scowling, mustached young men there. I didn't like the fact that they saw us go down. They might gang up and approach us on the tell. At how many yards would I order them to stop, and, if they did not, run to the side away from the tour group, pull the pistol and shoot in the air? And if that didn't work? If they didn't stop, if the soldiers didn't come? I would shoot again in the air. And if that didn't work? I would get down on one knee and aim for the legs. And if the gun jammed? So my fantasies went—not there at the tell, for there I was busy with ancient reality—but in front of the mirror shaving in Jerusalem or Tiberias five or six hours earlier. In fact, we always passed and they did nothing, cowed, accepting, hating. Waiting. We went to the temple and looked beyond the auto repair and the stone cutting, the sweating young men, at great Ebal, and across to Gerizim, and entered the romance of these mountains.

"Cursed, who moves his neighbor's boundary!"

"Amen!"

They never ganged up. I read the curses to pilgrim amens, talked about the earth, the lack of earth, the function of belief in one God, how the children of Israel experienced this God, but always with an eye out to my left, where I expected they would come from if they came.

We pictured the tribes of Israel gathered on those slopes, and the hoped-for kingdom of heaven gathered there, at a moment in history when a whole cowed city of one hundred thousand was gathered there. People who did not rise, who did not say No, who did not gang up, who did not come from right or left.

And I could stand there, a Jew, because these words and others like them had preserved my people so that we could come back out of dispersion—a thing unique in history, indeed, but creating an anomalous situation: two peoples, each with its felt just claim to the same land.

Would I, in their place, have had the courage to rise up, to sacrifice a measure of safety and comfort for a dream of freedom? I don't know. I could only hope so. But they did not rise up. Nineteen years of King Hussein, twenty years of us. So what was there but to despise them? Though again: I did not know I despised them. And what was there but to despise myself, for agreeing to join, with my little pistol, the forces that cowed them? And all so that I might lead the multitude to Shechem, and stand between the mountains, and listen for the holy, with an eye out to the left.

I did not know that I despised myself. I did not know how limited, how basically phony, was the exaltation I felt there until at last they did rise up: all these people, these formerly passive, quaint, and obedient people, angry, pouring into the streets, standing up against our soldiers. A vast assertion of humanity. I saw it on TV, as the rest of the world did, though it was happening just a few miles down the road. But that was unburdening. That was exaltation: when I understood that I could no longer safely lead the multitude to Shechem.

We demeaned them. We still try to, more than ever, like the prisoners caged here. And that one who knew Hebrew cried out: he would not be demeaned. We demeaned them and were demeaned. It was, and still is, demeaning to live in this country. For we share the same humanity with them. When they used to let themselves be cowed, and we thought it good—thought that they were behaving just the way they should—then we were agreeing that freedom is not essential. Thus our own humanity became something else, something to which freedom is not essential. Now they have risen up, have reasserted the necessity of freedom, but we, by trying to put them down, continue to represent a quasi-humanity to which freedom is not essential.

18

Sunday night. Cell.

AMI HAD ME STAY for flag raising and inspection this morning, and afterward he called me over. As usual, I hoped it would be word of my immediate release. But he pointed to the narcissus bed and said, "Feel it."

I bent over and felt the red earth. It was dry.

"You had all Sabbath to give them water," he said.

I wanted to say, "I didn't know it's my job." But it would not help to argue. No doubt, since I had planted them, I was supposed to feel a fatherly responsibility. I said:

"I saw how red the soil is and I thought it was wet." This was true. I had glanced.

"Did it rain?"

"I guess I thought someone else was doing it."

"Well, I guess you shouldn't have. Now they're dying."

I looked concerned.

"I hope not."

"I leave for one day and the whole place falls to pieces. Well, water them. Maybe you can save them."

He went into the station.

Some little boy in me curled up in a ball. I took a black plastic wastebasket and went into our cell compound to our bathroom for water. I was coming back—I had not quite reached the outer cell gate with it—when a policewoman smiled at me. She stood in the doorway of the storeroom opposite the jailers' little office. She held papers in her hand—more girl than woman still, with perfectly straight brown hair to the shoulders, the kind that flips at every jiggle and jiggles at every flip.

"*Kol ha-kavod,*" she said.

I stopped. It means "All honor to you," "Hats off!" "I salute you."

"My sister read about you in the paper. She called me. She says to tell you *kol ha-kavod* too."

I thanked her and walked back to the narcissuses. The little boy uncurled.

THEN I WENT to Mercy's kitchen. We had to wash everything down so it would be spotless for the next crew: refrigerators, burners, the white-tiled walls, the racks. No breaks today. I soaped the blue dishes in coffee-brown water, throwing them into the rinsing sink. Then I moved over and rinsed, while Uzi and Obadiah brought more. The men are complaining, Uzi said, that the blue plastic cups are not rinsed enough. Many are down with the runs. "They're just kvetching," he said, to soften the blow. But he really thought so, I could tell, and considered it my fault.

He stacked the blue cups which I had finished, loaded them into a big pot of water, and set it on a burner. I rinsed more, not searching out the cigarette burns—or trying not to, just very lightly skimming. He began stacking them for a new pot.

"This is just in case," he said. "We don't want to pass it on to the new ones."

Obadiah dumped the last in, and I finished. Then we started washing the tiled walls. Passing back and forth to get clean water, I glanced at the cups changing shape.

"The cups are melting, you know," I told Uzi.

He went over and looked.

"That's all right," he said.

But he turned off the burners.

"We'll just let them soak awhile."

With rags we lifted the hot, full pots and slid them, one behind another, into a niche between our rinsing sink and the oven. Stacks of slowly smiling mouths.

Monday night. Cell.

Lunch was our last meal to work, and the biggest, because many of the new guys had arrived early. Just as the orange dishes started to come back, the water stopped. It took us about an hour of futzing around (the sinks already full with the big meat pans, the orange dishes piling up anyhow on the counters, on the cutting tables, finally on the floor) to find out that a pipe had broken somewhere off in the wilderness. Uzi and I—and Kobi, when he could be found—wound up carrying everything over to the police side, where they had water. This meant loading the dishes into the biggest pots and hauling them through the gutted building, squeezing around a cement mixer there, to an extra, troughlike sink outside the police kitchen. We filled it with suds, and I wedged a pot for rinsing under a faucet. Uzi soaped, being faster. But he had to search down the trough to find the dishes, and it slowed him. I got to glance at him therefore, and in this unaccustomed setting, I saw him as a trusted old Roman slave and I his pet boy.

It took us most of the afternoon. We said good-bye, pledging to say good-bye again before he finally left. But a half hour later he showed up in the cell and sat down on Yigal's bunk. He said how much he had enjoyed working with me, and I thought that he had come to say the last good-bye. But then he said that the new kitchen crew had not arrived, and they had been ordered to stay for one more meal, but the good news was that they had water again, and would I mind helping with dinner?

I shook my head.

"I'm tired," I said. "You guys are going home. For me it just goes on."

He was shocked. It was not like me. This was not the pet boy they had come to love. In working hard there I had wanted to shake up their stereotypes, to show that a refuser could be a good worker, good soldier. Instead I had legitimated them. If I, even I, work in their Jericho kitchen, then it is all right for them to work here. In that case it is all right for the troops whom they feed to be here—and if *that* is all right, then it's not all right for Palestinians to throw stones at the troops, which makes it all right for the troops to go out and capture and jail them. I koshered the kitchen. I koshered the whole operation.

I did not say any of this now. I am no man for confrontations. I just said I was tired. Which I was.

Uzi stood and repeated that it had been good to work with me and that this was good-bye then. A sad figure. He seemed to need me somehow—I'm not quite sure how—but not merely to help with the load, or to kosher his kitchen. I said I would come and say good-bye to all.

I ate on the police side, waited half an hour, and went over. Kobi came and shook my hand.

"I may not agree with you," he said, "but I respect you."

Then he went to the dairy fridge and came back with a Coke and a Hershey bar. From the *shekem*, he said. It was my first Coke in the two weeks. I leaned back against a cutting table and sipped it slowly, alternating small bites of chocolate. Freedom: the possibility to buy a Coke. Kobi crossed his hands upon his belly and watched, beaming.

Uzi worked at the sinks, his cigarette dangling. He made a great clatter. The blue cups wobbled on the counter where he threw them. Would not take shape.

When I had finished, I went to him.

"Good-bye, Uzi."

He turned, wiped his hand on his thigh and shook mine.

"You were an excellent worker. I said, 'Do something,' and you did it. I never had to go out looking for you." A little speech. A little coldness. Was that the sum?

"I was slow," I said.

"You were one hundred percent," he said.

"Thanks again for looking after me."

"Think nothing of it." He turned back to his work.

"Where's Mercy?"

"Gone. He was sorry not to see you."

I went back to the cell and was told that someone had stood outside and called my name a couple of times. That may have been Mercy.

Mercy had said he would leave his address and he did not. Maybe that's why he came by, if he did. But then he could have left it with someone to give me. Or he was miffed at me for not doing the last meal. And of course there is the fact that I, in my usual inconsiderate style, had forgotten to offer him mine. Not that we would ever have used them.

Tuesday night. Cell.

Yoni left this morning. I was picking up wrappers and cigarette butts in front of the outer cell door when he came from the police station, all set to go, duffel bag over one shoulder—small and wiry, still a bit trembly (the Revenge has laid him out the last few days). We shook hands.

"I'm glad to have met you," he said.

This had feeling in it. It caught me off guard. The direct, glad look in the brown eyes. I said that it was mutual and that I hoped he would have no trouble being received back into his unit, but if they kicked him out they didn't deserve him. This I had said before, of course. It was the only thing I could think of. I shrink before the expression of male tenderness.

There had been nothing deep and personal between us. The one philosophical talk. But somehow I had meant something to him. What then? Who is this *me* whom he is glad to have met? I get the picture of a large figure, like no one he has ever known, a man who thinks, who lives in accordance with what he thinks, who has the courage and strength to stand alone, if necessary, against a whole society, but whose humanity is not reduced to a posture. Well, this much is true: I think, and my humanity is not reduced to a posture. But the same humanity flinches before a tender male eye.

Yigal and Dror also left this morning. They did not find me to say good-bye. I was of no account to them.

Three empty beds. A smaller circle now. Shlomo, the two Gadis, Danny, Barak.

BARAK IS a quiet one, but it takes spirit to get twenty-one days for arguing about not having shaved. He is small and fair—actually not so small, but he hangs around with Danny, so he seems small. Orna has a crush on him. I eat all meals on the police side now, so I see these things. We are already at table when she comes in with Miri and the others. Her head twitches like a bird's. If she sits deliberately with her back to him, she'll twist around ten times during a meal. Dark laughing glances. I have grown used to the idea of that sign above her bed, and again I find her attractive. But it is more distant now. A dull nudge. (One would rip it down, of course. Ripping it down has itself become part of the fantasy.) Once upon a time—it seems like two minutes ago—such glances were directed at me. I sit not far from Barak. The hand has moved on.

Wednesday night. Cell.

Only at night can I write now. I work even less than in the kitchen, but there I could count on the breaks and I knew about how long they would be. Here they can call me any minute: to sort uniforms at the quartermaster's, or wash vehicles, or collate forms. I know now what that servant felt in *Miss Julie*—at the disposal of the master's bell. Could play that part now. But I have, nonetheless, a secret weapon:

Cheever. I bear him on my thigh, as Zeus did Dionysus. Between calls he is reborn red and fat. Only after dark, when the outer door is locked, can I enter enough of a trance to write.

The beds are full again. Two were brought in while we slept last night.

In the morning the two would not get up. They kept the brown blankets over their heads. The rest of us shaved, dressed, and folded our blankets. Udi came back to check. He made as if to kick the one on Yigal's bed, but then he returned his foot to the floor, bent over, and yelled, "Get up!"

There came a mumbling from under the blanket. An adjustment. Stillness.

Udi bent again, this time to where the head would be, and shouted, "Get up!"

That could take the eardrum out, I thought.

Now a voice came. "You yell at me again . . ." It trailed off. He had somehow returned to sleep.

Udi raised his foot again to kick. But he put it down. I had seen Rafi kick once—not Yigal, but the bed frame with Yigal on it. Udi didn't have it in him. He turned to us.

"Go to breakfast. These guys are gonna get an extra week."

When we came back from breakfast they were still asleep. We had morning cleanup.

Mostly I have missed this part. I used to go right from the police mess to Mercy's kitchen. Danny, who is monitor now, assigns me the southeast quarter of the big yard, from the club to the police station and across to the barricades. I carry the black plastic wastebasket and pick up cigarette butts, candy wrappers, cans, whatever. Bend, stoop, pick. Straighten. Search. Yet here's a butt. Bend, stoop, pick. Straighten. Search. He feels it in his sacroiliac. But on Long Island they used to say: Oh my sacraliliac!

They, not I, for I was a boy. Now I have a sacred lily too. Why sacred? (Bend, stoop, pick.) That is where the Uncanny taps. You get the willies there. *Mysterium tremendum.* (Bend, stoop, pick.)

At the moment it is mere dry age that taps. Two minutes ago I heard my mother say, "Your father's laid up. His sacraliliac." Between his sacred lily and mine, so little has really happened. My life could be put in a small bag—an ancient leather purse, thong-tied—and hung on a yardarm alongside others. And of that little there is less that actually functions now. Vast stretches might merely have been dreamed. This is partly a consequence of too much moving around. . . .

Such are the reflections as I bend, stoop, pick. I spend five minutes on half a line of Eliot's: ". . . the butt-ends of my days and ways." It has seized my brain like a grappling hook, yet I cannot remember the start.

I dump my basket in the garbage can.

"Cap-tain, cigarette."

Would that be Suleiman? Mahmoud?

A dark figure between the tin sheet and the jamb. I set down the basket and stretch my hands out as if cuffed and shake my head.

It is different in daylight. Easy to make resolutions in the safety of one's bed.

I take up my basket and go back to picking.

"Cap-tain, cigarette."

If it were my boss, then I would bring him. Or if it were Smilansky's worker, asking in Hebrew. It's this primitive "Cap-tain" I can't stand.

Like the beduin kids coming up to us after we've hiked Wadi Qilt. The whining voices: "Money! Give me money!" Like automatons. Child zombies. A nightmare of children. Not stopping. Clinging. Not to be put off.

"Cap-tain, cigarette."

My back is turned. Bend, stoop, pick.

The jailers would catch me. Lengthen my term. All for what? His smoking habit.

These are not my boss.

Bend, stoop, pick.
The walls are very thick.

And here's a butt.

Some have lipstick. Orna's. She alone wears it. They are not heel-flattened, hers. I look over a section which I think I have cleaned, the corner by the club, and discover more. Not hers. Dusty old butts, pressed into the grain of the asphalt. Those who came before me missed them. I would not expect others to be as thorough, as pedantic as I. Danny, who gave himself the other half of the yard, is rigging up the hose. No sacred lily there.

"He feels it in his sacraliliac." He is of course me. In college thirty years ago I first noticed the "he." Going to the drawer for a pair of socks, I'd hear, "He went to the drawer for a pair of socks." But that was adolescence. I lived my life as a novel being written. This method preserved, against so much evidence to the contrary, a sense of destiny. (If life is a novel, there must be an Author.) I am not sure how or when that stopped, or why the tense changed. Now it is a chorus of crones, wings whirring at my back. How dispassionately they examine, comment, like nurses above the ether. "He feels it in his sacraliliac." Long Island crones. They measure out the thread.

Bend, stoop, pick. It can easily give me the willies, this kind of work. The dishwashing was all right, though, maybe because of the company, water, large motions, clatter, radio. It's these niggling tasks that get me. The infinity of dirt and butts. The lack of distraction. I can talk with my internal Thous, but the conversation can't go very far, because the mind's bound to a body and the body is doing something else. And this something else is something infinitely stupid. It's as if I were imprisoned in someone else's stupidity. Infinitely at the disposal of an infinite stupidity.

When I do not get the willies, it is because I link up what I am doing in an implicit chain of in-order-tos, and then it feels related, however distantly, to that unknown but (I hope) benevolent destiny over which the crones have charge.

I remind myself why I am here. Each butt, a decoration. I shall take them home, and let the kids color them, and pin them on my uniform.

But I can feel how easily, if I did not remind myself, it could slip over. When the implicit linkup is not there—and I am not distracted—my body becomes noticeable. The fact of my body: I think that's what gives me the creeps.

The sense of destiny distracts me from the here and now of the body. And it seems to allow infinite time. As long as destiny is not fulfilled, Death cannot come (or so it seems) to pluck the sacred lily.

"Cap-tain! Cigarette!"

Right across the yard. They will hear from the office. I put down the bucket and stretch my arms toward him again, as if cuffed.

Noga shuddered. Noga hasn't lost the capacity to feel. As for me, I go to jail for them. Let them be satisfied.

I could, of course, just sidle over there and toss in a handful. Could go as if to empty the bucket. My back to the office. Through the aperture. Danny, but that's all right. Yes, but later, Taxi Driver. He would check that cell. "Where did you get these butts?" Some of them with lipstick. That they should put their lips where she put hers! And she, wishing death to the Arabs! A neat revenge.

Yes, but the revenge I want—or so I have learned in the course of many a rocky relation—is not political. If I threw them her butts, it would be part of my general revenge against women. When I was ten, I kicked my girlfriend in the shins. The teacher upbraided me in front of the class. And I can still remember why I did it: because they entice me, because they get through the interstices, because they do not leave me in peace.

It is the women who shaped my sense of destiny. I do not, of course, remember. I piece this together from what others have told me, from the interpretation of dreams, and from what I see among children.

The foundations consist in the Thous I played, bestowing a counterfeit "me."

But that is not enough to explain the sense of destiny. We have Stage Three.

At first I could play the male and female both. But then came an age when the anatomical difference seemed important, and I refused to play the female.

The longing for the banished Thou continued, and there was still this actual female, my mother, who had been my first Thou. How should I deal with her now? Since I could not play her anymore, how should I reduce the enticing sting of her otherness? How control my longing?

Thus arises the first ambition: where I cannot identify, I must possess!

And then all those teachers.

Culture translates the first ambition, and redirects its force. The mother of childhood reappears as school (alma mater), and later as firm, or country, or the literary world, and so on. Beyond all projects, beyond that cross section of the world which is to be conquered, stands a lost Thou—the parent with whom I refused to identify—and beckons me forth.

Ambition arises where identification fails. And once the sense of destiny is established, then other persons—already depleted once—reappear as means or obstacles or decorations, or else they just don't count. To feel for them becomes impossible.

Identification and ambition: these do a prison make.

Am I confessing only for myself? Or for all human beings? I wouldn't do this in public, if I didn't think it was for many.

There are those who, lacking a sense of destiny, prefer to fit themselves into another's or to adopt one ready-made. The effect is the same: the flight from the body, the flight from longing, the flight from each possible Thou.

Such then is my prison. Its walls are embedded in the foundations of character. I have become it—is there anything left to be freed?

Well, not so fast. There are the children. My self and not myself, they thaw the frozen heart. But the range of feeling is limited. Ambition distracts me even from them.

Needed: a cure of the ground. But so radical a cure, it would have to undermine the old identifications, and pull ambition down.

Who shall play the tune of enchantment backward—in my case forty-six years?

Impossible.

Rafi appears bringing one of the new ones along by the elbow and a broom in the other hand. A small tanned fellow with a mocking smile. Ashamed to be pushed around. His shirttails are out, and the hat is perched anyhow. Rafi hands him and the broom over to Danny and goes into the station. Danny lays the hose down still spurting and brings him past me into the club. Then Danny comes out, looks at me, raises his eyes to heaven.

I say: "He's going to sweep it all out here where I've cleaned."

Danny considers.

I ask: "Where's a dustpan?"

"Forget it. You've finished. Just leave it."

He goes back to his hose. He likes hosing.

Now that he's said to forget it, I feel like forgetting it. I stretch, rubbing internally the holy bone. The butts he sweeps out will be tomorrow's.

I go to the narcissus bed. They have survived my Sabbath neglect. I never planted anything before. Amazed to see the little green sprouts. So that really happens.

A few butts among them. Hadn't noticed earlier. I've developed an eye for butts.

Some of the bulbs have shoved themselves up above the dirt. Or the water washed the dirt away, one or the other. I start sweeping dirt back onto them and picking out the butts. To the left, the unplanted half, there are even more. In the evenings the smokers sit on the bench in front of this bed and toss the butts back behind them.

That's it: "To spit out all the butt-ends of my days and ways." The essence of prison is to cut one off. As a butt spat out. This cut-off state seems more acute in my Jericho jail, but that is because I am stripped here of the illusion of not being in prison.

And if I seem, nonetheless, a man who feels for others, it is because I behave for the most part as I know I would feel—*feel* I would feel—were it not for my prison.

Subjunctive living.

I pick the butts from my narcissus bed.

And if he were to call again, and if I were to bring them, I would bring them subjunctively.

If one could say, as Jesus did in the garden, "Not as I will, rather as You will"—if one could say that to the person one loves and mean it from the bottom of the soul, as Jesus is said to have meant it there at Gethsemane, for he sweat blood in saying that to God—why, that would be the confession of the dependence which one always, before this, tried to escape. It would be, in other words, redemption.

Easy to say. Bend, stoop, pick. Not as I will, rather as you will.

In meaning it, he earned the title Paul gave him: the second Adam. The first, by biting into the fruit of another garden, had said, "Rather as I will"—he had cut himself off from the father. This biting of the fruit I view as a symbol: one tries to get control of the source of one's being by taking the Thou inside. Thus we win an illusion of self-sufficiency, but we have cut ourselves off from the tree of life and are banished.

Then comes Jesus: "Father, may this cup pass me by. But not as I will, rather as You will." He, the perfect human being, could say that from the deepest parts and open himself to the Thou. The second Adam undoes the trespass of the first.

The problem is, how can *we* get the benefit of *his* having done that? How can I manage to do what he did—and be redeemed from the prison I have become?

"There is no way," wrote Kafka. "What people call a way is merely wavering."

There is no way. For a quarter century I sought it, without knowing the way to a way, and I suppose at some point I must draw myself up (I am older than many of the wise ever got) and take a stand in this matter, on the basis of my own poor experience, and say: it is not to be sought. There is nothing to be done.

Wanted: a cure of the ground.

Wanted: the false self splayed out on a cross. But will anything be left to live?

Jesus went up to Golgotha and was crucified, and three days later, we are told, he rose from the dead. The first part, the crucifixion, was already decided by his prayer in the garden. This prayer he could make, but I cannot—not from the deepest depth. Yet the crucifixion of the false self is nevertheless a possibility, since it does not depend on me.

> *I can nail my left palm*
> *to the left-hand crosspiece, but*
> *I can't do everything myself.*
> *I need a hand to nail the right,*
> *a help, a love, a you, a wife.*

That is the end of an Alan Dugan poem, "Love Song: I and Thou."

The crucifixion of the false self, then. But the false self, which has ruled the roost for so long, may be all that there is. Hence the importance of the faith in Jesus' resurrection.

To psychologize the Gospels is a form of Christian heresy. By refusing that dimension, Christianity lost redemptive depth. To the question, "How can we get the benefit of Jesus' self-sacrifice?" they answered by eating and drinking him—that is, they identified with him. The supposed rite of redemption merely repeated original sin. Jesus was internalized. He walks with them and he talks with them. But if the deeper gospel is true—if this prison built by me, this mechanism for producing a delusion of self-sufficiency, is that from which I need to be redeemed—then no one can go to the cross for me.

Where is the way to Golgotha? How shall I get crucified? There is no way. Nor would a single crucifixion suffice. If anything of me survived it, I would surely crawl back into prison, as the disciples went back to fishing. What is needed is not a way, rather a succession of Golgothas, little crucifixions meted out. Training in freedom. Perhaps that is a function of marriage. The Dugan poem suggests it, and I can think of no more likely place. Of course one has to know how to *use* a good crucifixion. An art as yet untried. Hungry enough, one could develop perhaps an alertness to potential Golgothas. One could develop, as for butts, an eye.

BEND. Stoop. Pick.
   Not as I will, rather as you will.
   Oh sacred lily!

19

Thursday night. Cell.

JERICHO HAD ITS FIRST rain this morning, the "former rain" of Deuteronomy. I heard it in sleep, and when Udi came dripping in to yell, "Get up!" there was the smell of his wet poncho rustling by me before and after—cold drops on my temples—and upon slightly awakening, slightly distinguishing, the fainter smell of wet cement after seven dry months. The others continued to sleep. They would sleep ten more minutes anyhow. I took my shaving stuff, got into my shoes and my coat with the hood, poked my head out and saw the reflection of the spotlight broadened and rippled in our little courtyard. The drain had backed up. It drummed on my hood, slashed through the light beam, stippled the new pool. It seems so strange after so long to have water coming down from the sky. Untoward. One wants to shout, "Hey! What's going on?" One had forgotten. It seems like a personal act. To be blunt and honest—no irreverence intended, but the honest truth— my first thought is that someone up there is making water and we should run for it. Then comes maturity. You remember what this is. You put your hand out in wonder, in welcome, and smell the earth or cement.

I tried tiptoeing around the edge of the pool, but it turned out there was no edge. My Rockports got soaked through. Wet feet for the day.

It put me in a good mood, though. Danny arrived barefoot to shave beside me, and I taught him the bugle song that my Marine Corps dad used to sing when we lived in a trailer in Camp Lejeune in World War II.

Oh! How I hate to get up in the mor-ning . . .

We tiptoed back singing it. I gave him the end of a blanket. The technique for folding requires two. So we stood in the middle folding and singing, as the others shook off sleep.

Oh! How I'd love to remain in bed . . .

The new ones remained as yesterday, the shape of whales. But the others stood up, and by grunts and glances, paired off. It lends a human touch, to start the day with a pas de deux. The result each time is a compact cylinder about the size of a large muff with sixteen folds at both ends. Two people together have done something perfect.

Udi did not come back to check. Perhaps he didn't want to get wet. Or more likely he didn't want to find the two asleep and be caught in the same position as yesterday, a foot indecisively raised. We sat around and listened to the hiss.

"Won't have to hose down today," said Danny.

No butts. No car washing. They would find things for us to do, but it afforded a happy illusion nonetheless. The routines would be suspended, and it would take them time to come up with new ones.

We sent out a dove to see if the kitchen had opened. Gadi the Lazy. He came back. No olive branch.

"How come *they* get to sleep?" asked Shlomo.

"It's bad for morale," I added.

They had not worked yesterday. They had wandered around the base finding females to joke with.

Danny made a sign with the back of his hand, fingers raised and closed around. In New York it would provoke a fight, but here it means "Wait."

We sent the dove. He returned and said, "Ten minutes."

I bore Dionysus.

"What is that book?" asked Shlomo.

"Stories."

"Horror stories?"

"No."

"I only read horror stories."

"They're in English anyway, you dummy," said Barak.

"He could read them and tell us," said Shlomo. "Couldn't you?"

I had the sensation of standing on the edge of a vast empty pit.

"Sure," I said, "but they're not."

I began to read silently, and then it occurred to me that I might put a brainteaser to them.

"You come to a fork in the road. There are two gates, one to life and the other to death, but they aren't labeled. Two guards sit on a bench to the side. One of them has to tell the truth, the other has to lie. You don't know which guard is which. You are allowed only one question to one of them. What's the question?"

"I've heard this before," said Barak.

"Then don't say."

"You think I remember?"

I had to repeat it a few times, and then they sat back to think. I propped my two muffs for a backrest and thumbed through Cheever. Not bad: to listen to the first rain, read a story. No guilt, since there's nothing to be done.

They made a few attempts. We sent the dove and he did not come back. We went to eat.

At breakfast they kept trying. "Put yourself in the situation," I said. Shlomo kept wanting the answer. The others insisted that there had to be more information. I said, "One has to lie. The other has to tell the truth. That's a lot of information." "But you don't know which is which!" they said. I repeated: "Put yourself in the situation."

The women came in. More than the usual twitching. The first rain would do that. They outteased my brainteaser.

Gadi the Cheerful made avocado salad. He had brought small wet lemons from the tree. We spread it on bread. The police-women wanted some—"How about some of that guacamole?" Danny stretched his big body, twisted around to them, and with full cheeks shook his head.

"Very bad for cops."

But then he scraped off half of it onto a blue plastic plate and passed it down to Gadi, who took it over.

He winked at me and said, "Have to keep on their good side."

Udi came to the head of our table and told us the jailers' courtyard was flooded too. "So get squeegees," he said. "It's time."

The sky had lightened, the rain had eased. In the cell those two were still on their bunks.

Danny sent me to the jailers' courtyard. As soon as I shoved the water out into the yard it flowed back in. He put Shlomo out there with another squeegee. Shlomo caught from me what he could, shoving it on, to a place where it would flow by itself toward the big drain. Most came back, and it kept drizzling.

"No end to this!" I shouted.

He came up to me.

"Give me the answer. I won't tell."

I hesitated. He looked so desperate.

"You go to either one of them—it doesn't matter which—and you ask, 'Which way would the other guy tell me is the way to life?' The way he points to will be the way to death."

He looked stunned.

"Go think about it."

We went back to shoving the water.

THE RAIN HAD STOPPED, the sun was shining, and we were still shoving and sweeping. While I was in the doorway, sweeping it out, a policewoman came from the station with a bucket. She dumped soapy water on my narcissuses and went back in.

"Did you see that?"

"She's been doing that," Shlomo said.

"Why didn't you tell me?"

We went over there. Each bulb sat in a puddle of suds.

"What does she think she's doing?" I said. "You know her?" He did

not. It was not the one who had smiled at me, but she had the same
kind of jiggly brown hair.

"Maybe we'll switch places," I said.

"Do you have any more brainteasers?"

"No."

We switched. But I couldn't both catch water from him and see
down the hall. When she came out again it was too late to stop her. Miri
was walking by.

"Those are Ami's narcissuses," Miri said to her.

"I know," she said. "That's why I'm doing it."

She laughed, jiggled her hair, and went back in.

Miri was walking by on tiptoe through the water, shaking her head,
smiling sadly.

"That's evil," I said.

She stopped on tiptoe and looked at me. I nodded toward the
narcissuses. Eyes blue as ink. As if to ask, "Are you surprised?
Don't you know that this exists?" But also compassion, just the
hint of a frown between the brows—Poor boy! You have just discovered evil, which I have lived with untiring for ages, and will you,
fragile boy, bear up under the great knowledge? But of course she
would not be thinking that. She would be thinking—Poor man! Stuck
here, prisoner here, away from wife and children—is this what
you came to this country for?—you don't deserve this—how hard it
must be! Her throat is full, more than Botticelli would have allowed.
But a face that can express so much compassion in a look, one
searching look, must not be forgotten. I already have such a face
from thirty years ago. Otherwise I would have taken Miri's right
then and put it in my pocket next to Cheever, to keep, to pat in hard
times, to draw out at night before sleep and look at and be borne
upon the waves.

She was about to say something, but she canceled it and smiled
and turned. Then she turned back.

"David's having a birthday today."

"Who's David?"

"You know, the tall one. The one you freeze for. Try to get alone
after lunch, you and Danny. I'll bring you some cake if I can."

"Do I have to freeze?"

She laughed and tiptoed away, watching the water.

"It's all coming *back* to me!" yelled Shlomo.

"Sorry, sorry."

AMI DID NOT mention the narcissuses. He noticed, but apparently there is some sort of feud on. After flag raising and inspection he sent Shlomo and me to the quartermaster. We sorted shirts according to size, tying each bundle of ten with the sleeves of the undermost. There were also American shirts, which we put to the side.

"Have you gotten any American hats in?" Shlomo asked.

"I've gotten no hats at all," said the quartermaster. "I'm really short on hats." He is a tall, thin boy with an olive face.

On the upper half of the door is a window, so that soldiers can come and exchange there. When we had sorted for about an hour, Rafi stuck his head in.

"Have you seen those clowns?" he asked me.

"Which clowns?"

"The new ones."

"You mean they're awake?"

"I'll kick their ass."

He vanished.

The quartermaster sat on a high stool and looked out the window.

"Must have escaped," he said.

I said: "They're wandering around the camp. That's what they did yesterday."

"So what's he upset about?"

"His commander's here," I said.

"Oop."

"Having a birthday."

"Oop. Oop."

Shlomo put the brainteaser. The quartermaster took it in, then shook his head as if waiting for more.

"That's it!" said Shlomo triumphantly.

The quartermaster tossed the brainteaser to a shelf on his right.

It would sit beside Shirts, Extra Large. He turned again to the window.

"Look at him run. Like a duck. They'll get their own ass kicked. They'll wind up in jail with you."

We finished the shirts and started on the pants.

"So what's the answer?" he asked me.

"I don't know."

He looked at Shlomo.

"All right. I give up."

Shlomo kept sorting.

"You have to put yourself in the situation," he said.

"Who gives a shit."

He lit a cigarette and looked out the window.

"They've found them."

I stood up. Ami and Rafi each had one. They were parading them from the police kitchen in the direction of the yard.

We finished the pants, and he told us we could go.

"Do you want the answer?" Shlomo asked.

"Sure," he said.

"Do you have an American hat?"

"I told you. No hats."

"No hat, no answer."

The quartermaster shook his head and shut the door on us.

"He doesn't have any," I said.

"If he really wants the answer," said Shlomo, "he can take from someone. He knows where to find me."

We rounded the corner with the idea of going to the cell, but the middle gate was locked—it consists of bars only—and there, shut in, was the one from Yigal's bed, hatless, unshaved, stalking about our courtyard.

He paced the wet perimeter, arms swinging—he held a screwdriver. He paced, a prowling fury, from the cell away to the toilets, then across, then back toward us to the middle gate, and as he crossed toward the cell again, he reached out with the screwdriver and caught the bars, strumming. I would have liked some dry socks. So we stood there, not knowing what to do. This middle gate had never been locked before. He had the thing timed: rip-clang, away, across, back, rip-clang. But when he saw that we had not moved, he stopped by the gate and rubbed the edge of the screwdriver against one of the bars.

"How's it going, boys?" he said.

"Fine," I said. "Wet feet."

He glanced, then went back to sharpening. "You need boots. I'll get you some."

"It's all right."

"What size do you wear?"

"That's the problem. Thirteen."

"It's no problem. This afternoon you'll have them."

"I could use some socks," I said. "From the bag under my bed."

"That's an interim solution. What you need is a major solution."

Rafi came out of the small office.

"Ezra," he said, "give me that."

"You watch out, I'll give it to you."

Rafi smiled.

"We're finished," I said to Rafi.

"Go to the club. I can't put you here."

We started moving. The club would be good—I could read. If I asked to go in and get socks, he would think of something.

But he called us back.

"Do you have an extra razor, one of you?"

Ezra stopped. He stroked his chin with his right hand and waved the blade: no, no.

"No," said Shlomo.

"No," I said.

Rafi went back into his office. We started toward the club. Halfway across the yard we heard the strum.

AN HOUR LATER he was still doing that. Hadn't missed a beat. They gave us a covered jeep to wash. I hate this work. Shlomo took the outside and I the cabin.

I hate it. You cannot do a good job, because a good job would be infinite, since dirt is infinite. In this case infinity was caked. We did it with paper towels. There are no rags on the police side. In Mercy's kitchen, yes, but that connection is broken.

These are hard, coarse paper towels. You wet one, it shrivels into a ball. You make a streak, and you take another, wet it, make another streak, but between the streaks there is still a line. The sun blasted. No trace of the rain. I was glad now for the hat. I kept saying it over to myself, in time with his strum: "I'm glad I've got this hat." It made me almost queasy, but I could not stop. My idling brain.

That was on the passenger side. But when I went around to the driver's side, I was out of the sun, and here I determined to stay. I would work like a miniaturist. I would get every speck. I would change the water twenty times to do the seat. Twenty more for the floor. O Vengeance! For I worked with my back to the police station, and I knew that they'd be watching me from the window. "Is he still there? What's he doing to that jeep?" They would call the honcho over, the birthday boy. He would look with that all-boring look of his and not be amused. He would recognize this style of resistance. You want to use me like a slave, then you're gonna get it. I could already feel the eyes hot upon my back. Burned two small holes in my shirt. The dirty wet paper balls piled up on the asphalt beside me. This would cost the army. Better to have brought it to a carwash. I went to the storage niche next to our bathroom for another roll. I would not stop. I would be buried first in wet paper balls.

My father used to set me to work like this. Mowing the lawn, for example. We had a hand mower. Everyone else had a gardener. In mowing a lawn, you do one row and then you come back on another, but you don't want to leave a strip in between, so you overlap. My father stormed down on me from the house one day. "Three times you go over the same damn row!" He had been watching from a window. He grabbed the mower and furiously showed me how, then left it and strode back in. He was not very often mad at me, but such are the times one remembers. I had not thought he might be watching. Maybe that's where I got this idea.

They would never put me on a vehicle again. I could sense the beam of rage between my shoulder blades. Happy birthday.

I would give the excuse that I am a philosopher. I do not merely wipe up dirt. I seek truth in a grain of dirt. This they cannot take away from me. Even in solitary, Cheeverless, I would seek it in the dust. They may order me to shut down my mind, but even I have no power to do so. So I am happy to clean their vehicle, but I must do it this way. Such is my nature.

"And what is truth in a grain of dirt?" he would ask.

"Truth . . ."

In this fantasy Pilate waits. I begin to explain my philosophy. His rage transforms to rapture. He rips off the towels and dips them for me. Then we change places. I rip and dip, and he wipes, examines, throws. Others come from the station. "What has happened to our commander? His birthday cake is getting cold." "Start over for them," he says. "Oh it will be boring for you to hear it again," I say. "No," he says. "I want to hear it again. These are the lectures we should have had in the evenings." So I start again, and they too are enraptured, rip and dip, wipe, examine, throw. It will be the cleanest jeep you ever saw.

"So truth," I conclude, "is simply life as it is, when you are not fleeing from it."

"But in a grain of dirt?" he says. "Am I fleeing from this dirt?" He looks at the smudge on the wet paper ball. Alas, poor Yorick.

"In the mode of truth," I say, "you are taken completely out of yourself, but in such a way as to be given back to yourself."

"And this dirt is supposed to do that?"

I am silent. Better think of something. They will pelt me with paper balls. The paper pelting of Stephanos.

"Dirt," I say. "Well, how do we get to dirt? There comes a time early on—eight months or so—when the child turns away from its parents. It seems more interested in things, toys—but only as long as its mother or father or someone like that is near. It is learning to work on things and get itself back from the results, as if the re-sults were responses. All right, now let's say I'm the father. My presence animates things, and sometimes the child turns to me to make sure I am in tune. The things are like extensions of me—they got their first significance during play with me; I endow them with my spirit, you might say. But a difference is, they are still there when I, the father, go away. So a time comes when I can leave, and the child can still get itself back from things, as long as it believes that I remain in tune, wherever I may be. This belief is the first faith, you might say. And the dialogue with things is the beginning of art.

"Of course you can say that the belief is wrong, that the absent mother or father is not always in tune, is not always thinking about the child and what it might be doing. If the child were to agree with you, it would lose faith. And at some point it does lose faith. That's when it identifies with its parents, setting up images of them in its head, talking with them there. Then things become mere things. Technique replaces art. But was the child wrong to believe? Doesn't the absent mother or father remain, in some deep sense, in tune? It is a question of faith."

They have stopped cleaning. They are quite still. Bewildered. The commander, dully looking ahead, tries to catch up with it. Orna, flustered, angry, twitching, rips at her paper ball. I shall have to pick up those shreds. Miri, puzzled, a bit disappointed, fearful for me. Did Stephanos have a Miri?

"The dirt," I continue. "Yes, well, that would have to do with art. Children can play for hours at the edge of a puddle. Just as I've been cleaning this jeep."

But it is such a long row to hoe, from here to there, from this smudge on a paper towel to the truth. Poetry in a grain of grime. The absurd presumption: that with this next swipe the world might be transformed. Where there is no way, there are no shortcuts. An enormous amount would have to be done—undone and done—for the grime to become so interesting as to take me out of myself and give me back. Out of the prison and back free. Most of my education would have to be undone. The society which promoted that education would have to be undone. In such a society this army camp would probably not be here. There would be no occupation, no intifada. I would not be wiping this dirt at all.

The actual commander appears at my side. I freeze.

"At ease," he says. "Stefan, don't make a doctorate of it."

"Yes, commander. It's hard to know when to stop, commander."

"Well, that's enough already. It all comes back anyway."

"Yes, commander."

"You've done a good job. It just has to be good. Not perfect."

"Yes, commander."

EZRA AND THE OTHER ONE were penned up again after lunch. Rafi gave me forms to collate in the club, regulations for the Allenby Bridge. I could hardly object, since I myself still pick up tour groups there. I sat with my back to the skeletal banquet. I put five piles on a bench and a stapler at the end.

Danny and Barak came in.

"We're waiting for the cement to dry," said Danny.

They are making a duck pond in the entrance-courtyard of the rooms they are restoring.

They pulled up chairs across from me. No problems with the banquet.

Rip-clang.

"There he goes," I said.

Danny said: "He's sharpening that screwdriver to stick it in the officer who sent him here."

It made me wince.

"Against Rafi maybe. For cooping him up."

"No. He has an understanding with Rafi. Rafi had to coop him up. He knows that." He leaned forward and put a hand on the paper where my hand was. "Get this. They know each other. This Ezra's a gang leader. They're from the same neighborhood. It's very tricky for Rafi, follow?"

"What about the other one?"

"Under Ezra's protection."

I nodded and he removed his hand. He too started to collate. Barak received from us and stapled.

"So how are your twins?"

His face darkened. "They're good."

"What twins?" asked Barak.

"Goats," said Danny. "I've got goats."

"You've been working together all this time, and you haven't told him about your goats."

"We sing when we work."

He handed a sheaf on in silence. Then he said: "After we talked that day I wrote the longest letter in my life."

"Did she get it?"

"I don't know."

"It takes a long time. The censorship."

"I didn't send it that way. I never thought I could write such a letter. It was philosophical. You know, I didn't really remember what you said, except about the octopus people. But you set off all kinds of ideas in me, and now I can't remember them either. I should have made a copy."

"Just ask her to show it to you Monday."

He is getting out Monday.

"She probably didn't keep it. Probably thinks I'm nuts."

"Interesting, not nuts."

"Nuts."

We worked. I guessed from his face that she had started with someone else.

Rip-clang.

"It must be hard"—I filled the silence—"if you're interested in someone, and she's with someone else, in an isolated situation like that."

"Sure it's hard."

"On the kibbutzim, for example."

"It's murder. I grew up in kibbutzim."

"In college it was like that. We had a hundred and fifty students in the whole place. A nice small college isolated up in New England. The planners never thought of that. I mean: the measures people have to go through—a boy of eighteen or nineteen—to sit in the same dining room with the girl he loves and the guy who's got her, eating. All of them, eating. Even you, eating. Two or three times a day. It's enough to distort you for life. Do you know about Prometheus?"

They had not heard of him.

"He's from Greek mythology. A Titan, something between man and god. He stole fire from the gods and gave it to man, so Zeus punished him by having him tied to a rock. An eagle came and ripped his liver out and ate it, but overnight his liver grew back, so again the same thing next day, and so on forever. That's the way it was. There was lots of liver too. Liver and pork chops. I ate pork chops in those days."

"This guy's got stories," he said to Barak.

Miri appeared in the doorway with three pieces of chocolate cake on paper plates. She smiled slyly. I rose and froze. She laughed.

"At ease."

She left it with us. We ate it slowly with our fingers. The icing was cold and smooth. The inside was just the right sweetness and just the right texture.

"Go on," said Danny.

"Let's just enjoy this cake."

20

Friday night. Cell.

FILLED THE MINYAN. They need me tomorrow. "If you don't come, there won't be a service," said the leader. I shall be called to the Torah. No escape.

Then came dinner, news, and partying. While the others hobnobbed in the yard, Danny came to me and talked about his life. Those are his secrets, I may not repeat them. I lay on my bed, propped on an elbow. He sat on the floor on the other side of the doorway: long legs drawn up, arms wrapped about the shins, the close-cropped head upon his knees. Someone in the Nachal had cut his hair perhaps. Or the reverse: the legs stretched out, the back stretched—he would rub it against the jamb. Gray eyes gone earnest. He kept it chronological, stabbing at events like fish. He hit a few. Once Miri walked by in our small courtyard, smiled at me coming and going. His legs were stretched out then, and she would have seen only the boots, great brown ziggurats.

It is not for me, I keep having to remind myself. I am not in college anymore. Mine was the avuncular piece of cake. And her patrolling, not for me. A blink ago, yes. But the blink includes two marriages, a doctorate, two children, a change of country, ten years' guiding—all, all reduced now, in the serene actuality of her boredom, her quick and passing smile. A Friday night with nubile maids and randy youths.

What stops me too from swimming in this element? Thirty years, a leather purse hung on a yardarm. It falls into the sea. I am back, just back from the college play. That was me—Friar Laurence. Had a tonsure cut from a pink rubber ball. Put sallow on. Made jowls with a liner. Pushed my legs like a man of eighty. So here I am. Have not quite got the silver out of the sideburns. Couldn't erase the jowls entirely. The lines in the forehead—effective. This hesitation in every movement, the seeming frailty, stiffness—it was always a part of my character. The toenails gone with fungus, the sharper features, pee-broken sleep, the bad breath after bad nights are all . . . all incidental, like the bump of fat I had removed last year from my shoulder. Or like the pain in the ball of my right foot. Into the sea with them, and I am back: Steve Langfur, just down from his room, to sit on the grass in front of the dining hall of a Friday night, digesting pork chops, talking with Amy Baumgarten about her life, her love, the ill done her, stroking her long black hair.

We found back then, to talk about, the same kinds of things which he now finds to talk about. The words of thirty years ago have disappeared, but these words are like them in intensity, in apparent freight of meaning for a life. The words of thirty years ago were water after all. They are as forgotten as river water, near a bank where one sat with a friend and talked. Now I sit with Danny. The bank has not changed much. Water eddies in about the same places. The water itself—recycled through the heavens, like the pain of which he speaks, through the generations. Where did we get all those words? Where does Danny get them? As plentiful as drops in the Dan. If the others had not come, he could have gone on deep into the night, even till dawn and breakfast, as we used to—I suppose because the ultimate confession lies always beyond reach. Or no, it is not confession exactly, what he does, what we did. The source is rather an enormous sense of possibility. That is the real difference in our ages. One confesses then too—the problems, blocks, the traumas that might have caused them, the hard knot of the personality—but one does so in the deep faith that it is possible to change. Fundamentally. And that the change can occur before dawn, that the others will see it at breakfast. Or in a semester, or during the summer break, or in a year.

Even the deepest wound seems healable. It takes a long time to discover that the wound was fatal after all.

But he gives me hope. If I could go back in memory to the river of thirty years ago . . . If I could play the tune backward to the point where I went wrong . . . If I could dip my hand in the stream and change its course . . . The bare facts cannot be changed, nor what they meant to me, but if I could unfreeze the meanings, let the facts impinge again, let them mean differently this time . . . If the return were sufficient, a real working through . . . The mature man, impinged anew by old facts, would take a different course.

The others came in. He stopped. Went back to his bunk. I felt satisfaction. Except for this the relations here have been so ghastly thin. Mercy, for example. A pat on the shoulder, a squeeze of the elbow, a platitude, an off-color joke. I suppose I single out Mercy because I sensed with him the possibility for more. But why did I sense it? The aquiline nose perhaps. Like my guide-teacher's nose. Or his quiet authority in the kitchen perhaps. Like my father's. No question but that I "projected" my father onto him. He's my age, but it didn't stop me. I saw Mercy, I don't see myself. I see partly, sometimes chiefly, with the eye of a small boy. So Mercy, his encouraging pat and his joke: a "father figure."

The trouble with the language of psychoanalysis is its tone. But that is everything.

How much goes into the relation with my son. How much that I do not remember must have gone from my father to me. Benny probably won't remember the catches, football, Frisbee, ambushes, floor games of baboons and gorillas, boxing, embracing, or my clenched teeth and the little ancillary signs of my frustration, that I cannot somehow fix this thing in a Faustian freeze, a fist. But it does get fixed. Out of the flowing, uncatchable exchange is formed somehow a content. That is the thing he will find later in his Mercys, as I found it here in this cook, so that the mere working side by side in a kitchen, the occasional pat, the off-color joke were enough to give a sense of fellowship and fulfillment. They contained the catches, football, fishing expeditions, which I never in fact had with this Mercy, but which we had with our fathers and give to our sons. Time is gathered in the pat on the back.

The relation, externally so thin, has depth—and there is truth in this depth, contrary-to-fact truth. What other vehicle does my mostly forgotten father have?

"You have projected your father onto Mercy." The assumption is that the relation with my father is one thing, belonging to the past, and Mercy is someone else, belonging to the present. To project, therefore, is to distort the real Mercy and miss him.

Well, yes, granted there is bad projection. Here the image one projects is hardened, fixed—in identification, the repetition hardens it. When that image collides with someone you meet, it obfuscates, distorts, overwhelms. A nemesis, grinding present into past.

But bad projection is possible at all only because each encounter *is* a gathering of time. If I sense my father in Mercy, that may be bad. Or on the contrary, if the conditions are right, it may be the deeper Mercy I am able to sense, even in this thin and passing relation, because of my lost father.

A Mercy free of all "projection" would be penny-thin to me, would not be Mercy. He would not appear with this horizon of potentiality. It is the shade of a lost Thou which lends each present person such horizon. They alight, the long forgotten, now on this one, now on that one, with great fluttering wings. They are the shadows which give dimension, so that this particular passing person appears *as* person, appears as harboring much more.

There is no escaping the ghosts, once one is old enough to have them. They must inform.

THIS THOUGHT ABOUT MERCY, this image of the fluttering wings, is the best I can do—at least for the time being—when it comes to that woman in the paper. When they asked me what I could say to her, I didn't answer. In fact, I knew an answer. *The* answer even. But it was cold and heartless, and I couldn't have said it to her.

The answer I knew begins with a Talmudic story. A woman named Bruria lost both her sons on one day, unexpectedly, while her husband (a famous sage) was off in the study house. She put them in the bed and laid a cover over them. When her husband returned, she said, "A stranger came by. He left two pearls with me for safekeeping. He'll be here any minute, but they are such beautiful pearls. I don't want to give them back." The sage became angry: "What kind of thing is this? You must!" So she took him to the bed and showed him their two sons.

This story has a flaw. One should not be attached to pearls, but one should be attached to children. And isn't it inhuman, cold and heartless, so quietly to give them up? It seems so—but it seems so to us who are not in the condition of Bruria.

Life is not owed me. Of the people who are important to me, not one of them is owed me. Yet we say "my son," "my father"—and this "my" carries the fullest weight a possessive pronoun can. But Bruria, we are to understand, would not have uttered so heavy a "my."

I shall try to imagine Bruria's way with her sons when they were alive.

I have written about the relation of I and Thou from the standpoint of a child toward its parent. I wanted to get it pure—before identification complicates everything. But consider the parent. Myself as parent. I am no Bruria, no saint. I am a walking dyad—worse, a synagogue of identifications and unknown longings, a minyan to myself, or more than minyan, for there are women in me too: I am protean, I am, as the demoniac said to Jesus, "legion." A clunking chatterbox. Then to us a child is born. From the standpoint of this child I am a Thou. I am absolutely important to it (more responsibility than I, with my complications and ambitions, really want). And so I need not fear: if I were to pour myself out to the child, it would respond, and I would receive myself back, in something like the primordial manner of I and Thou.

There is a limit to the child's capacity. I am so much more than it can comprehend. I do not get my whole, complicated self back. But the old anxiety—that those I need will not respond in kind—has no place in the relation with a child. With everyone else, yes, the defenses work constantly, but here they are pointless. It makes no sense to identify with the child or to view it in terms of some project (it has no place inside my work world, though it may motivate my work). Its glance or word strikes something in me which is not part of the defensive mechanism. It opens up the fatherhood in me. Thus life is awakened, feeling is awakened. Of course this is not all of me. Yet something has escaped my defenses, is alive. It is a taste of life in a world only half alive. This is a principal reason why our children are so intensely precious to us.

The I-Thou relation is the necessary and sufficient condition for being a self (although of course it depends on the fulfillment of prior conditions). In this sense it is an absolute. When I say that Bruria's attachment to her sons was absolute, or that mine to my children is, I mean that the quality of the I-Thou relation pervades it. But this absolute attachment can include a kind of nonattachment, as when Bruria compared her sons with pearls.

I know how strange, how mystical that sounds. But there is nothing paradoxical here. By "nonattachment" I mean not-holding-on. There is a sort of attachment which does not require holding on—which requires, in fact, that one not hold on. For the attempt to hold on is the attempt to reduce otherness.

If I could live in such a way that I receive myself from a Thou—and when no Thou is there, receive myself again from the things we have shared—if I could live thus, why, then, my attachment to the beloved would be absolute, but on the other hand, my "my" would have the lightness of Bruria's.

In this sense our children may be likened to pearls which have been left for safekeeping.

But I do hold on. I am not Bruria. I am Legion, who learned long ago to play the parent unto myself. The I-Thou relation seems to be *in* me. Lip service to mortality aside, I seem to myself, most of the time, immortal and invulnerable.

The child, however, is vulnerable. I made myself as if invulnerable, but I cannot do the same for the child. (Dip the baby in the Styx, there will still be a place on the heel.) Exactly at the point, therefore, where the light of the I-Thou relation comes again into my life, I again become vulnerable. Nor can I cure this. The old techniques do not work. I cannot incorporate the child into the mechanism of my self-sufficiency. So now I find myself outside my burrow—out there with this vulnerable child.

I am not Bruria. How shall I not try to hold on when the rest of my life is a system for holding on?

Precisely with regard to a child, whom I cannot bring into the system of defenses, the "my" becomes heavily possessive, insistent, strident.

The story of Bruria, deep as it is, does not then do much good. For it is the truth, but we are not in the truth.

To that woman whose son was kidnapped, or to that man in Beit Jalla who saw his son gunned down, it does not do to say, "God did not owe you this son, who brought you much happiness. You were thankful when you were with him, and you found that sufficient, infinitely more than you deserved. You knew that he might be taken away, yet you were able to live with him in the fullness of joy. Now it has happened. It is natural to grieve for the loss of so much happiness. But wait for what else life may bring. It may someday again be good to be alive."

All this would be true, if one lived in truth. But one does not, and it does not do. The child had gotten through in ways that other people, who are not one's children, cannot. They cannot *because* one is defensively cut off, *because* one is not Bruria. It will not do to speak to a mourner as if he or she were a saint.

That much I knew already, when Gadi the Lazy asked me about philosophy. But it would not do.

Now comes this thought about Mercy: how the shadow of my mostly forgotten father fluttered above him, giving him depth. The thought does not provide anything more to say to the woman in the paper, or to that father in Beit Jalla. It shows, though, something which many people already intuitively know: why a certain kind of presence can console. As Mercy bore the shade of my father, so do people bear the shades of the mostly forgotten Thous who once gave life and who have the power now to keep the grieving person in the stream of life and carry him or her through. The chief thing is the being-with. Each person is a nodal point for the gathering of time. But the mourner's absent Thous, who seek to become present in me, are those who gave life—who comprehended him or her. I cease to be a nodal point when I say or do something which makes it clear that I do not comprehend. Thin and fragmentary though the relation be, I must—by confirming the intensity of the grief—be with him, be with her, so that the absent Thous can again be with him, with her too—not in some fantasy apart, but connected to the stream, to the thin trickle that goes on. It does no good to say, "Know that as life flowed between you and your son, so life can flow again between you and others." In practice it will probably not flow thus again. But because we visit and bear with us the shades of the old, life-giving Thous, there is still a flow of life. Even so mighty a grief cannot entirely stop it.

21

Saturday night. Cell.

THE YEMENITE READ the Torah passage this morning. I was
appointed fifth to bless. Ordinarily I would have sat there in suspense awaiting my turn, but this Yemenite swept me away. I had my
Bible open to the page—it started with God's visit to Abraham at
Mamre under the terebinth trees. ("Abraham sat in the opening of his
tent in the heat of the day, and behold, three men stand across from
him" [Gen. 18].) I could just barely follow. It is a different Hebrew to
hear, not like everyday speech, not like the Yemenite's everyday
speech either. It glides without effort, hurdling the consonants. A
vowel, nasally intoned, barely reaches purity, then blends into the
next. It is like a zither playing the Torah. The two bearded officers
(different bearded officers this Sabbath) stood on either side of the
table, each in his tallit (we all wear them in the morning—even I had
a borrowed one), trying to follow in their Bibles. Their function was
to correct him if he made a mistake, for the Torah has no vowel
markings. They did not correct him and probably could not. There
was nothing to hold on to. It was like being swept along by wind and
current and grabbing for branches to stop, to rest—but the branches
come off in your hand. Nothing left but to give yourself up. The
ornate black letters in our Bibles were like the useless branches.
They had, it seemed, little or nothing to do with this current. If you

245

made an effort to connect them to it, you were lost—it had gone on. You jumped two lines, three lines, listening for "Abraham" to hook up to the letters for Abraham, and then you thought maybe you had heard it and went forward on that hypothesis to hear and see if the next sounds fit—but you could not be sure—only yes! There it was! Or was it? You could not be sure. But you went on, letting your eyes glide almost arbitrarily over the black serried chessmen, fancy soldiers on the bank of the river that bore you along—don't ask them for help—the song blows right through them.

We knew the stories of course. They knew them because they are Orthodox, and I because I am a tour guide. But to hear these stories this way—! It must be a Hebrew less altered by travel and exposure. This Abraham was different, as dark perhaps as the concentrating curly-bearded Yemenite. That was generations of study and devotion there ("And you shall teach these words diligently to your children . . ."): to be able to read five chapters of Torah in a traditional music and dialect like a river.

I sat at my table in the back corner. I kept a finger of my left hand in the prayerbook at the blessings—I would not trust memory when my turn came—and with a finger of the right hand I made a swipe at following. I had often been at Mamre—the traditional Mamre, for no one knows where it was. No "terebinths" there today. A tuft of grass, I remembered. It came to mind amid the black-clad, quick-parading soldiers. It surfaced greenly and hugely among them, but I could not hold on to it—I had to quick-march with them—on to Sarah in the tent and God's announcement, "I shall return this time next year and your wife Sarah will have a son"—hidden laughter in the tent; she is old, her husband old—and God's response: "Why did Sarah laugh? Is anything too wonderful for God?"

And stop. The Levite (we had no Cohen, no priest, so a Levite got first turn) kissed the last word of that passage with the corner of his tallit, rolled the Torah shut, and said the after-blessing ("who has given us the Torah of truth and planted eternal life in our midst"). Amen. The second stood up. Approached. The Yemenite opened the scroll and placed the pointer on the first word of the next. The second kissed and blessed. Amen.

"And Sarah denied it . . ." the river took up, as if the blessings had not occurred in time. There was no seam. Only the Amen between eternity and time.

And on toward Sodom. "Shall I hide what I am about to do," said the Lord, "from Abraham, who will become a great and enormous nation, in whom all the nations of the earth will be blessed?" There is no attempt to render, by some inflection of the voice, this bargaining over the fate of Sodom. The music is oblivious to the content.

Stop. The after-blessing. The third arises.

Two angels now. Lot is sitting in the gate of the city, as Abraham had in the opening of the tent. He too welcomes them. A righteous man. But the river leaves no time for these old thoughts—or only time to wave at them in passing. The men at Sodom gather at Lot's door. The angels smite the crowd with blindness. They warn Lot to flee to the mountains.

Stop. Kiss. Shut. Blessing. The fourth is called. I review the blessings in my prayerbook. The stomach turns. The throat constricts.

Take shelter there, they said. So that town is known as Zoar, little place. An oasis on the Jordanian side, on the southeast end of the Dead Sea, a green spot amid the badlands. It has borne that name at least since Jeremiah. So Sodom would have been down there, in those badlands still reeking of sulfur. Lot's wife looked back and turned to salt. Conveniently by the modern road. We get out and take her picture. From the north like Queen Victoria. Ho-ho-ho. Must leave this business. I don't like mentioning Queen Victoria, but I don't like myself when I don't mention her—my self-righteous, prissy restraint. Where are they? Probably up in the cave above Zoar. Lot's daughters have gotten him drunk. There is no man left alive, they think, to come to them in the accustomed manner, so they make him drunk and sleep with him to get his seed. From these unions derive the Moabites and Ammonites, who probably had a different version.

I have leaped out ahead. At least I think it is ahead. I perch upon the start of the next chapter, waiting for "Abraham." I miss him. I hear "Abraham," but it must be farther down. They are at Gerar. Can never find Tell Gerar. He presents Sarah as his sister. Cannot find them. I jump to the next chapter, perch there. My turn is coming. Constriction: chest, throat. Heartbeats. Trembling in the knees. Cold. I hear and see the word *pakad*—"visited." I have found them, thank God. "And the Lord visited Sarah as He had said and did to Sarah as He had said. And she conceived and bore a son to Abraham in his old age . . . Isaac. And Abraham circumcised Isaac his son at eight days old as God had commanded him."

Stop. My turn. Dimly I hear the after-blessing.

"The fifth will rise!"

The fifth rises, fairly floats over to them with his prayerbook. "You don't have to know anything," I say to myself. The Yemenite, seen from the side, is sharp-looking, energetic, attentive, like a runner held back, awaiting the gun. He does not have this self-consciousness because he is devoted to something beyond himself. Thus he can flow. But I, a dull and muddy-mettled fellow, am so turned back upon myself, I can hardly move. I operate the crane that moves me.

None of this is perceptible, thank God—unless to the invisible ancients. The bearded officers have merely glanced up from their books. The others, seated about in white silk, the garb of the generations, have not begun twisting and staring.

He opens the scroll and places the silver pointer, the end of which is shaped like a hand, upon the first letter of the next word. "And Abraham . . ." The crane takes up the corner of my tallit, lifts it, and then brings it over to touch the "and." It brings the corner to my lips. I kiss the corner. Shall this purify my lips? Do I roll the scroll shut now? The crane effects this. No one objects. I am doing things right. It opens my prayerbook—no one gasps.

"Bless the Lord who is blessed."

My voice is fuller, surer than I would have expected. I gain confidence from it. I become the crane.

They mumble the response, except the officer on my right, who says it with a certain aggressive charge:

"Blessed the Lord the blessed forever."

I repeat that and read on:

"Blessed are You, O Lord, Our God, King of the universe, Who chose us from among all peoples and gave us His Torah. Blessed are You, O Lord, Who gives the Torah."

"Amen," they say.

"Amen," sings the Yemenite, rolling it open, finding the word. "And Abraham . . ."

I hold the handle of one roller. The real thing. The black letters hand-penned. The silver pointer pauses—now here, now here. Not a current. Hand over hand lightly from branch to branch. Now that the pointer shows me where his voice is, I can hold on to him and fly. We fly, indifferent as clocks, through Sarah's happiness. Yitzhak—Isaac—it means laughter. At his weaning feast she sees the son of Abraham and Hagar, an Egyptian maidservant. He is making fun. "Banish that woman and her son," she says, "so that her son won't inherit with mine." The thing seems very grievous to Abraham. The song does not grieve with him. It did not rejoice—why should it grieve? All is well known. All is accounted for. Blessed. "And God said to Abraham, 'Let it not be grievous to you, and do what Sarah tells you with the boy and your maidservant, for it is in Isaac that your seed will be called. But I shall also make a nation from the son of your maidservant, for he is your seed.' And Abraham arose in the morning. . . ."

That son is Ishmael; "God heard." The Arabs are supposed to be his seed. "Our cousins," we call them—and they us, for they accept the lineage. A wave to them in the next room. They are stretched out on the cement floor. They hear the nasal intonation, coming thinly through. They cannot know what it is. The Yemenite reads on my behalf—I want them to know. A wave to you, fellow prisoners, cousins. With one hand only, from the Torah scroll. "Ishmael! His story!" I must hold on or drown.

". . . bread and water and gave them to Hagar, put it on her shoulder, and the boy, and sent her, and she went, and she wandered in the wilderness of Beersheba. And the water in the bottle was finished, and she put the boy under one of the bushes. And she went and sat down across from him at a distance, about a bowshot away, because, she said, 'I don't want to see the boy die,' and she sat there and raised her voice and wept. And God heard—"

Heard you, Ishmael!

"—the voice of the child, and an angel of God called to Hagar from heaven, 'What's the matter, Hagar? Don't be afraid. Get up, take the child, and hold him in your arms, for I shall make a great nation of him.' And God opened her eyes and she saw a well of water and she went and filled the water bottle and gave the child to drink. And God was with the boy, and he grew and settled in the wilderness and became an archer. He lived in the wilderness of Paran, and his mother took him a wife from Egypt."

The pointer rests. I (it is I now, but I am a crane) put the corner of my tallit there, bring it to my lips and kiss it. I roll the scroll shut and take up my prayerbook. Find the place. I go to speak, but nothing comes out. No voice.

"Blessed are You," prompts the officer on my right.

"Blessed are You," I find myself saying, "O Lord our God, King of the universe, Who gave us the Torah of truth and planted eternal life in our midst. Blessed are You, O Lord, Who gives the Torah."

"Amen."

"The sixth will rise."

I start to go, but the officer on the right stops me and shakes my hand, looks into my eyes. A large, good-natured man. I smile a broken smile. I am no good at this, I want it to say. I'm sorry I'm no good at this.

They need my prayerbook, for it is open to the blessings. The sixth does not know them. A Frenchman, I think. He too has been hauled in.

Abraham and Abimelech at Beersheba. A dull story. I have read it to tourists there, oh, thirty times, in order to explain the city's name.

"The seventh will rise."

A tall brown man. Ethiopian perhaps. He too needs my prayerbook. The officer helps him gently.

The officer's forehead is high, sallow, gleaming. It slopes back, narrowing. His jaw is broader. The line of the beard, which is silver in small curls, slants straight from jowl to ear. It parallels the forehead. A sleek look. His eyes are smart and mischievous. Jacob's eyes.

The other across from him—more serious, a slightly hounded look. The beard still reddish. It follows the jawline in an L.

The Ethiopian is close to the Yemenite, so I back up a bit to get a look at the pointer.

The silver hand begins to shift. "And it came to pass after these things . . ."

This will be the binding of Isaac. So this too today.

" 'Take your son, your only, whom you have loved, Isaac, and go to the land of Moriah, and raise him up there as a sacrifice on one of the mountains I will show you.' And Abraham arose in the morning and saddled his ass, and took the two servants, and Isaac his son, and cut wood . . .''

The voice does not quaver, nor did Abraham waver.

"And Isaac said to Abraham his father, he said, 'My father!' and he said, 'Here I am, my son.' ''

Oh they knew that then too. Then too a son was a son. There is nothing like a son.

"And he said, 'Here is the fire and the wood, but where is the lamb for the sacrifice?' ''

As Benny would ask. Trying to be helpful, reminding his forgetful father.

"Stale bread," I say to him, knocking on my head. "Stale bread here."

"No, Daddy!"

" 'God will see to the lamb for the sacrifice, my son,' and they went on together. And they came to the place which the God had said to him, and Abraham built the altar there and arranged the wood and tied up Isaac his son and put him on the altar above the wood. And Abraham stretched forth his hand—"

The silver hand does not flinch either.

"—and took the knife to slaughter his son . . .

" 'Abraham! Abraham!' ''

His hand, uplifted, stops. The silver hand shifts on.

" 'Here I am,' says Abraham.

" 'Do not stretch forth your hand against the boy! Don't do a thing to him. For now I know that you fear God. You did not withhold your only son from me.' ''

He sees the ram caught in the thicket and he sacrifices it instead. Then the angel of the Lord calls out to him a second time:

" 'Because you have done this thing, and have not withheld your only son from me, I will bless you greatly and multiply your seed like the stars in the heavens, like the sand on the seashore, and your seed will take over the gate of its enemies. And all the nations of the earth will be blessed in your seed, because you obeyed me.' ''

He goes on to the births in the family of Abraham's brother. They are like surgeons at the table. The Yemenite is chief. The silver hand, his scalpel. Or it is like a circumcision. The same concentration. The swift sureness.

Stop. The Ethiopian reads the after-blessing. The sleek one is ready to help him. Not necessary. They shake hands. Great warmth there. I too feel it. Here this Jew is brown, and that Jew white. This Jew is African, that Jew European. The Yemenite, Arabian. The others in the minyan are Moroccan, Polish, French—it is so small a crowd, everyone has taken part in this Torah service. We are brothers bound by this scroll, this story, black on white. That promised seed. I receive my prayerbook and return to my place in the back.

The Yemenite himself does the blessings. He repeats, to close it, the passage about births in the family of Abraham's brother.

Or in their white shawls now, from this distance—like priests presiding over sacrifice. It must be just so.

The police side cook goes to lift the Torah, and we stand up. He sits, balancing it upright on his knees. We sit. His head is erect. The Moroccan halo. The dark planet. A small, wizened, whiter, older brother—I take him to be Polish—dresses it. We adorn the scroll like a woman. At other times we kiss it, dance with it—ten men, at least ten, and a very important woman.

He is doing the blessings for the reading that follows the Torah portion. This week it is Elisha and the woman of Shunem. One can see the village clearly from Tell Jezreel. "There is Shunem, where the prophet Elisha told a barren woman that she would give birth to a son. She did, but the son died. So she sent for Elisha, and he went up to the room and lay upon the boy and breathed into his mouth, and he came back to life." Again, the children.

Abraham was willing to sacrifice his son. I find that hard to conceive. I would not be willing. The relation with this particular person here, this Isaac, is itself ultimate and absolute. There is nothing higher. But of course the story seems to want to say, "There *is* something higher."

I cannot accept that. There is indeed a divine dimension. But the divine refers us to one another, not to itself.

That could be the point of the story. At first it seems to set the divine claim against the human bond, but at the last moment it annuls the opposition.

The issue is sacrifice. There is nothing like a child, for a child restores the dead adult to life. That is part of the meaning of these stories (Ishmael, Isaac, the son of the woman at Shunem). On the surface it is the children that are restored to life. But the stories have such power because our own children are so important to us, and they are so important because they restore *us* to life.

Our children are vulnerable, so we are vulnerable in them. The whole mechanism of defense arises to engulf and protect the child—hence the weight on the word "my" in "my son," "my daughter." This smidgen of truth and life—a pleasing irritant. When we play I clench my teeth.

God says, "Take your son, your only, whom you have loved," meaning your son who is wrapped in the "my." One must be willing to give that son up in order to be with one's son as he is. This is what Abraham does on Moriah.

AS WE STRODE through the yard on our way to the mess hall, where we would bless God for the Sabbath wine and bread, and then have lunch, we heard:

"Cap-tain, cigarette."

It came from the cell on the left. The same guy, no doubt. I walked just a step behind them, and I noted a stir in the striding group. The Orthodox do not smoke on Sabbath. The prisoner did not know that, or did not realize, despite the yarmulkes, that these were the Orthodox, whom he had been hearing for two hours.

It came again. The sleek one with mischievous eyes—I shall call him "Jacob," since Jacob was mischievous—just turned his head to them and shouted, "Don't throw stones!"

We went around past my cell over to the mess. The police side cook brought bread and wine. Jacob blessed God the Creator of wine to our "Amen." We washed our hands in the ritual manner. Jacob uncovered the bread, blessed God, broke it, ate and distributed. We ate it and renewed our unity. Then the police side cook brought us an early lunch of chicken. It had been kept warm in the oven, for there is no cooking on Sabbath. The officers sat across from me and tore into the food. Jacob asked me:

"Were you able to follow?"

"Just barely."

"Beautiful, no?"

"I felt back at Sinai."

He shook his head and chewed.

"Not back that far," said the reddish-bearded one.

"Sinai, no," said Jacob. "The Temple. Second Temple."

The other waved his empty fork in doubt.

"I have a good authority," said Jacob. "My wife's uncle is a musicologist."

"It's possible, that's all."

"They were very isolated, down there in Yemen."

We fell into silence and ate.

Later we did the afternoon service, where he read from the start of next week's portion: the burial of Sarah. Then we went back to the mess for a little meal, "the third feast" it's called. Sabbath is to be a day of joy, and so on this day, at least, no matter how poor you are, you are supposed to take three meals.

It turned out to be the same as dinner (which is the same as breakfast), only earlier: stale bread, white cheese, the plum jam. But the cook added halvah as a treat. We said the blessings. We had become by this time a little group: the group of this Sabbath in Jericho. The officers sat across from me again.

"Did you know," I asked them, "that Hillel lived in Jericho?"

Hillel was a sage from the time of the Second Temple. He is famous for having said: "If I am not for myself, who will be for me? But if I am for myself alone, what am I?" And, "If not now, when?"

"How do you know that?" asked the red-bearded one.

"We did a refresher course for guides here. The guide said so. The house of Hillel may have been an actual house in Jericho."

"I'd like to see the source on that."

"I'll look it up and send it to you. If you'll give me your address."

He nodded. "Later."

They do not write on Sabbath.

My colleagues trooped in, pulling off their hats: Danny and Barak, Shlomo, the two Gadis. Not Ezra and his sidekick, though. It was odd to see them from another table. Even hatless they looked like prisoners. It was perhaps the plainness of the uniforms, the lack of accouterment. They pulled the chairs from beneath the table with a lot of noise. In this place where the others, reservists, police, all knew each other, had a function together, they were each a functionless stranger in a small and functionless band of strangers. Danny saw me, waved briefly. I smiled back.

We returned to the synagogue and did the evening service, in which we declared that Sabbath was over. There was wine and a braided, double-wicked candle for Havdalah, a ceremony which marks the transition from the holy to the profane. Jacob lit the candle, and someone turned out the light, so there was only the one sputtering flame. We gathered around it. Ten ancient sorcerers.

Jacob poured the wine to overflowing, so that the week should overflow with blessings. The police side cook brought sprigs of rosemary and gave one to each of us. Jacob intoned:

"Here is the God of my salvation. I shall trust in Him and not be afraid. Yah is my strength and song, and He shall save me. And you shall draw water with gladness from the wellsprings of salvation. . . ."

There were more verses in this vein. Then he lifted the tin silvery goblet:

"I raise the cup of salvation and call out in the name of the Lord."

He blessed God the Creator of wine. Then he blessed God the Creator of perfumes, and each sniffed his sprig. It was to restore our spirits, since the extra soul which had accompanied us through the Sabbath was now departing. He blessed God the Creator of light, and each held his fingers to the candle and looked at the nails, so as to use the light, thus marking the transition to the workaday world.

"Blessed are You, Lord our God, King of the universe, Who distinguishes between holy and profane, between light and darkness, between Israel and the peoples, between the seventh day and the six days of work. Blessed are You, Lord, Who distinguishes between the holy and the profane."

He drank deeply. Then he passed it around, and each took a sip. And should I sip? This distinction between Israel and the peoples—I know I understand it quite differently from the way they do, quite to the contrary: that the peoples are our reason for being, that we are the servant.

The cup came to me and I sipped. Our deepest bond is perhaps unknown to all of us, but I wager my version is close. From this bond I sipped.

Jacob dashed out the candle in the overflow of wine that was in the saucer. We filed out in darkness, I the last.

"Close the door," someone said to me.

I closed it.

This time it was the Palestinians from the bad cell on the other side.

"Water! Water!" they cried in Hebrew.

They had shoved the corrugated tin sheet off at an angle, despite the heavy tire, which remained in place. They had squeezed three large plastic cola bottles through the bars. They held them out.

In fact, I had not seen a guard all day.

"Water! Water!" Always twice. The word lends itself to being called out twice. *Mayyim! Mayyim!*

I was behind. I stopped. I wanted to see. But I knew they wouldn't.

Brown arms in the electric light. Hagar's children. They waved the bottles as the nine walked past.

"Mayyim! Mayyim!"

The nine kept talking together as they strode. Some interesting topic. A sense of ease, of release. Jacob was carrying it on.

They rounded the corner.

THE NINE BACKS. I was not surprised. Wanting, hoping to be surprised, and not surprised. Joking together. Bearded Jacob, turning to the others—turning his head to the left, away from the cell, carrying it boisterously on . . .

And if they—at that moment, in that place—were not the Jewish people, who then?

The tenth man?

The tenth man: I will tell you what he did. He went into the police office, knocking politely. A kid sat there. Some kid he had never seen before. Writing at the desk.

"Yes?"

"I want permission to give them water."

He looked up. Hesitant.

"No permission."

"They haven't had water all day. Not since yesterday afternoon."

"You don't know that."

"There's been no guard all day."

"That's not our business."

He resumed writing. The tenth man stayed. He looked up.

"Yes?"

"I want to give them."

"They get water when they're supposed to, and they know it. Now go to where you're supposed to."

The tenth man went out and stood by his narcissus bulbs. He looked across at them. They did not cry out. They held the plastic bottles toward him through the bars. Almost a threat.

It occurred to him: What's it all been about?

He went and took the bottles and filled them at the coolest faucet he knew, down by the police side kitchen.

I could always say, he thought, it's for the flowers.

Epilogue

I WAS RELEASED ON SCHEDULE the next morning. There was no new order waiting for me. Two weeks later one came, but it was for foot patrol duty in West Jerusalem, something I could accept. Six months after completing this service I received a notice of discharge—a routine sort of notice, though a few years earlier than the norm. I did not ask why. I did not argue.

What attracted me to this country ten years ago was the sense of community. Well, there are people with whom I still feel that possibility. But it is no longer the old sense, the old bond that included all of us, no matter our politics: the people of Israel in the land of Israel. My ideal of community was and is of something founded in rightness and extending beyond itself, as the I-Thou relation, in order to endure, must extend beyond itself. I once thought that way (I blush to say it) about the people of Israel in the land of Israel: that basically, despite aberrations and regressions, it was a community which stretched out its hand to its Arab neighbors. Thus our Declaration of Independence put the matter. I believed this, and so did a lot of other people. To some extent we were naive, no doubt. But to a greater extent the fall has been a real one.

Today I can no longer think about the people of Israel in the land of Israel without also having the picture of those nine backs and the heads turned to one another in relaxed and animated conversation.

We continue to live here. Noga and the children are rooted here after all—in love and friendship, in the weather, the food, the holidays, the language. I guide now and then. It is a beautiful country.